NOVELS OF THE
EIGHTEEN-FORTIES

NOVELS OF THE
EIGHTEEN-FORTIES

❦

KATHLEEN TILLOTSON

OXFORD
AT THE CLARENDON PRESS

Oxford University Press, Amen House, London E.C.4
GLASGOW NEW YORK TORONTO MELBOURNE WELLINGTON
BOMBAY CALCUTTA MADRAS KARACHI CAPE TOWN IBADAN
Geoffrey Cumberlege, Publisher to the University

FIRST PUBLISHED 1954

REPRINTED LITHOGRAPHICALLY IN GREAT BRITAIN
AT THE UNIVERSITY PRESS, OXFORD
FROM CORRECTED SHEETS OF THE FIRST EDITION
1956

NOTE TO SECOND IMPRESSION

I HAVE taken the opportunity to correct a few minor errors, and also to set right a mistaken attribution of two reviews in *Fraser's* to G. H. Lewes.

K. T.

BEDFORD COLLEGE
UNIVERSITY OF LONDON

10 *March* 1955

PREFACE

THE plan of this book ought to explain itself, the whole of the first part being introductory; but some of my principles of selection need to be made clear at the outset. My book is not what is sometimes called a 'decade-study'; I do not refer to all the main preoccupations of the time, but only to those that seem especially relevant to the novels. And, though I hope I am never careless of chronology, I do not proceed through the decade year by year, but risk generalizations, some of which are perhaps more applicable to the late eighteen-forties. I have sometimes gone to other decades, especially the fifties, for illustrative material, but my general policy has been to reserve this for the footnotes. I have not attempted a survey of all the novels of the forties, but rather of those kinds of novels and contemporary views about novels (assumed or expressed) which contribute to our fuller understanding of the great novels of the period. The four novels chosen for detailed study are some of those which I believe stand to gain most from such an exploration of 'background'; they are novels which are essentially 'of' the forties as well as 'for all time'. With that intention, I was precluded from choosing the novel which on other counts demands full-length treatment—*Wuthering Heights*. This novel, which speaks so clearly to our generation, hardly spoke at all to its own. Then, since the forties produced no historical novel of any distinction, I say the less about that

kind of novel; and I give only a partial account of the
'novels of fashionable life', which could not be
adequately treated without taking in the eighteen-
thirties. They may have as much merit as the minor
religious novels, of which I say more; but in this
particular decade they are farther from the centre.
I have not mentioned all the novels that I have read,
but they have contributed something to my general
conclusions.

The introductory section is intended to set the four
chosen novels in a firmer relation to their time; in the
second part, that relation is deliberately less emphasized. There, the four novels are placed in an order
not chronological, but I think logical. Each of them
called for a slightly different approach, but in all I
have wished to make clear the main centres of interest
and also the quality of the art which created them.
For unlike some modern critics I believe these
novelists were artists, true and not 'spoilt'.

The ground plan of this book and the choice of the
novels in the second part survive from a course of
inter-collegiate lectures delivered in the University
of London in 1949. The draft of the lectures has
been much enlarged and almost entirely rewritten;
and I have tried to take account of new material published up to 1952. To the numerous biographical and
less numerous critical studies of the novelists which
have appeared in the last twenty years, many of
which I regard with respect, I have found little
occasion to refer; I was concerned to ask different
questions. My approach naturally led me rather to

nineteenth-century biographies and memoirs, and to
nineteenth-century criticism, especially as it appears
in the periodicals of the time, still too much neglected.

To modern editions of the novels my indebtedness
is limited to a mere gratitude for their existence. We
have virtually no edited texts of Victorian novelists,
and no means, short of doing the work ourselves, of
discovering how (and why) the original edition
differed from the text we read. A small but not trivial
example is the chapter-titles of *Mary Barton*; they
affect the reader's response and one would like to
think them Mrs. Gaskell's; but they appeared in no
edition published in her lifetime, and I have found no
evidence of their origin.

My specific obligations to published works are
duly recorded in footnotes; but to some I owe the
kind of stimulus that cannot thus be acknowledged
adequately. Among these are Mr. Michael Sadleir's
writings on Victorian fiction; Professor Gordon
Ray's annotation of Thackeray's letters; Professor
J. W. Dodds's book on Thackeray; several articles
on Dickens's methods by Professor John Butt (sup-
plemented by his correspondence and conversation);
Mr. G. M. Young's *Portrait of an Age*, and his unpublished Clark lectures delivered at Cambridge in
1940. Less definable, but not less gratefully remembered, are my obligations to the interest (and
sometimes the ignorance) of many undergraduate
students, and to the encouragement of several col-
leagues. Of the latter I wish especially to thank Dr.
William E. Buckler, of the University of Illinois,
who attended the original lectures and kindly com-

mented on my first attempts to revise them; and Miss Mary Lascelles, who read a draft of the fifteenth section in Part I and encouraged me, generally and at particular points, to develop my argument further. My colleague and husband Geoffrey Tillotson heard and read my work at various stages and preserved me both from particular errors and from general despair. I am also indebted to his writings on the nineteenth century, published and unpublished—but not (to my loss) to his forthcoming book on Thackeray, which was written later than mine.

Thanks to the staff of the British Museum Library are customarily general and formal, but my gratitude includes many well-remembered particulars—as also to the libraries of the University of London and of Bedford College. But indispensable as libraries are, the possession of books is equally so, and here I have been especially assisted by my husband's infallible eye for the likely second-hand catalogue or bookshop. And it was thanks to my father, Eric Constable, that I grew up among the classics of the last century. He read part of this book, and I hope recognized that it was essentially dedicated to him; as it now is to his memory.

K. T.

BEDFORD COLLEGE
UNIVERSITY OF LONDON
      16 *May* 1953

ACKNOWLEDGEMENTS

FOR permission to quote from copyright material I wish to thank the following: Messrs. Hodder & Stoughton and the executor of Clement Shorter for quotations from Charlotte Brontë's letters in Clement Shorter's *The Brontës: Life and Letters*, and Basil Blackwell for quotations from *The Brontës, their Lives, Friendships, and Correspondence*; the Brontë Society for quotations from its *Transactions*; the Yale University Press for quotations from John Chapman's diary in Gordon Haight's *George Eliot and John Chapman*; and the Harvard University Press and Mrs. Hester Thackeray Fuller for quotations from *The Letters and Private Papers of William Makepeace Thackeray*, edited by Gordon N. Ray. I also wish to thank the Director of the Victoria and Albert Museum for permission to quote from Dickens's manuscript 'number-plans' in the Forster Collection, and Mr. J. H. Mozley for permission to quote from unpublished letters of Harriett Mozley.

CONTENTS

NOTE ON EDITIONS
AND REFERENCES

In quoting from the novels of the eighteen-forties I have used the first edition in volume form, but have given references to chapter and not page, and where the chapter numbering was not continuous throughout the work, being broken by volume division, I have altered it in accordance with modern reprints.

ABBREVIATED TITLES
of Works Frequently Referred to

[WALTER] BAGEHOT, *Literary Studies*—Everyman edition, 2 vols., 1911. [1st edition, 1878; some essays previously collected in *Estimates of Some Englishmen and Scotchmen*, 1858.]

B.S.T.—Brontë Society, *Transactions and other publications*, Bradford, 1898– .

CROSS—J. W. CROSS, *George Eliot's Life*, 3 vols., 1885.

DICKENS, *Letters—The Letters of Charles Dickens*, edited by Walter Dexter, 3 vols., 1938 (The Nonesuch Dickens).

FORSTER—*The Life of Charles Dickens* [originally issued in 3 vols., 1872–4, and revised for the two-volume edition of 1876] *by John Forster*, ed. J. W. T. Ley, 1928.

GASKELL—ELIZABETH C. GASKELL, *The Life of Charlotte Brontë* (1857; 3rd edition revised and corrected, 1857).

S.H.B.—*The Brontës, their Lives, Friendships, and Correspondence*. 4 vols. (Shakespeare Head Brontë, Oxford, 1932).

THACKERAY, *Letters—The Letters and Private Papers of . . . Thackeray*, collected and edited by Gordon N. Ray, 4 vols., Cambridge, Mass., 1945–6.

THACKERAY, *Works—The Oxford Thackeray*, edited by George Saintsbury, 17 vols., Oxford [1908].

TROLLOPE, *Autobiography*—ANTHONY TROLLOPE, *An Autobiography*, 2 vols., 1883.

PART I

INTRODUCTORY

§ I

It is now, I think, too late to talk about 'Victorian novels'; their range is too vast and vague to lead to any useful generalization. So vague, indeed, that the common reader's picture of the Victorian novels is a phantasmagoria of stage-coaches, Barsetshire, women in white, and Hugh Thomson illustrations; and a class of undergraduate students, invited to expose their knowledge of the field, will begin by happily hazarding Jane Austen and *Jane Eyre*. The secrets of chronology are well guarded by some popular critics and some modern reprints, which also commonly deprive the novels of their preliminaries and even their full titles. These instances may be extreme; the wanting information can be found; but there remains, at any level, the insuperable difficulty of doing critical justice to the novels of sixty-three years in a single book. (No one would attempt it for the fifty-three years of our own century.) The time has surely come to break up 'the Victorian novel' into manageable segments; not by novelists, or categories, or phases, but simply by concentrating upon a decade or so at a time. Replaced in their original context of time and opinion, the novels may be found to make better sense, to take on values new to us, which modify or substantiate the old. At the same time, in attempting to recover something of the contemporary eye, the perspective of distance need not be rejected. My ultimate purpose has been to learn more about particular novels and their time, and about the novel as a 'kind', by looking rather more closely than has been customary at the novels of an early decade, the eighteen-forties.

§ 2

I shall begin by briefly indicating some of the available material, proceeding from the more to the less known; to say 'novels of the eighteen-forties' is not automatically to call up the names of the works even of major novelists, or their place in those novelists' careers; and still less the threads that unite them, threads often running through long-forgotten novels but contributing to the whole design. But I am, of course, reminding rather than informing; for this is a decade in which the reader of Victorian novels can easily be made to feel at home.

The novelists whose complete work chances to fall within the pale of this single decade are few; but the work of the Brontës very nearly does so, with *The Professor* (written by 1846), *Wuthering Heights*, *Agnes Grey*, and *Jane Eyre* (1847), *The Tenant of Wildfell Hall* (1848), and *Shirley* (1849).

Dickens, writing from 1833 to 1870, is represented by five novels: *The Old Curiosity Shop* (1840–1), *Barnaby Rudge* (1841), *Martin Chuzzlewit* (1843–4), *Dombey and Son* (1846–8), and *David Copperfield*

(1849–50); besides two travel-books and five Christmas stories. Thackeray is seen nearer the beginning of his shorter career, with *The Luck of Barry Lyndon* (1844), *Vanity Fair* (1847–8), and *Pendennis* (1849–50), besides many sketches and stories. Of other considerable and still-famous novels the forties give us Mrs. Gaskell's first novel, *Mary Barton* (1848); Kingsley's first novel, *Yeast* (1848); Disraeli's three middle and most famous novels—*Coningsby* (1844), *Sybil* (1845), and *Tancred* (1847). These remind us that the *roman à thèse* is already establishing itself; and to them may be added two out of many novels on the religious problems of the day: Froude's *Nemesis of Faith* (1849) and Newman's *Loss and Gain* (1848). Other now-famous names are absent, or appear faintly: only the first two and least characteristic of Trollope's fifty or so novels belong to the forties: *The Macdermots of Ballycloran* (1847) and *The Kellys and the O'Kellys* (1848). The Trollope who was famous in the forties was Anthony's mother, Frances, nineteen of whose hundred novels fell in these years. Wilkie Collins did not begin to publish until 1850: Charles Reade and George Meredith a few years later. And as yet there was no such person as 'George Eliot': by 1849 Mary Ann Evans was just beginning to hope for a literary career as journalist, critic, and translator; she had published only her translation of Strauss's *Leben Jesu*, and had abandoned her one attempt at fiction after a single chapter.[1] She was already a critical reader of con-

---

[1] Cross, ch. iii (Mrs. Bray to Miss Hennell, 25 September 1846), and ch. vii ('How I came to write Fiction').

temporary novels[1] (notably of *Jane Eyre*) and was soon to be a critical writer. For her, as for Thackeray, an important stimulus came from impatience with the follies and stereotypes of the modern novels she read: nearly coincident with her beginnings as a novelist is her anonymous essay in the *Westminster Review* of 1856. It was called—in that less polite age—'Silly Novels by Lady Novelists'; and it supplies more than one text for the forties. Of that decade, the most popular 'lady novelist' was Mrs. Gore, who published twenty-four novels—a fertility excelled only by the 'solitary horseman' novelist G. P. R. James, whose score is twenty-eight. Yet even of these two the importance is attested by the parodies provided by Thackeray in *Punch's Prize Novelists*— with which most readers now may be content, and fairly so, for they are as accurate as absurd. Others deserve, for a variety of reasons, more serious attention: the diverse talents of, for example, Samuel Warren, Mrs. Marsh, Geraldine Jewsbury, Lady Georgiana Fullerton, and Marmion Savage, were limited, but estimable as well as marketable.[2] Minor popular novels have much to tell us of the nature (and size) of the contemporary novel-reading public; they show what expectations had been built up in the minds of readers and hence how far the great novelists could afford to defeat those expectations. The crime novels of Ainsworth and Lytton are a

[1] She had reviewed one novel, Froude's *Nemesis of Faith*, for Bray's *Coventry Herald* in March 1849 (Cross, ch. iii).

[2] This may seem a random choice, but I have selected those authors whose books are most prominent in advertisements and reviews, and which I myself have read.

necessary part of the context of *Oliver Twist*, *Catherine*, and *Barry Lyndon*; the high-life or 'silver fork' novels increase our understanding of those who react against them, especially of Thackeray. And when, for example, a prolific and popular minor novelist changes his groove, as Lytton did with *The Caxtons* in 1849, he testifies to the establishment of a major change in subject matter: from extravagant romance to domesticity, from the extremes of high and low life to the middle class.

One other kind of novel popular in the eighteen-forties is still being read today (or was yesterday); but most modern readers will have been unaware that they were reading minor novels of the eighteen-forties when they read, for example, *The Tower of London*, *Old St. Paul's*, *The Last of the Barons*, *Masterman Ready*, *Children of the New Forest*, and *The Pathfinder*. While some books descend from the library to the schoolroom, others ascend, perhaps even to the confines of the British Museum Reading-Room. Many works intended primarily for the young of the eighteen-forties are now read only by the closer students of the period—such as the five earliest stories of Charlotte Yonge, *Abbeychurch*, *Langley School*, *Scenes and Characters*, *Henrietta's Wish*, and *Kenneth*; Harriet Martineau's admirable *The Crofton Boys*; the earlier tales of Elizabeth Sewell; and that neglected minor masterpiece Harriett Mozley's *The Fairy Bower*, with its sequel *The Lost Brooch*. Such examples are enough to remind us that the line between tales for the young and novels is a wavering one; it was indeed felt to be specially so in the forties, and all these books rightfully belong to the history of the novel.

§ 3

My subject is English novels—not American novels, nor other European novels. The exclusion of American novels is at this date defensible. It is perhaps the last decade in which this is so: for though the earliest novels of Herman Melville, *Typee*, *Omoo*, and *Redburn* were published in the late forties I do not find that they were much noticed in England; and Hawthorne—the earliest American novelist to be taken seriously by contemporary English critics—published his first novel, *The Scarlet Letter*, in 1850. Perhaps typical is a patronizing, even contemptuous article on contemporary American literature in *Blackwood's*; Poe's tales and Hawthorne's *Mosses from an Old Manse* are alone commended.[1] The great invasion of the English public by the American novel begins a few years later with *Uncle Tom's Cabin* and *The Wide, Wide World*.[2] In the eighteen-forties, with the single exception of Fenimore Cooper (widely read, and by men as well as boys) the direct relevance of America to a survey of the novel in England is limited to piracies (in both directions), arguments about copyright, and Dickens's pictures of American society in *American Notes* and *Martin Chuzzlewit* (which Carlyle said set '*all* Yankee-doodle-dom blazing up like one universal soda-water bottle').[3] But

[1] November 1847.
[2] See Nassau Senior's *Essays on Fiction* (1864), p. 450.
[3] Sir Charles Gavan Duffy, *Conversations with Carlyle* (1892), p. 245.

there are signs of things to come. In 1844 Henry
James paid his first visit to Europe: at that time he was
only a year old, but before the forties were out, I am
sure, he was reading English novels; visiting England
in 1870 he was reminded by the English countryside
of 'the opening chapters of half-remembered novels,
devoured in infancy';[1] and those early impressions put
him on firmer ground when in the eighteen-sixties
he became a reviewer of English novels, including
Our Mutual Friend and *Wives and Daughters*.

A more comprehensive study would need to include the influence of French upon English novels
at this period. French novels were much read in England at this time by men and independent women—
one shop in the Burlington Arcade, Jeffs's (the shop
where Miss Evans first met Mr. Lewes) sold nothing
else[2]—and their influence on the English novels is
not negligible: 'George-Sandism' is a recognized
label. Contemporary critics draw comparisons not
only between Charlotte Brontë and George Sand, but
between Thackeray and Balzac; they review recent
French novels;[3] they also discuss the vexed question
of the 'limitations' of novelists in the two countries.
These last tend to be rather wistful in tone: as for
instance this from a review in *Fraser's*:

If we are to make a choice between prosy decent books and

[1] *Letters*, ed. Percy Lubbock (1920), i. 28.

[2] [G. H. Lewes], 'Recent novels; French and English', *Fraser's*
(December 1847).

[3] Sometimes with reprobation; see *Athenæum* (1847), pp. 543–4, 809.
Blackwood's in November 1849 announced that it would not continue to
review French novels 'until a manifest improvement takes place' (p. 619).
Like *Fraser's*, it had hitherto reviewed them regularly.

vicious books that are written with sprightliness and skill, we are, of course, bound to prefer the former. There is no room or excuse for hesitation. But we cannot help regretting . . . that our English novelists . . . should not be able to make [morality] a little more amusing.[1]

But the conscious insularity of which Matthew Arnold was later to complain was growing stronger,[2] especially after 1848, the year of revolution. An early philistine is Tennyson's 'Tory member's eldest son' in *The Princess* who exclaims:

> God bless the narrow seas!
> I wish they were a whole Atlantic broad.

He is the ancestor of Mr. Podsnap, who

considered other countries a mistake, and of their manners and customs would conclusively observe 'Not English!', and presto they were swept away.[3]

But it would be absurd to confuse Dickens with his creature; by the date of *Our Mutual Friend*, he liked living in France, was conversant with the French theatre, and anticipated one of Taine's criticisms by pointing out the hypocrisy of those readers who contrasted Scott's 'uninteresting' heroes with those of French novelists; the former, like his own, '*must* be presented to you in that unnatural aspect by reason of your morality'.[4] Thackeray, who had lived in Paris

---

[1] October 1851, p. 375.

[2] Mrs. Gore in her preface to *Cecil . . . a Coxcomb* (1841) complains of those 'Tartuffes' who 'every now and then raise a cry of infection, as for the plague or cholera, and establish a *cordon sanitaire* as in the instance of the modern French novelists'.

[3] *Our Mutual Friend* (1865), ch. ix.

[4] Forster, vi. 3; vii. 5; ix. 1. The letter quoted was written 15 August 1856.

in the thirties, knew contemporary French literature well; he reviewed French novels,[1] translated part of a novel of Sue's, had some tenderness for Dumas and was perhaps directly influenced by Balzac. Charlotte Brontë borrowed a 'bale of French books . . . upwards of 40 volumes' from the Taylors in 1840, and found them 'clever wicked sophistical and immoral'.[2] In 1849 Mary Ann Evans was finding 'the psychological anatomy . . . of early married life' in George Sand's *Jaques* 'quite preternaturally true'.[3] There was little 'Podsnappery' among English novelists and novel-readers of the forties.

§ 4

My subject is English novels—not English novelists. This is partly dictated by the chronological limits; the work of none of the novelists I treat, save of Emily and Anne Brontë, was confined to the eighteen-forties, and three out of the four novels selected for closer study were, in some sense, first novels. Although I suggest the relation of novels to the novelist's whole career, I do not survey that career; and although I have often drawn on biographical material, my approach is not primarily

[1] 'On Some French Fashionable Novels', in the *Paris Sketch Book* (1840). See also 'Jérome Paturôt' (*Fraser's*, September 1843; *Works*, vi) and reviews in the *Foreign Quarterly Review* (1842–4). Thackeray's attitude towards the French is well summarize'd in J. W. Dodds, *Thackeray* (1941), pp. 47–54.

[2] *S.H.B.*, i. 215. Their titles are unknown; they did not include Balzac, whom she did not begin to read until 1850, and thought inferior to George Sand (iii. 172).

[3] Cross, ch. iii (letter of 9 February 1849).

biographical. Such an approach, except in very skilled hands (Johnson's, or Forster's), is apt to side-track criticism; it has certain dangers, especially for this period with its deceptively full documentation, and especially at our distance of three generations when families have begun warily to release skeletons from cupboards. The margins of Victorian novels may easily be filled with 'chatter about Harriet'—about Ellen Ternan, Mrs. Brookfield, M. Héger; but this is surely an evasion of the critic's responsibility. Where biography may legitimately help us is in the closer defining of the social and literary tradition in which the writer worked, the class from which he sprang, the books which he read and admired. At particular points where the novelist draws more directly than usual on his personal experience, it may help to explain what seems to interrupt his usual detachment; but even there it should be the last and not the first resort. Again, when a novelist begins to write novels only in middle age we may look to 'biography' for an explanation. It is obvious that for particular novels, such as *David Copperfield* and *Pendennis*, biography may have even more relevance. In more general ways a knowledge of an author's life can help us to define qualities which we perceive independently in the novels: for instance, the instability of Dickens's childhood, his years of experience as a Parliamentary reporter, his life-long passion for the theatre. The circumstances of Thackeray's life may possibly help to account for the gradual invasion of the satirist by the moralist—for the shift from 'Pen and Pencil Sketches of English Society' to 'Vanity

Fair'. He seems to admit the change in a letter of 1847:

A few years ago I should have sneered at the idea of setting up as a teacher at all . . . but I have got to believe in the business, and in many other things since then,[1]

and he told a friend who asked how he found out his true vein that he found it when his misfortunes began.[2] Again, Mrs. Gaskell was thirty-eight when she published her first novel—almost her first publication. Its preface alone shows that this is an example of a convergence of particular experiences which pressed upon the mind and compelled expression. As it happened, it also released a fine artist. With the Brontës the interconnexion of work and life is, at one level, only too obvious;[3] the critic's problem is to distinguish between fact and speculation, and what is still more difficult, between the less and the more critically relevant. There is here the special circumstance of a mass of early unpublished writing, forming a kind of bridge between the author's inner life and the novels; accordingly, in my study of *Jane Eyre*, I have found it necessary to deal more fully with the novelist and her history than elsewhere. But there too I hope *Jane Eyre* itself firmly occupies the centre of attention.

The general emphasis upon novels rather than novelists will have the perhaps surprising effect of

---

[1] *Letters*, ii. 282.   [2] *Letters*, iv. 378 (Appendix XVIII).

[3] 'The question has scarce indeed been accepted as belonging to literature at all . . . the fashion has been, in looking at the Brontës, so to confound the cause with the result, that we cease to know, in the presence of such ecstasies, what we have hold of or what we are talking about' (Henry James, *The Lesson of Balzac* (1905), p. 65).

making us more closely resemble the novels' first readers. Although they might hope to 'see Dickens plain' at York Gate, or Brighton, or Broadstairs, they really knew much less about his life than we do. When *David Copperfield* came out, its autobiographical references were only vaguely guessed; and often guessed amiss; it was thought, for instance, that the writer might be a native of Yarmouth.[1] *Mary Barton* was not only a first novel but was published anonymously; there was the initial interest of guessing the author's sex. Most readers scarcely knew Thackeray's name when they met it on the cover of *Vanity Fair*. Nor had they any idea who were Currer, Ellis, and Acton Bell—men or women, one or three. Again this did not restrain them from wild guesses; the rumour ran that *Jane Eyre* was the work of a discarded mistress of Thackeray's.[2]

On the other hand, in order to confront these novels with the eyes of the eighteen-forties, as well as our own, we need more equipment than ignorance about the lives of the novelists. It will be necessary first to consider such matters as the status of the novel at this time; the relation of author and public, especially as seen in certain methods of publication; the areas of exploration allowed and forbidden to the novelists.

[1] *Fraser's* (December 1850), p. 704. There is, however, a biographical notice in Charles Knight's *Cyclopædia of Biography* (6 vols., 1858), and perhaps earlier ones.

[2] Letter of Jane Carlyle to Thomas Carlyle, 14 January 1848 (first printed in L. and E. Hanson, *Necessary Evil* (1952), p. 360). This is the earliest record of a persistent rumour; see also Thackeray, *Letters*, ii. 441, 697.

§ 5

One reason why the novel is particularly interesting in the eighteen-forties is that it was in process of becoming the dominant form. In the eighteen-forties critics began to say what they continued to say more forcibly for the next forty years or so, that the novel was the form of expression most suited to the age—'the vital offspring of modern wants and tendencies'[1]—that it had become what the epic and the drama had been in previous ages:

The novel is now what the drama was in the reigns of Elizabeth and James I;[2]

and

The ground once covered by the Epic and the Drama is now occupied by the multiform and multitudinous novel.[3]

People were very conscious of progress and change; they were beginning to be interested in extinct forms of life, 'vestiges of creation', and by analogy put the epic among them. In 1842 Tennyson, refusing to write an epic, comments,

> Nature brings not back the mastodon
> Nor we those times.[4]

When a Victorian poet did approach the epic, as

[1] *Prospective Review* (1850), p. 495.

[2] Op. cit. (1849), p. 37. This writer anticipates that the novel will 'be the form in which much of the poetry of a coming time will be written'.

[3] *Christian Remembrancer* (April 1848), p. 405; and cf. *Blackwood's* (October 1848), p. 462. Carlyle had said the same thing much earlier: 'We have then, in place of the wholly dead modern Epic, the partially living modern Novel' ('Biography', in *Fraser's* (1832), collected 1839).

[4] 'Morte d'Arthur', in *Poems* (1842).

Browning did in *The Ring and the Book*, he was obviously affected by the novel: Browning first offered the material to one novelist, Miss Ogle;[1] and another, Henry James, has told us how he would have used it.[2] And what is true of *The Ring and the Book* is true of innumerable narratives in verse, the outstanding instance of which is Clough's *Bothie*. How far the novel really was taking over the original functions of drama and epic is a larger question into which I am not entering. The decline of the drama, as has been often said, assisted the rise of the novel, and it is probable that some of the novelists in our period, notably Dickens, would have enjoyed being dramatists had the conditions of the theatre, financial and otherwise, been more favourable.

The dominant literary form of an age has its dangers as well as its rewards. It tends to attract talents, especially minor talents, that in other ages would have found other media or perhaps not literary media at all; some of the 'silly' lady novelists, as George Eliot suggests, would at other periods have stuck to letters, diaries, and gossip. Especially in the eighteen-forties did it attract writers with an axe to grind: 'Whoever has anything to say, or thinks he has . . . puts it forthwith into the shape of a novel or a tale.'[3] The significance of this mass of propaganda novels must be considered later; it is enough at present to mention one extreme, if obscure instance—

---

[1] H. W. Griffin and H. C. Minchin, *Life of Robert Browning* (1910) p. 229.

[2] 'The Novel in *The Ring and the Book*', in *Notes on Novelists* (1914).

[3] *Fraser's* (November 1850), p. 574. See below, pp. 115 ff.

Mrs. Frewin's anonymous tale of 1849, *The In-heritance of Evil, or The Consequences of Marrying a Deceased Wife's Sister*. But this kind of novel is only one among many; within the novel, there is as yet no dominant type, but a surging variety of material and method, new fashions jostling old, new ground broken in time, place, purpose, and social class.

The demand for novels was larger than ever before.

Novels [said a writer in *Blackwood's*] are not objected to as they were; now that every sect in politics and religion have found their efficacy as a means, the form is adopted by all.[1]

The general embargo on novel-reading had gone except in a few circles—it was a freedom which was later to forge its own fetters. Looking back from the seventies, Trollope noted that in his youth in the twenties 'the families in which an unrestricted per-mission was given for the reading of novels were very few, and from many they were altogether banished'.[2] Queen Victoria, we may remember, was allowed to read no novels in her youth except Hannah More's: her first real novel was *The Bride of Lammermoor*. In 1847 *Fraser's* said that thirty years earlier

every novel came into the world with a brand upon it. The trail of the Minerva Press was over all. . . . To the largest part of the reading public . . . the novel, like the pole-cat, was known only by name and a reputation for bad odour.[3]

By the eighteen-forties the change was complete. It was Scott more than any other novelist who had been

---

[1] October 1848, p. 462.

[2] *Autobiography*, ch. xii. The *Saturday Review* (24 February 1866) referred to the change as 'wonderful'.

[3] *Fraser's* (September 1847), p. 345.

responsible, and through the breach that he had made rushed Dickens.

§ 6

Besides the wide popular demand, we may note the beginnings of serious criticism of novels; in the quarterlies and the monthlies several novels would be reviewed together in a long article, and the critics tried, with varying success, to sift, group, and generalize on the mass of current fiction. The most interesting novel-criticism is to be found in *Fraser's*; the outstanding reviewer, here and later in the *Westminster Review* and the weekly *Leader*, being George Henry Lewes.[1] But *Blackwood's*, the *Prospective*, the *North British Review*,[2] and many other periodicals also took novels seriously. It was difficult for critics to keep pace, and it is not surprising that they did not get very far in establishing critical standards; they had very little tradition to guide them. Even now we can hardly be said to have an adequate aesthetic of the novel. The few accepted formulas are tools that as often as not break in our hands: as Virginia Woolf said, writing in 1927,

if fiction is . . . in difficulties, it may be because nobody grasps her firmly and defines her severely. She has had no rules drawn up for her, very little thinking done on her behalf. And though rules may be wrong and must be broken, they have this advantage—they confer dignity and order upon their

---

[1] For details, see Morris Greenhut in *Studies in Philology*, xlv. 3 (July 1948), 491–511; and Anna Kitchel, *George Lewes and George Eliot* (1933).

[2] To which one contributor was Nassau Senior, who collected his reviews in *Essays on Fiction* (1864).

subject; they admit her to a place in civilized society; they prove that she is worthy of consideration.[1]

This lack of a 'place' may be the novel's own fault, in that it has 'swallowed all formulas'. Certainly there is no Aristotle, no Johnson, no Coleridge in this field of criticism, though the critic of novels can learn from all of these. (It is noteworthy that Arnold, the greatest Victorian critic, never writes about English novels.) Not that we lack *writing* about novels—we have historical surveys, studies of particular novelists, or strings of them; but all are largely descriptive, and hardly attempt to provide a critical system. Some of the materials for constructing such a system may be found in Flaubert's letters; some in Henry James's reviews of novels, articles on novelists, and in his classic essay 'The Art of Fiction'—whose date and occasion, however, somewhat restrict its scope. Restricted also, this time by the creator's bias, are the prefaces he wrote for his novels in their collected form. But James was asking the right questions; his criticism must be the chief source of any future aesthetic of the novel—as it is already of the critical system of Mr. Percy Lubbock in his *Craft of Fiction*.

One reason for the comparative poverty of criticism of novels and the lack of dignity which Virginia Woolf ascribed to fiction is the difficulty of detaching the novel as art from the novel as pastime, or, to use Collingwood's terms, 'art proper' and 'amusement art', one arising from imagination and the other from make-believe. It is some such distinction that underlies the epigram 'Literature is a luxury, fiction is a

[1] *The Moment and Other Essays* (1947), p. 90

necessity'—a distinction perhaps to be borne in mind
rather than enforced (how many day-dreams of writer
and reader get into *Jane Eyre*?). There is something
in common in the reader's response to whatever
novels he enjoys, on whatever level. Where does the
devotee shade off into the addict? We had better
admit that in all novel-reading there is an element of
indulgence. Hence, partly, the endeavours of many
early nineteenth-century parents (and a few at all
periods) to ban it entirely, for abstinence is found
easier to enforce than temperance. Any lines that are
drawn will seem absurd—the prohibition of novel-
reading in the mornings, or on Sundays, the allowing of Scott but not Dumas, of three-volume novels
from Mudie's but not 'railway novels' from W. H.
Smith. Macaulay's father forbade novel-reading to
his daughters in the daytime 'except during Tom's
holidays', and compared it to 'drinking drams in the
morning'.[1] The control of novel-reading was as tick-

---

[1] G. O. Trevelyan, *Life and Letters of Lord Macaulay* (1876), ch. i.
The classic instance of prohibition in the mid-nineteenth century is that
in the home of Edmund Gosse in the fifties; the only fiction he read before
the age of eleven was some pages of a sensational novel which he found in
the lining of an old trunk. In his later boyhood, when his father had re-
married, one or two curious exceptions were made: Michael Scott's *Tom
Cringle's Log*, and the novels of Dickens but not Scott (*Father and Son*,
1907, chs. ii, ix, x). Gosse's parents were Plymouth Brethren; in other
Dissenting circles, the single exception was *Uncle Tom's Cabin* (Nassau
Senior, *Essays on Fiction*, 1864, p. 436). The situation in Anglican house-
holds is reflected in Charlotte Yonge's novels (e.g. *Scenes and Characters*,
1847, ch. iii; *The Young Stepmother*, 1856–7, ch. iv; *Magnum Bonum*,
1879, ch. lx).

'Railway novels' made their appearance in the late forties; one popular
series was Routledge's *Railway Library*, a shilling series of reprinted fiction starting in 1849. W. H. Smith secured a monopoly of the bookstalls
on the London and North-Western system in 1851, and by 1862 had

lish as the control of sweetmeats. This was indeed a
favourite analogy: Trollope said that people read
novels 'as men eat pastry after dinner—not without
some inward conviction that the taste is vain if not
vicious'.[1] 'Oh, delightful novels, well-remembered!'
exclaimed Thackeray, 'sweet and delicious as the
raspberry open tarts of boyhood';[2] and again, 'Novels
are sweets'—with the significant addition, 'All people
with healthy literary appetites love them—almost all
women;—a vast number of clever, hard-headed
men.'[3] One of such men was Henry Crabb Robinson, inveterate novel-reader, as his diary records, for
seventy years. 'A novel to me,' he says (repeating
Zachary Macaulay's sterner image), 'is like a dram
to others.' He read novels whether he liked them or
not, the mark of the true addict: 'I have unluckily
entangled myself into reading Shirley which I do not
much like.' At the age of ninety, in 1865, he was re-
reading *Vanity Fair* in bed: 'But reading by candlelight is so dangerous if I hold the candle in my hand.'[4]
Or there is William George Clark, reviewing a new
novel by an unknown author:

We took up *Jane Eyre* one winter's evening, somewhat
piqued at the extravagant commendations we had heard, and

covered most of the important railways; his care in selecting books earned
him the nicknames of 'The North Western Missionary' and 'Old
Morality' (Herbert Maxwell, *Life and Times of the Right Honourable
William Henry Smith, M.P.*, 2 vols., 1893, i. 52 ff.; on 'railway novels'
generally, see Charles Knight, *Passages in a Working Life* (3 vols. 1864–5),
iii, ch. i.   [1] *Autobiography*, ch. xii.

[2] *Roundabout Papers*, 'On a Peal of Bells'.

[3] Op. cit., 'On a Lazy Idle Boy'.

[4] *Books and their Writers*, ed. Edith Morley (2 vols., 1938), ii. 805, 693,
816.

sternly resolved to be as critical as Croker. But as we read on we forgot both commendations and criticism, identified ourselves with Jane in all her troubles, and finally married Mr. Rochester about four in the morning.[1]

But the fact itself is both commendation and criticism. This pleasure, this indulgence in sweets and pastry, this 'dram-drinking', which starts as an obstacle to serious criticism, is perhaps itself the main critical principle. As Trollope says, 'The novelist may not be dull. . . . The writer of stories must please, or he will be nothing.'[2] And he finds support from a very different novelist, Henry James: 'The only obligation to which in advance we may hold a novel . . . is that it be interesting.'[3] Criticism begins when this interest is subjected to cool examination: what do you reread in bed by candlelight when you know who marries whom and what is behind the black veil?

§ 7

One important difference between the reading public of the eighteen-forties and that of today is the much less obvious gaps separating different grades of novel-readers. The position today is indicated in a remark from a recent survey of the novel since 1939:

I have written as an intellectual addressing other intellectuals; one tract of fiction I have therefore omitted: the best-sellers.[4]

[1] *Fraser's* (December 1849), p. 692; compare Thackeray, in *Roundabout Papers*, 'The Last Sketch'.

[2] *Autobiography*, ch. xii.   [3] 'The Art of Fiction' (1884).

[4] Henry Reed, *The Novel since 1939* (1946), p. 7.

Such a remark could not have been made in the eighteen-forties, when almost all the great novels were best-sellers, either at once or within a few years, and have remained so. The obvious obstacle to any such distinction in the eighteen-forties is, of course, Dickens, whose highest achievements stand, like Shakespeare's, on the broadest possible base of popularity.[1] With the possible exception of Emily Brontë, the eighteen-forties produced no novelist who was both great and esoteric. Writing in *Blackwood's* in 1855, Mrs. Oliphant was to note that Hawthorne made the mistake of addressing an intellectual audience, when 'the novelist's true audience is the common people—the people of ordinary comprehension and everyday sympathies, whatever their rank may be'[2]—in other words, Dr. Johnson's 'common reader'.

It was to this public that Dickens addressed himself, one might think with no principle in mind except the traditional advice of the old actor: 'Make 'em laugh; make 'em cry; make 'em wait.'

§ 8

In the forties the author had several methods of getting his books into the hands of the public.[3] Three

[1] His novels reached even the illiterate; Mrs. Hogarth's charwoman, who lodged at a snuff-shop, attended a monthly tea at which the landlord read the new number of *Dombey* to the assembled lodgers (Forster, v. 7).

[2] 'Modern Novelists—great and small', May 1855, p. 565.

[3] Little attention has been paid to these—relatively little even by bibliographers. But see Michael Sadleir, *Trollope a Bibliography* (1928); *XIXth Century Fiction* (2 vols., 1951); *Victorian Fiction* (catalogue of an

such methods are illustrated by the four novels studied in Part II, and a fourth by Kingsley's *Yeast*.

The commonest material form in which a reader of the eighteen-forties met a new novel, as at almost any time in the nineteenth century, was that taken by '*Jane Eyre: An Autobiography*. Edited by Currer Bell'. This novel was in three small 'post octavo' volumes—like David Copperfield's first novel, 'compact in three indiwidual wollumes'[1]—the usual format for novels since about 1830. By modern standards the volumes seem small and squat—like bound Penguins, but with better margins and more lead between the lines. Their most surprising feature is their price—a guinea and a half for the three. Surprising, until one realizes the dominance of the circulating libraries, and their interest in keeping book prices high.[2] Then as now, very few people *bought* new fiction in volume form; and of these, fewer still would feel inclined to buy a novel by an unknown writer—really unknown, for the poems of Currer, Ellis, and Acton Bell, published in the previous year, had only two buyers and three reviews. But after reading early reviews of *Jane Eyre*, the reader would probably order a copy of it from his circulating library.[3] By the eighteen-forties

exhibition arranged by John Carter and Michael Sadleir, 1947); Graham Pollard, *Serial Fiction* in *New Paths in Book Collecting* (1934). The *Cambridge Bibliography* is erratic in noting the original form of publication, especially for minor novelists.

[1] Ch. li.

[2] See Michael Sadleir, *Bibliographical Aspects of the Victorian Novel* (1937) (typescript in British Museum), and the sources referred to above.

[3] It was advertised in the *Athenæum* (13 November 1847), p. 1162, as 'Now ready at all the libraries'; a review in *Tait's Edinburgh Magazine* (May 1848), pp. 346-8, says that few circulating libraries are without it.

the circulating library was everywhere—Thackeray's
verses were apt:

> In the romantic little town of Highbury
> My father kep a circulating library.[1]

And the subscription rates were very moderate—for
new novels only one guinea a year. The separate
volumes made for convenience of fireside reading,
and for sharing among members of a family; though
it would be exasperating to finish volume I, which
ends at the point where Jane rescues Mr. Rochester
from his blazing bed, when one's elder sister had not
quite finished volume II. For the three-volume form
matched a formal literary design: in many novels the
structural divisions are as clear as the three acts of a
play.

Less common were novels in two volumes. One of
these was *Mary Barton*. It was included in a well-
known series, 'Chapman and Hall's Series of Original
Works';[2] although anonymous, it might be more
likely than *Jane Eyre* to take immediate buyers, for its
sub-title, 'A Tale of Manchester Life', was in 1848
highly topical; and its price was eighteen shillings.

The publication of a new novel in one volume was
rare; the unpopularity of this form with publishers
(again, thanks to the tyranny of the libraries) may

---

[1] *Letters*, iv. 356.
[2] This had originated in 1843, as 'Chapman and Hall's Monthly
Series', an interesting compromise between part-issue and volume publication; novels were announced, and a few published, in four monthly parts
at three shillings each. Sadleir has shown that this was 'a conscious attempt to break the conventional fiction-price and fiction-format', defeated,
like earlier ventures, by the dominance of the libraries (*XIXth Century
Fiction*, ii. 132).

have been one cause of the rejection of Charlotte
Brontë's *The Professor*. The one-volume form normally signalized a cheap reprint, usually appearing
two or three years after first publication;[1] it seems
also to have been used for certain special types of
novel, perhaps less likely to find favour with library
subscribers—religious novels[2] and tales intended to
appeal to younger as well as older readers.[3]

In the same year as *Mary Barton* another method
of publication—that of the magazine serial—is
illustrated by the fifth novel mentioned above. In
the July number of *Fraser's Magazine for Town and
Country*, a half-crown monthly of independent views,
appeared anonymously the first instalment of *Yeast:
or the Thoughts, Sayings and Doings of Lancelot Smith,
Gentleman*; it was concluded in six instalments (rather
less than Kingsley had intended) by December. So
for fifteen shillings the reader had good value.

But if the would-be novel-reader had no library
subscription, and took in no magazine, he could still
have his new novels. In any month of 1847, he
might see in the bookshops, in paper wrappers,

[1] The *Parlour Library* (1847–63), an early venture in cheap fiction
series, in shilling volumes of 'about 320 pages', published monthly, included 'works of fiction, by the most celebrated authors'; most of its early
volumes were reprints or translations, but vol. i and vol. xi were new works
by the Irishman William Carleton. It was advertised as 'universally proclaimed by the press of Great Britain, the cheapest ever published'
(*Athenæum*, 11 December 1847, p. 1284).

[2] *Loss and Gain* (1848), *The Nemesis of Faith* (1849).

[3] Examples are Harriett Mozley's *Louisa* (1842), Charlotte Yonge's
Abbeychurch (1844) and *Scenes and Characters* (1847); these overlap with
the first group and, like *Loss and Gain*, were published by Burns, who
also included new religious fiction in his series, *The Englishman's Library*.

greenish blue or bright yellow, for only one shilling, the
current monthly parts of *Dealings | with the Firm of |
Dombey and Son | Wholesale, Retail, and for Exporta-
tion | By Charles Dickens* and *Vanity Fair | Pen and
Pencil Sketches of English Society | By W. M. Thackeray.*
That was the form in which these two novels made
their first appearance; and it was that form which so
greatly extended the novel-reading public, by the
simple device of spreading and lowering the cost—
the total cost for a work equal in length to a 'three-
decker' came to £1. No wonder that a critic of 1851
remarked (prematurely, however) that the three-
volume novel was ' "going out with the tide", being
superseded by the periodical novel, a cheaper article'.[1]
In other ways these two forms of publication—magazine serial and part-issue—increased the popularity
of the novel. The suspense induced by 'making 'em
wait' was intensified by being prolonged—to see
what happened next the reader had to wait a month
at a time. All novel-readers know the temptation to
turn to the end: here is a confession of Thackeray's
(a double confession):

> In the days of the old three-volume novels, didn't you
> always look at the end, to see that Louisa and the Earl (or
> young clergyman, as the case might be) were happy? If they
> died, or met with other grief . . . I put the book away.[2]

But during publication in parts there was no end to
turn to—which some readers found an added pleasure: Disraeli's Lord Montfort, for instance:

> I like books that come out in numbers, as there is a little

[1] *Fraser's* (January 1851), p. 75.   [2] *Philip,* ch. xxiii.

suspense, and you cannot deprive yourself of all interest by glancing at the last page of the last volume.[1]

Often the end was not even written, perhaps not predetermined: for this and other reasons, publication in parts induced, as I hope to show, a kind of contact between author and reader unknown today.

In the eighteen-forties neither of these forms of publication was quite new. The monthly part as a method of publishing new fiction had become established only in the late eighteen-thirties; but its ancestors are found in two very different types of part-issue common in the eighteenth and early nineteenth century. First, the very cheap part-issue of reprints of popular fiction now famous from Hazlitt's reference:

The world I had found out in Cooke's edition of the British Novelists [1792] was to me a dance through life, a perpetual gala-day. The sixpenny numbers of this work regularly contrived to leave off just in the middle of a sentence, and in the nick of a story, where Tom Jones discovers Square behind the blanket. . . .[2]

Secondly, there was the expensive part-issue of new and finely illustrated works, often architectural and

---

[1] *Endymion* (1880), iii. 1.

[2] 'On Reading Old Books', *London Magazine* (February 1821); collected in *The Plain Speaker* (1826). Besides Cooke's series there was *Harrison's Novelist's Magazine* (1780–8), and in our period a well-known and remarkably cheap publication, the twopenny weekly *Romancist, and Novelist's Library* (1839–40, 1841–2). See further Pollard, op. cit., pp. 259–61, and Sadleir, *XIXth Century Fiction*, ii (Section 3), pp. 135–7, 141–5. Of these series, Edward Lloyd's weekly part-issues of sensational new fiction are the obvious descendants.

topographical. Fielding refers to such publications in
Joseph Andrews:

> Homer was the first inventor of the art which hath so long
> lain dormant, of publishing by numbers; an art now brought
> to such perfection, that even dictionaries are divided and ex-
> hibited piecemeal to the public.[1]

If fiction was published with illustrations in this way
—'raffish colour-plate books of the *Tom and Jerry*
type',[2] the emphasis was on the illustrations. It is an
offshoot of this second type that we find when, late
in 1835, the publishers Chapman and Hall planned
with an artist called Seymour 'a series of cockney
sporting plates of a superior sort' to be accompanied
by letter-press and published in monthly parts. The
scheme hung fire for a while, until they thought of a
young author who had written a series of sketches of
cockney life in the *Monthly Magazine* and *Morning
Chronicle*, and put before him the general notion of a
'Nimrod club of sportsmen'. The young author knew
little about sport, and asked for a freer hand and a
wider range of English scenes and people; as a concession he would keep the general idea of a club—
'My views being deferred to, I thought of Mr. Pickwick'—and *The Posthumous Papers of the Pickwick
Club* were accordingly begun.[3] The artist died suddenly after the second number, and his place was
taken by Hablot K. Browne ('Phiz') who was to be

---

[1] 1742; ii. 1. These continued throughout the nineteenth century; by
the forties they were often of a cheap, 'useful-knowledge' type, like
Charles Knight's *New Orbis Pictus.*

[2] Sadleir, *Bibliographical Aspects of Victorian Fiction* (unpaged).

[3] Preface to cheap edition, 1847; quoted Forster, i. 5.

long associated with Dickens. In this type of part-issue the artist is normally the dominating partner. But by the accidents of the publishers' choice of author and the first artist's death, the balance between writer and artist was changed, and it was not as a series of superior plates accompanied by letter-press that even its earliest readers thought of the *Pickwick Papers*. The letter-press so caught the public interest that it not only fairly launched Dickens on his career, but initiated a virtually new method of publishing fiction, and established in the public the habit of buying novels as well as borrowing them. Only a limited demand was expected: the binder prepared 400 copies of the first number, but by the time the fifteenth was reached, over 40,000 were required.[1] Dickens leapt into fame: everyone read *Pickwick*. Emily Eden, the sister of the Governor General, found it 'the only fun in India', and read it in numbers 'not more than ten times';[2] Alexander Bain read it in his Natural History class 'out of the professor's sight';[3] Dr. Arnold complained to his neighbour Wordsworth that his boys at Rugby thought of nothing but 'Bozzy's next number';[4] Captain Brown in *Cranford* was run over by a railway train while reading his copy of the current number.

[1] Forster, ii. 1; T. Hatton and A. H. Cleaver, *A Bibliography of the Periodical Works of Charles Dickens* (1933), p. 6.

[2] *Miss Eden's Letters*, ed. Violet Dickinson (1919), p. 298. She says, 'there has been a Calcutta reprint, lithographs and all'.

[3] *Autobiography* (1904), p. 53; account of the winter session 1837-8 at Marischal College, Aberdeen.

[4] *Letters of William and Dorothy Wordsworth: the Later Years* (1939), iii. 1120; and cf. Arnold's letter to Cornish, 6 July 1839, in Stanley's *Life*, ch. ix.

After such success, it was natural that Dickens should retain this pattern of publication as a kind of trade-mark. For eight of his novels, the pattern is uniform—a shilling monthly part of thirty-two pages, generally with two plates,[1] the work completed in twenty monthly parts issued as nineteen, the concluding part being a double number at two shillings. Throughout the period of Dickens's working life, from 1836 to 1870, when he died after writing the sixth of the projected twelve numbers of *Edwin Drood*, the monthly part-issue was a fairly popular method of distribution.[2] The public liked it for its cheapness and perhaps also for its particular qualities of suspense. The publishers liked it for various financial reasons—high circulation, spreading and elasticity of costs, payments from advertisers (each part carried extra leaves of general advertisements), independence of lending libraries. The author liked it both for its large financial rewards—which reached him while he was

[1] Except for *Pickwick*, Nos. I–II.

[2] Examples include a few novels of Mrs. Trollope, Ainsworth, Marryat; most of Surtees; Thackeray's *Vanity Fair* and *Pendennis*. After 1850 there are *The Newcomes* (1853–5) and *The Virginians* (1857–9), Trollope's *Can You Forgive Her?* (1864–5) and *The Way We Live Now* (1874–5). The failure of *The Vicar of Bullhampton* (1869–70) in this form marks the decline of the part-issue. A new modification appears with George Eliot's *Middlemarch* (eight five-shilling parts at irregular intervals in 1871–2) and *Daniel Deronda* (1876). This form was imitated by Trollope's *Prime Minister* (1875–6).

Part-issue was not confined to novels; the greatest autobiography of the century, Newman's *Apologia*, was published in eight weekly parts, and Browning's *The Ring and the Book* in four monthly volumes, on the stated grounds that he wished people 'not to turn to the end', but to have 'time to read and digest . . . but not to forget what has gone before' (*William Allingham A Diary*, 1907, p. 181).

writing—for reducing the risk of piracy, and for the warmth of contact with his readers.

In the end one cheap form of publication devoured the other; the part-issue was driven off the market by its rival the magazine serial. When *Macmillan's Magazine* and the *Cornhill*, costing a shilling[1] instead of half-a-crown, were founded in 1859–60, the doom of the part-issue was in sight; for the reader could now get his instalment of a novel and much else besides at the same price.[2]

The history of the magazine serial is a much longer one, extending through the eighteenth century to our own day and adorned by great names such as Meredith, Hardy, and Henry James. Reprinted fiction had appeared in eighteenth-century magazines; the first new novel to appear in that form was Smollett's *Sir Lancelot Greaves* in *The British Magazine* (1760–1). Later, in the eighteen-thirties, Marryat had several serials running; *Oliver Twist* ran through twenty-four numbers of *Bentley's Miscellany*; and by 1840 serials are usual in the half-crown monthlies; *Fraser's*, for example, had Thackeray's *Catherine* (1839–40)

---

[1] An earlier venture in the field was *Douglas Jerrold's Shilling Magazine* (1845–8) with serials by Jerrold, R. H. Horne, and others, as well as articles, short stories, reviews, and poems. According to Jerrold's biographer (Blanchard Jerrold, *The Life and Remains of Douglas Jerrold*, 1859, ch. x) this was at first successful, but fell off later because Jerrold had so many other irons in the fire. But in any case it was probably too radical, and too 'low', to offer a serious challenge to the half-crown monthlies in that period.

[2] See Trollope, *Autobiography*, ch. xv. Serials in the *Cornhill* included *Framley Parsonage*, *Lovel the Widower*, *Philip*, *Romola*, and *Wives and Daughters*; in *Macmillan's*, Hughes's *Tom Brown at Oxford*, and Kingsley's *Water Babies*.

and *The Luck of Barry Lyndon* (1844). At first, they tend to be shorter works than the novels issued in parts—may even, like Thackeray's *Shabby Genteel Story* (1840), be long short-stories completed in about six instalments. Cheaper and more specialized periodicals also carried serials; several early tales and novels of Charlotte Yonge, for example, appear in the monthly *Magazine for the Young*, the *Churchman's Companion*, and a little later in the *Monthly Packet* under her own editorship.

At a still lower rate, the new popular weekly papers were providing serial fiction for the masses. At the price of a penny, the reader could have his fill of serial romance, along with much improving and informative matter, in (for example) the *Family Herald*, *Lloyd's Penny Weekly Miscellany*, or *Reynolds' Miscellany*. The interest of these serials may be mainly sub-literary;[1] but such periodicals helped to prepare the way for Dickens's twopenny weekly *Household*

[1] They tend to reflect fashions that were dying out in serious novels; many are historical, others 'Gothic', like Reynolds's *Wagner, the Wehr-Wolf*, others again pseudo-Society like *Julia Tremaine*. But they should not be confused with the later 'penny dreadfuls', deliberately aimed at the juvenile market. James Malcolm Rymer (identified in the British Museum catalogue) also wrote *Varney the Vampire* (published in weekly part-issues) but his several serials in *Lloyd's Penny Weekly Miscellany* are not particularly horrific. Of these, *Ada, the Betrayed* was a favourite of the schoolboy D. G. Rossetti, along with two historical serials by Pierce Egan —*Robin Hood* and *Wat Tyler* (W. M. Rossetti, *Dante Gabriel Rossetti, his Family-Letters, with a Memoir*, 2 vols., 1895, i. 82). The cheap romantic fiction of the forties and fifties offers a virtually unexplored field to bibliographers and literary and social historians. The competition between it and cheap instructive series is described by Charles Knight, in *The Old Printer and the Modern Press* (1854), and *Passages in a Working Life* (3 vols., 1864–5).

Words, started in 1850, with Mrs. Gaskell as an early contributor.[1]

So far as the reader was concerned, there was little difference between periodical serializing and monthly part-issue;[2] but the author ran the risk of subservience to editorial policy. Later instances of this will spring to mind—the trouble which led to the withdrawing of Trollope's *Rachel Ray* from *Good Words*, Hardy's difficulties with *Tess* in the *Graphic*. But the less strict standards of 1848 already provide one instance: the editor of *Fraser's* asked Kingsley to shorten *Yeast*[3] because some readers were threatening to cancel their subscription. Kingsley had to comply, but published the complete version in book form with further additions in 1851. There was no such drawback when the editor wrote his own serials, as Dickens did later when he ran *Hard Times* in *Household Words*, *A Tale of Two Cities* and *Great Expectations* in *All the Year Round*. (But Dickens was severe with contributors, and had particular difficulty with Mrs. Gaskell over *North and South* in 1855:[4]—'If I were Mr. G. O Heaven how I would beat her!' The difficulty here was aesthetic—Dickens's insistence that each weekly instalment should end at an arresting point, a tough order especially for so leisurely an author.)

[1] *Lizzie Leigh* (1850), *Cranford* (1851–3), *North and South* (1854–5).

[2] The part-issue was of course longer than the monthly magazine instalment, and that was longer than the weekly instalment; and the shorter the unit, the greater the emphasis on 'climax'. Dickens often chafed at the restrictions of the weekly instalment; see Appendix I, pp. 314–15 below.

[3] *Charles Kingsley; his letters and memories of his life*, edited by his wife (1877), ch. vii; letter to John Conington, 19 December 1848.

[4] See A. B. Hopkins, 'Dickens and Mrs. Gaskell', *Huntington Library Quarterly*, ix. 4 (August 1946), pp. 366–76.

§ 9

Serial publication, as I have said, induced a close relation between author and reader—in Thackeray's words, a 'communion between the writer and the public . . . something continual, confidential, something like personal affection'.[1] Dickens showed his own awareness of it in his prefatory note to the concluding number of *Dombey and Son:*

I cannot forego my usual opportunity of saying farewell to my readers in this greeting-place, though I have only to acknowledge the unbounded warmth and earnestness of their sympathy in every stage of the journey we have just concluded.[2]

And so did Thackeray in his preface to *Pendennis* when it was published in book form:

in his constant communication with the reader the writer is forced into a frankness of expression, and to speak out his own mind and feelings as they urge him. . . . It is a sort of confidential talk between writer and reader.

(This has an obvious bearing on Thackeray's apparent garrulity.) The prolonging of this intercommunication over eighteen months or more enforced the effect of contact; there was a sense of long familiar association—in which, as one reviewer said, a 'sort of tenderness' came to be felt even for the 'covers of the monthly instalments'.[3]

[1] 'A Box of Novels', *Fraser's* (February 1844); *Works*, vi. He is speaking, with his usual generosity, of Dickens.

[2] Cf. Albert Smith's farewell in *The Pottleton Legacy* (1849), referring to 'the continuous intercourse from month to month . . . establishing a tie which is not willingly broken'.

[3] Review of *Dombey* in *The Sun* (13 April 1848). George Eliot was

The response of the public to each instalment was lively. Each number, said a contemporary critic,

is anticipated with more anxiety than the Indian Mail, and is a great deal more talked about when it does come.[1]

Evidence of such talk exists abundantly; contemporary letters and memoirs testify to the buzz of excited discussion between the numbers in mansion and parsonage, college and cottage. 'Will Nelly die? I think she should , writes Lady Stanley to her daughter-in-law.[2] Some of this buzz reached the author in letters—it is the beginning of 'fan mail'.[3] One admirer wrote to Dickens, to 'counsel him to develop the character [of Sam Weller] largely—to the utmost'.[4] The original of Miss Mowcher in *David Copperfield* wrote to protest, so that the character is altered between chapters xxii and xxxii.[5] Thackeray received complaints that *Vanity Fair* contained too much Amelia, and entreaties that Laura in *Pendennis* might marry Warrington, and that Clive Newcome might marry Ethel. ('What could a fellow do? So many people wanted 'em married'.)[6]

Publication in numbers also afforded evidence of

'convinced that the slow plan of publication [of *Middlemarch*]' was 'of immense advantage . . . in deepening the impression' (letter of 4 August 1872).   [1] *Fraser's* (January 1851), p. 75.

[2] *The Ladies of Alderley*, ed. N. Mitford (1938), p. 2; letter of 27 January 1841.

[3] And like fan mail it is found at all literary levels. The author of *Ada, the Betrayed* thanked 'over two hundred ladies and gentlemen' for their letters (*Lloyd's Penny Weekly Miscellany*, 1843, No. 52).

[4] William Jerdan, *An Autobiography* (1852), iv. 364.

[5] Cf. Forster, vi. 7, and K. J. Fielding in *The Listener* (9 July 1951) with new letters.   [6] *Letters*, iii. 465 n.

fluctuating sales, and to this Dickens was especially alert. When sales fell for the early numbers of *Martin Chuzzlewit* (perhaps because he had lost readers over the previous experiment of *Master Humphrey's Clock*),[1] he sent Martin to America, and watched them revive a little; when they rose again after the introduction of Mrs. Gamp, he provided more of her. Thackeray cared less for such evidence, but was not less conscious of it. The fact that 'subscribers left him' when Pendennis was shown as meeting temptation probably strengthened him in his determination. But to Dickens declining sales brought a sense of insecurity, not only financial but creative. The accounts after the second number of *Our Mutual Friend* showed a fall, and this left him, he said, 'going round and round like a carrier pigeon, before swooping on number seven'[2] (the number he was then about to write). But the stimulus of rising sales was a much more usual experience, carrying him forward on a wave of confidence. It was not the mere desire for money, nor even the mere desire to please, though he felt both strongly; rather the sense of a sympathetic, applauding public seems to have been profoundly necessary to him. The editing of cheap weeklies, the producing and acting of plays (not for money but for charity), and above all, the public readings from his books, tell the same story. These readings, first thought of in 1846, were begun

---

[1] Forster, iv. 2. A modern scholar has attributed the fall to *American Notes* (Ada B. Nisbet, 'The Mystery of *Martin Chuzzlewit*', in *Essays . . . dedicated to Lily B. Campbell*, University of California Press, 1950).

[2] Forster, ix. 5; letter of 10 June 1863.

in 1853, and continued against all advice, friendly
and medical, until the year of his death—for which
they were at least partly to blame. Nothing could
compete with the intoxication of actually *seeing* the
audience responding, with laughter and tears, even
swoons and fits, to Sam Weller and Mrs. Gamp, little
Nell and Paul Dombey, Bill Sikes and Nancy. But
though this became an almost morbid satisfaction,
it sprang from a need he felt as a literary artist, a
need of which I believe serial publication first made
him conscious. In the serial-writer's relation to his
public there is indeed something of the stimulating
contact which an actor or a public speaker receives
from an audience. Serial publication gave back to
story-telling its original context of performance, the
context that Chaucer, for example, knew and exploited (the units of his narrative are often like serial
instalments, and his confiding yet reserved relation
with his audience is often like Thackeray's). The
creative artist, as R. G. Collingwood has said, requires an audience whose function is not merely
receptive but collaborative, even 'concreative'. 'It is
a weakness of printed literature that this reciprocity
between writer and reader is difficult to maintain.'[1]
Thanks partly to serial publication it was less difficult
in the nineteenth century than now, and the novelists,
especially Dickens, drew some of their strength
from it.

It is obviously a condition of this reciprocity that
the novel should be written, as well as read, in instal-

[1] *The Principles of Art* (1938), pp. 323–4; and see the whole chapter
(xiv).

ments, month by month; while his public is reading, the novelist is writing; each number comes to the reader fresh from the author's mind, glistening with baptismal ink. 'The following pages' says Dickens in the preface to *Pickwick*, when this practice still had novelty, 'have been written from time to time, almost as the periodical occasion arose.'[1] He had no need to say it later; it was assumed, as by the innumerable readers who wrote hopefully to beg a reprieve for little Nell. This hand-to-mouth method of composition, at first sight so perilous, was habitual with both Dickens and Thackeray (except in *Esmond*); it accounts of course for their both leaving novels unfinished at their death, *Edwin Drood* and *Denis Duval*—novels partly published, but with little more in the writer's desk than had been printed. Such a method made great demands on the novelist, and the letters of both Dickens and Thackeray are strewn with references to the agony of working against time. Dickens's more exacting contracts early in his career sometimes obliged him to be writing two serials in the month, devoting a fortnight to each; after 1843 he usually contrived to be writing hard for one fortnight and spending the other, not of course in rest (for he never rested) but on other activities. During the 'writing' fortnight he would accept no engagements ('I am always a prisoner, more or less, at this time of the month')[2] and his iron will and rigorous method kept him invariably up to time. He wrote on uniform-sized 'slips', and knew how many should go

---

[1] Preface to 1837 edition.
[2] *Letters*, ii. 13; letter of 10 February 1847.

to a number;[1] on the few occasions when he mis-calculated there was a last-minute dash to the print-ing-office—once at least from the Continent—to cut or to add. (The cancelled passages still exist in proof state, and a few have already been published.[2]) But the dread of failing outright in his obligations is rare. In the autumn of 1846 the double demands of the early numbers of *Dombey* and of the promised 'Christ-mas Book' nearly defeated him. And he had once a bad moment of panic in a stationer's shop at Broad-stairs when he overheard a lady inquire for the latest number of *David Copperfield*; she was told that it would appear at the end of the month; and he knew he had not as yet written a word of it; 'Once, and but once only in my life, I was — frightened!'[3]

For Thackeray, on the other hand, panic was con-stant—he usually left his writing till the eleventh hour, having formed as a journalist the habit of working with the printer's boy at the door:

Towards the end of the month I get so nervous that I don't speak to anybody scarcely.

I always have a life-&-death struggle to get out my number of *Vanity Fair*.[4]

[1] Dickens's methods were first studied by John Butt, 'Dickens at Work', *Durham University Journal*, xl, No. 3 (June 1948); see also the same writer's 'Dickens's Notes for his Serial Parts', *The Dickensian*, xlv. 3, No. 291 (June 1949).

[2] John Butt and Kathleen Tillotson, 'Dickens at Work on *Dombey and Son*', *Essays and Studies by Members of the English Association*, N.S., iv. (1951), pp. 77–78, 92; John Butt, '*David Copperfield*: From Manuscript to Print', *R.E.S.*, N.S., i. 3 (July 1950); *The Dickensian*, xlviii. 4, No. 304 (September 1952), xlix. 1–2, Nos. 305–6 (December 1952, March 1953).

[3] W. Charles Kent, *Charles Dickens as a Reader* (1872), pp. 45–46.

[4] *Letters*, ii. 311, 346.

No wonder Charlotte Brontë refused her publisher's suggestion that she should write a serial on the grounds that she had neither the necessary confidence nor the 'unflagging animal spirits'.[1] Once only did Dickens and Thackeray fail their readers. Dickens suspended both *Pickwick* and *Oliver Twist* in 1837 when his young sister-in-law Mary Hogarth died; *Pendennis* ceased to appear for three months in 1849 during Thackeray's serious illness—anxious inquiries poured in, and the finished work is dedicated gratefully to his physician.

§ 10

The practice of serial publication did not go uncriticized. 'Art will not endure piecemeal generation'[2] is a judgement of the fifties; earlier, there were objections to 'novel-writing in scraps against time'[3] and, more pungently, to 'the monstrous anomaly of a twenty-month's labour and a piecemeal accouchement'.[4] Reviewers were not quite disinterested; part-issue put them in a difficulty. If they reviewed the novel during publication, they risked premature judgement; if they waited for completion, their criticism might well be superfluous.

[1] *S.H.B.* ii. 161; letter of 14 December 1847.

[2] *North British Review* (October 1855), p. 350; and see *Blackwood's* (April 1855), p. 455.   [3] *Fraser's* (April 1840), p. 400.

[4] *Fraser's* (January 1851), p. 75. In that outspoken age, this seems to have been a favourite figure; compare Douglas Jerrold's letter to Dickens in 1846: 'You have heard, I suppose, that Thackeray is big with twenty parts, and, unless he is wrong in his time, expects the first instalment at Christmas' (Blanchard Jerrold, *Life and Remains of Douglas Jerrold*, 1859, p. 265).

But it is too readily assumed that serial-writing is damaging to the artistic unity of the novel. There are advantages as well as disadvantages; novelists and critics were well aware of the problem. Trollope saw that serial publication at least prevented any 'long succession of dull pages':

The writer . . . should feel that he cannot afford to have many pages skipped out of the few which are to meet the reader's eye at the same time. Who can imagine the first half of the first volume of *Waverley* coming out in shilling numbers?[1]

Here the advantage is clear: the serial novelist must arouse interest and display his main characters in the opening number. With the opening of *Waverley* we may contrast the opening numbers of *Dombey and Son* and *Vanity Fair*, each of which presents a scene showing the major characters at a crucial point in their lives, and indicating the forces of the coming conflict. But Trollope also saw the disadvantage to the novelist of being unable to revise an early number in the light of later requirements. He himself wrote serials, but was too cautious to do his writing month by month; he refused to start publication until the whole was complete, giving as his reason that:

An artist should keep in his hand the power of fitting the beginning of his work to the end. . . . When some young lady at the end of a story cannot be made quite perfect in her conduct, that vivid description of angelic purity with which you laid down the first lines of her portrait should be slightly toned down.[2]

---

[1] *Autobiography*, ch. viii.
[2] *Autobiography*, ch. viii. The exception to Trollope's rule of writing

A commoner criticism, which came from authors as well as critics, was that the design of the whole was apt to be sacrificed to the number-unit, and especially to the need of an effective close to a number. To 'provide a certain number of these [closes] at regular intervals', said Harriet Martineau, was 'like breaking up the broad lights and shadows of a great picture, spoiling it as a composition'.[1] In addition there was the danger of the too complete climax. After the death of Paul which concluded the fifth number of *Dombey and Son*, even Dickens's admirer, Francis Jeffrey, had his doubts: 'After this climax . . . what are you to do with the fifteen that are to follow?'[2] This anxiety was certainly shared by Dickens. At the head of his notes for the succeeding part he wrote: 'Great point of the No. to throw the interest of Paul, AT ONCE ON FLORENCE.'[3] Dickens had much more concern for the design of his novels than he is commonly credited with; and so had contemporary critics—'One of the great achievements in the art of the novel is unity'.[4] But the serial novelists in general were not careless of 'unity'; they did not expect to be forgotten when the instalments were complete; they meant their novels to be read and reread in book form. *Pickwick* might be criticized as 'a discursive

is *Framley Parsonage*, serialized in the *Cornhill* at Thackeray's request, and with characteristically inadequate notice.

[1] *Autobiography*, iv. 4. Cf. Crabb Robinson, *Books and their Writers*, ed. E. J. Morley, ii. 578.

[2] Lord Cockburn, *Life of Lord Jeffrey* (1852), ii. 407.

[3] Butt and Tillotson, op. cit., p. 82; from the manuscripts in the Forster collection at the Victoria and Albert Museum.

[4] *Fraser's* (October 1851), p. 382.

rambling narrative';[1] but Dickens said in his preface
that his care was to achieve two things; while every
number should be

to a certain extent complete in itself . . . yet . . . the whole
twenty numbers, when collected, should form one tolerably
harmonious whole, each leading to the other by a gentle and
not unnatural process of adventure.[2]

As he went on, Dickens learned more and more how
to keep the larger unit in mind. Although he wrote
from month to month he was not improvising, except
in detail. The whole pre-existed in his mind. 'The
design and purpose of [*The Old Curiosity Shop* was]
distinctly marked in my mind from the commencement.'[3] In *Martin Chuzzlewit*, he assured his readers
that he had 'endeavoured to resist the temptation of
the current Monthly Number, and to keep a steadier
eye upon the general purpose and design'.[4] His letters
show further that the creative period in the writing
came some months before publication: he was 'in the
agonies of plotting and contriving' *Chuzzlewit* in
November 1842. The first intimation of *Dombey* is
characteristic:

Vague thoughts of a new book are rife within me just now;
and I go wandering about at night . . . according to my usual
propensity at such a time, seeking rest, and finding none.[5]

This was in March 1846; in April, the 'new book'

[1] *Blackwood's* (April 1855), p. 455.

[2] Preface to 1837 edition. Compare his advice to Mrs. Brookfield in
1866 (*Letters*, iii. 461–2): 'notice how . . . the thing has to be planned for
presentation in these fragments, and yet for afterwards fusing together as
an uninterrupted whole'.

[3] *Letters*, i. 305.   [4] Preface to 1844 edition.

[5] *Letters*, i. 487, 740; for later novels see, for example, ii. 338, 649, 658.

was advertised for publication, to begin in October. Four months later he had written only the first number, but was able to outline the general plan of the whole novel in a letter to Forster, 'this is what cooks call "the stock of the soup". All kinds of things will be added to it, of course.'[1] Three months after that, the first number appears.

Dickens, it is clear, had for at least some of his novels the sort of prevision that Flaubert described:

Un bon sujet de roman est celui qui vient tout d'une pièce, d'un seul jet. C'est une idée mère d'où toutes les autres découlent.[2]

Whether or not that prevision came to him so easily as Bagehot supposed of Scott is open to doubt:

The procedure of the highest genius doubtless is scarcely a procedure; the view of the whole story comes at once upon its imagination like the delicate end and the distinct beginning of some long vista.[3]

His references in letters to 'violent restlessness', 'ghostly unrest', and 'hideous state of mind' in the period of incubation suggest a more uncomfortable process. But they make it clear that he underwent the true creative agony, not the mere bustle of the pot-boiler.

Unfortunately where Thackeray is concerned we lack precise evidence on the early planning of his

[1] Forster, vi. 2; see Appendix II, pp. 316–17 below.
[2] *Correspondance, quatrième série* (Paris, 1927), pp. 463–4; letter of 1861 [?].
[3] *Literary Studies*, ii. 161 ('The Waverley Novels', 1858). Scott's methods are described by Sir Herbert Grierson, *Sir Walter Scott* (1938), pp. 128–9.

novels. But we know that an earlier version of the
first eight chapters of *Vanity Fair* (then called simply
'Pen and Pencil Sketches of English Society') was
written early in 1845 and offered in vain to more than
one publisher;[1] the design must therefore have been
partly formed two years before publication.

The principle of design in single numbers, for
both Dickens and Thackeray, is evident even without the testimony of Dickens's 'number-plans' and
Thackeray's letters. If a modern reader knows where
the number divisions fall, he can readily find examples
in plenty, and perceive their relation to the whole. It
is part of the injustice done to Dickens and Thackeray
that no modern edition supplies such information;[2]
I therefore supply it for *Dombey and Son* and *Vanity
Fair* in an Appendix (p. 318).

Within a single number, the balance is held
between varieties of narrative method—summary,
description, and presentation—and also between the
fortunes of different sets of characters. In the sixth
number of *Dombey and Son*, for example, the interest
is divided between Captain Cuttle and Walter Gay,
Florence and her father: but with no loss of unity,
for both Walter's departure and her father's neglect
mark the decline of Florence's fortunes. In the

[1] Gordon N. Ray, 'Vanity Fair', in *Essays by Divers Hands*, Royal
Society of Literature, N.S. xxv (1950), 92–93. The manuscript of these
chapters is in the Pierpont Morgan Library.

[2] A fairly close analysis of *Dombey and Son* from this point of view is
given in Butt and Tillotson, op. cit., and of *David Copperfield* in John
Butt's articles in *The Dickensian*, Nos. 294–6 (1950).

The point at which a number begins is shown (for the novels in monthly
numbers) in T. Hatton and A. H. Cleaver, *Bibliography of the Periodical
Works of Charles Dickens* (1933).

eleventh number of *Vanity Fair*, the emphasis is first
on the rise in Becky's fortunes, then on the fall in
Amelia's; the close of chapter xxxvii, in which their
two young sons meet by chance in the park, supply-
ing the transition. A study of the way the numbers
end is particularly rewarding. The sinister suggestion of Diogenes's attack on Mr. Carker at the close
of the seventh number and of Mr. Carker's thoughts
about Mr. Dombey's second marriage at the close of
the ninth show Dickens's power of raising anticipation and using the emphasis of the number-ending
to draw attention to a piece of the pattern that might
be overlooked. Sometimes he places a clinching,
almost epigrammatic sentence at the close, as in the
first and (in the original edition)[1] the fifth numbers—
'Here's to Dombey and Son—and Daughter!' says
Walter, and Miss Tox echoes 'And so Dombey and
Son really is a daughter after all!'

It goes without saying that the endings do not
deal in the grosser kinds of suspense, familiar in the
old film serials. The surprises favoured belong to the
refined sort which includes the fulfilment of what has
been unconsciously expected. Perhaps the most
magnificent curtain-line of all comes at the close of
the fourth number of *Vanity Fair*. Becky is playing
some deep game, which has not been clearly revealed;
she has left Queen's Crawley and is staying in London with old Miss Crawley, with Rawdon in atten-
dance on his aunt. Old Sir Pitt comes to visit her:

'I say agin, I want you,' Sir Pitt said, thumping the table.
'I can't git on without you. I didn't see what it was till you

---

[1] See my note in *The Dickensian*, xlvii. 2 (March 1951), pp. 81 f.

went away. The house all goes wrong. It's not the same place. All my accounts has got muddled agin. You *must* come back. Do come back. Dear Becky, do come!'

'Come—as what, Sir?' Rebecca gasped out.

'Come as Lady Crawley, if you like,' the baronet said, grasping his crape hat. 'There! will that zatusfy you? Come back and be my wife. Your vit vor't. Birth be hanged. You're as good a lady as ever I see. You've got more brains in your little vinger than any baronet's wife in the country. Will you come? Yes or no?'

'O Sir Pitt!' Rebecca said, very much moved.

'Say yes, Becky,' Sir Pitt continued. 'I'm an old man, but a good'n. I'm good for twenty years. I'll make you happy, zee if I don't. You shall do what you like; spend what you like; and 'av it all your own way. I'd make you a zettlement. I'll do everything regular. Look year!' and the old man fell down on his knees and leered at her like a satyr.

Rebecca started back a picture of consternation. In the course of this history we have never seen her lose her presence of mind; but she did now, and wept some of the most genuine tears that ever fell from her eyes.

'O Sir Pitt!' she said. 'O Sir—I—I'm *married already.*'

After this the reader's instinct is to reread the April number to discover missed clues. Even if he guesses the identity of the man, he has a month in which to speculate on the likely results of the disclosure. At the beginning of the May number Thackeray teases the reader:

Every reader of a sentimental turn (and we desire no other) must have been pleased with the *tableau* with which the last act of our little drama concluded: for what can be prettier than an image of Love on his knees before Beauty?

It is not until the end of the chapter that the name of

Becky's husband is given. Unless the modern reader is aware of that month's wait, some of Thackeray's effect is lost.

Very different in its reverberation is another surprise ending, that of the ninth, the great Waterloo number. This number includes the farewells of Rawdon and George, the departure of the regiment, Amelia's suspicions of Becky's intrigue with her husband, the rumours that come about the battle, the comedy of Jos Sedley's plans of flight from Brussels, and the 'most expensive half-hour of his life', when Becky sells him the horses. Only in the closing paragraphs of the number do we move from Brussels to the battlefield. The two last sentences of the number bring the field and city together:

> No more firing was heard at Brussels—the pursuit rolled miles away. The darkness came down on the field and city; and Amelia was praying for George, who was lying on his face, dead, with a bullet through his heart.[1]

§ 11

In Dickens's farewell to his readers[2] at the close of *Dombey and Son* he acknowledged 'the unbounded warmth and earnestness of their sympathy'; and he chose the obvious example:

> If any of them have felt a sorrow in one of the principal incidents on which this fiction turns, I hope it may be a sorrow of that sort which endears the sharers in it, one to another.

---

[1] I do not know how soon Thackeray revised this famous sentence, deleting the opening 'The'; certainly by 1853.

[2] This becomes the Preface to the first edition (1848).

This is not unselfish in me. I may claim to have felt it, at least as much as anybody else; and I would fain be remembered kindly for my part in the experience.

He was referring, of course, to the death of Paul Dombey. He had set out to 'make 'em cry', and he had succeeded. Here is a well-known contemporary comment on the fifth number:

> Oh my dear dear Dickens! what a No. 5 you have given us! I have so cried and sobbed over it last night, and again this morning; and felt my heart purified by those tears. . . . Since that divine Nelly . . . there has been nothing like it. Every trait so true and so touching . . . and yet lightened by that fearless innocence. . . .[1]

The writer is Lord Jeffrey, the same who had scarified Wordsworth's *Excursion* in the *Edinburgh Review*. Something may be discounted for his nationality, and something for his years—he was now seventy-five— but on the whole, this is the response typical of Dickens's first readers.[2] And it is certainly not the response of the modern reader. The question suggests itself, How far are we, or how far is Dickens at fault—and not only Dickens but his first public? Our response is not of course peculiar to our own century: among the Victorians there were a few dry-eyed resisters. Henry Hallam confessed himself 'so hardened as to be unable to look on [the death of Paul] in any light but pure "business"'.[3] Fitzjames

---

[1] Lord Cockburn, *Life of Lord Jeffrey* (1852), ii. 406–7.

[2] 'We envy not the man who can read for the first time the account of the death of little Paul Dombey with a heart unmoved and an eye tearless' (*The Sun*, 13 April 1848); and see p. 52, n. 3 below.

[3] C. and F. Brookfield, *Mrs. Brookfield and her Circle* (2 vols., 1905), i. 255. Henry Hallam was the son of the historian.

Stephen complained that Dickens 'gloats . . . touches, tastes, smells and handles as if [the death of Little Nell] were some savoury dainty'.[1] Walter Bagehot in 1858 criticized Dickens's 'fawning fondness' for 'dismal scenes';[2] Ruskin in 1880 accused him of killing Little Nell as a butcher kills a lamb, for the market.[3] By the late nineteenth century the resistance seems to have been pretty general, judging from Gissing's cautious defence of Little Nell's death-bed in 1900: 'This pathos was true for them and for their day.'[4] His defence was on the right lines, the historical lines, for the response to such pathos must always be related to those changing things, manners and beliefs. In the eighteen-forties tears were shed more readily, and by men as well as by women. (Indeed any study of past literature soon discovers that the taboo on male tears is peculiar to our own century; and there are signs that it is even now on its way out.) At that time few would have agreed with Chesterton that while humour is of its nature expansive, pathos is in its nature confined.[5] We have also to bear in mind our other modern inhibitions, especially our inarticulateness on the subject of death (represented in 'No flowers. No letters'). The absence of a context for death in modern life, the lack of a setting of common belief—all this must impoverish its treatment in literature and the social impact of any treatment

[1] 'The Relation of Novels to Life', *Cambridge Essays . . . 1855*, p. 175
[2] *Literary Studies*, ii. 188–9 ('Charles Dickens', 1858).
[3] 'Fiction Fair and Foul' in *Macmillan's Magazine*; *Works*, xxxiv.
[4] *The Immortal Dickens* (1923), p. 199 (written as Preface for Rochester edition).
[5] Introduction to *Pickwick* (Everyman edition).

it receives. All that our own fiction can put beside the death of little Paul is the long-drawn clinical horror of the death of little Phil from tubercular meningitis in Aldous Huxley's *Point Counter Point*.

Dickens suffered from his imitators; he was initiating, not continuing a tradition. To put a child at the centre of a novel for adults was virtually unknown when Dickens wrote *Oliver Twist* and *The Old Curiosity Shop*. Further, the sufferings of children at this time have social relevance. Many of his readers had read the five reports on Child Labour which appeared between 1831 and 1843. Part of Gissing's defence is on these lines:

> Such pathos is called 'cheap' . . . in Dickens's day, the lives, the happiness of children were very cheap indeed, and . . . he had his purpose in insisting on their claims to attention.[1]

Some writers of the mid-century considered the age unduly sensitive—Bagehot, for example:

> The unfeeling obtuseness of the early part of this century was to be corrected by an extreme, perhaps an excessive, sensibility to human suffering.[2]

Dickens's pathos had its social purpose. Nell, Smike, Jo, even Paul are all in different ways social victims: as much as the Wilson twins in *Mary Barton*. With the pathos of their deaths is combined apportionment of particular blame:

> Dead, your Majesty. Dead, my lords and gentlemen. . . . And dying thus around us, every day.[3]

---

[1] *Charles Dickens, a critical study* (1898), p. 176.
[2] *Literary Studies*, ii. 190 ('Charles Dickens', 1858).
[3] *Bleak House*, ch. xlvii.

As it happens, in the case of Paul Dombey the historical grounds for defence are not the only ones to appeal to. There are also aesthetic grounds: stronger here than in *The Old Curiosity Shop*. Gissing was understating the case when he said, 'If the situation is to be presented at all, it might be much worse done.'[1] The pathos is in control because the scene is given from a limiting angle. We see with Paul's eyes, and not, until the close, with those of the author or the stricken onlookers. We see what Paul sees, the faces of friends appearing and disappearing through the more urgent visions of delirium; he is not self-conscious about his own death, he says goodbye, but —in contrast to Tennyson's 'May Queen' and Charlotte Brontë's Helen Burns—he makes no farewell speeches.[2] Dickens's use of poetic imagery as a means of releasing yet controlling emotion is the same sort as Shakespeare's. (Indeed, in comparison with Constance's lament for Arthur, Dickens is reserved.) The death of a child represents the extreme of pathos, but is incapable of treatment as tragedy; its expression, therefore, is found most appropriately in lyric, and when they touch it narrative and drama aspire towards that kind. This is true of the death of the child in Chaucer's *Prioress's Tale*, and in Spenser's *Daphnaida*:

> She fell away in her first ages spring,
> Whil'st yet her leafe was greene, and fresh her rinde,
> And whil'st her braunch faire blossomes foorth did bring,

---

[1] Loc. cit.
[2] Dickens's one instance of sentimental piety in a sick child's speech is in *Oliver Twist*, ch. vii (Dick's farewell to Oliver).

> She fell away against all course of kinde:
> For age to dye is right, but youth is wrong;
> She fel away like fruit blowne downe with winde:
> Weepe Shepheard weepe to make my undersong.

Dickens stands in less need of defence when he conveys pathos indirectly by means of a chance detail. In the sixth number, Paul's funeral passes down the street and is seen by the wife of a street entertainer:

The feathers are yet nodding in the distance, when the juggler has the basin spinning on a cane, and has the same crowd to admire it. But the juggler's wife is less alert than usual with the money-box, for a child's burial has set her thinking that perhaps the baby underneath her shabby shawl may not grow up to be a man, and wear a sky-blue fillet round his head, and salmon-coloured worsted drawers, and tumble in the mud.

There, the method is nearer Thackeray's; and it was in this direction—away from 'expansive' pathos—that Dickens moved in *David Copperfield*.[1]

Thackeray did not attempt to describe the death of a child, unless we count the episode in *Barry Lyndon*[2]—and this is removed from pure pathos by the ironies of Barry's narration. He was himself deeply moved by the fifth number of *Dombey*;[3] but in his writing he was protected from Dickens's

---

[1] Thackeray noted the change of manner in this novel: 'I think he has been reading a certain yellow-covered book and with advantage too' (*Letters*, ii. 531); so did F. J. Hort, in a letter of August 1849; 'exceedingly beautiful, with much extravagance pruned off. Without in the least ceasing to be Dickens, he has learnt much from Thackeray' (*Life and Letters*, 2 vols., 1896, i. 113).

[2] Ch. xix.

[3] *Letters*, ii. 266 n., quoting George Hodder, *Memoirs of my Time* (1870), p. 277.

dangers by his view that pathos should be 'very occasional indeed in humorous works'. (In 'humorous
works' he would include, as his lecture 'On Charity
and Humour' shows, both Dickens's novels and his
own.) He approved of his own comparison of Amelia
to Lady Jane Grey 'trying the axe' when she is
determining to send little George to live with his
grandfather, because 'it leaves you to make your own
sad pictures—We shouldn't do much more than that
I think in comic books'.[1] This comes well from
Thackeray, whose own pathos has an economy which
is rare in Dickens. At its finest (the death of George
Osborne, the death of old Sedley) it is of no time; it
has something nearer the 'sad earnestness and vivid
exactness' that Newman found in the classical poets.
And it is seldom exclusive of other emotions—
sometimes indeed armed against mockery by containing mockery. The rapidity of the transition might
often be expressed in his own words—'with one eye
brimming with pity, the other steadily keeping watch
over the family spoons'.[2] If he, too, is by modern
standards 'sentimental', he also, in Clough's words,
'sees the silliness sentiment runs into, and so always
tempers it by a little banter or ridicule'.[3]

[1] *Letters*, ii. 424–5. See also 'A Grumble about the Christmas Books'
(*Fraser's*, January 1847; *Works*, vi. 581–609).

[2] *Philip*, ch. xiv.

[3] Letter of 3 January 1853; *Poems and Prose Remains* (1869), i. 191.

§ 12

'They are a little broad, but she may read anything now
she's married, you know.'

Mr. Brooke, in George Eliot's *Middlemarch*, ch. xxx.

The novelist of the eighteen-forties was, then,
allowed more licence for sentimental pathos than
accords with modern taste; we generally assume
him, however, to have been much more restricted in
other respects. The death-bed might be public, but
not the marriage-bed. But before I consider how
far the novelists were seriously hampered by considerations of 'propriety' in this sense, a warning is
necessary against the popular foreshortening of the
Victorian age, against confusing the eighteen-forties
with the sixties, seventies, or eighties, or on the
other hand with the strictness of Evangelicals in the
early years of the century. It is too commonly supposed that Bowdler was a Victorian. He was, in fact,
a contemporary of Shelley. He is also too commonly seen as a mere censor, whereas he was rather a
popularizer. Many Victorian children met their
Shakespeare first in Bowdler's edition,[1] and were not
ungrateful. A tribute from an unexpected quarter is
Swinburne's:

More nauseous and more foolish cant was never chattered
than that which would deride the memory or depreciate the
merits of Bowdler. No man ever did better service to Shakespeare than the man who made it possible to put him into the
hands of intelligent and imaginative children. . . .[2]

[1] The complete edition was first published in 1818, the sixth edition in
1831.

[2] 'Social Verse', 1891 (*Studies in Prose and Poetry*, 1894, pp. 98–99);

Bowdler's expurgations were indeed moderate in comparison with those of some of his predecessors. In 1806 the Rev. James Plumptre had altered the second line of 'Under the Greenwood Tree' to

> Who loves to work with me.[1]

Such absurdities reappear in the eighteen-sixties, and novelists who were writing then as well as in the eighteen-forties serve to mark the change. It is in *Our Mutual Friend* that Dickens introduces Mr. Podsnap, with his abhorrence of anything that might bring a blush to the cheek of the young person. Podsnappery in all its fulness is a phenomenon of the sixties, and is probably related to the rise of the shilling magazines which extended the family reading of fiction still further. A surviving Victorian has said that,

the (largely imaginary) prudery and reticence of the Victorians is chiefly due to this habit of family reading. It would take a tough father to read some modern novels aloud to his children.[2]

One of those new shilling magazines, the *Cornhill*, rejected a story by Trollope,[3] and the editor responsible was, of all people, Thackeray. Trollope protested in vain against this 'squeamishness', reminding Thackeray of precedents, some very recent—

quoted in G. Lafourcade, *La Jeunesse de Swinburne* (Paris, 1928), i. 68.

[1] In *A Collection of Songs . . . selected and revised* (3 vols., 1806–8), i. 170. M. J. Quinlan, *Victorian Prelude* (New York, 1941), pp. 229–37 gives an account of Plumptre's expurgations.

[2] E. E. Kellett, in *Early Victorian England* (1934), ii. 48 n.

[3] 'Mrs. General Talboys', published in *Tales of all Countries*, second series (1863).

Effie Deans, Beatrix Esmond, Jane Eyre, and Hetty Sorrel—and added:

I could think of no pure English novelist, pure up to the Cornhill standard, except Dickens; but then I remembered Oliver Twist and blushed for what my mother and sister read in that very fie-fie story.[1]

But Thackeray remained firm—this was a new magazine and his business was to get and keep subscribers. The interesting point for us is that Trollope, a sensitive chronicler of manners, is noting a change. A change perhaps also in the attitude to Dickens, for it was also in the sixties that a headmistress escorted her girls out of the hall where Dickens was giving a reading from *Martin Chuzzlewit*; they left at the point where Mr. Pecksniff calls on Mrs. Gamp, and is mistaken by the neighbours for an expectant father. Presumably for the sake of the same young persons, Keene's illustrations to *Mrs. Caudle's Curtain Lectures* avoided the bedroom setting.[2] A reviewer of *Tom Brown at Oxford* remonstrated with the author for making his hero carry a girl who had broken her ankle: 'If this be muscular Christianity, the less we have of it the better.'[3] Ten years later Thackeray's successor, Leslie Stephen, begged Hardy to treat seduction 'in a gingerly fashion' in *Far from the Madding Crowd* and also cautioned him on *The*

---

[1] *Letters*, iv. 207.

[2] This new edition, a 'Christmas Book' of 1865, is noticed with amusement in the *Saturday Review* (2 December 1865), p. 712.

[3] *Athenæum* (30 November 1861), p. 72. Compare Hardy's enforced introduction of a wheelbarrow in the scene where Angel Clare carries the milkmaids in the serial version of *Tess*.

Hand of Ethelberta: 'Remember the country parson's daughters. *I* have always to remember them!'[1] Suppose we remember, in contrast, three country parson's daughters of a generation earlier; the Brontë sisters read, and wrote, as they pleased. Of the later age there are abundant examples from life—some within living memory—of prohibitions to daughters, who might not read the third volume of *The Mill on the Floss*, or any of *Jane Eyre*,[2] until marriage or middle-age, whichever came first. The apparent assumption was, in the words of Mrs. Lynn Linton (writing as an old lady in 1898), that 'knowledge of vice should come gradually in advancing age'[3]—the immediate instance of 'vice' in the manuscript novel criticized was the hero's squeezing the heroine's 'ungloved hand' in a hansom cab. Against this tyranny of the Young Person arise the famous protests of the eighties and nineties in the critical articles of Hardy, Henry James, and George Moore. It was in that period, too, that Samuel Butler gleefully recorded Festing Jones's *bon mot*, that Canon Ainger 'is the kind of man who is capable of bringing out an expurgated edition of Wordsworth'.[4]

But it is an error to refer this attitude back into the eighteen-forties. There were then—as far as my

[1] Hardy's recollections, in F. W. Maitland, *Life and Letters of Leslie Stephen* (1906), pp. 274–6.

[2] From many instances I choose one; Elizabeth Malleson (a lady of progressive views and a friend of George Eliot) read *Jane Eyre* aloud to her children some time in the eighties, 'entirely omitting Rochester's mad wife, and so skilfully that we noticed nothing amiss with the plot!' (*Elizabeth Malleson, 1828–1916*, privately printed, 1926, p. 90).

[3] G. S. Layard, *Mrs. Lynn Linton* (1901), p. 228.

[4] *Further Extracts from the Note-Books* (1934), p. 304.

knowledge goes—no similar instances of squeamish
editors, and fewer protests from readers and critics.
One, indeed, speaks strongly but vaguely:

> Almost any serial will give hints enough to an acute boy,
> [and] . . . guide him to the door with the red lamp.[1]

Perhaps the earliest general outcry[2] against a novel
on grounds of propriety came in 1853 against Mrs.
Gaskell's *Ruth*, in which a Dissenting parson helps
a seduced girl to pass herself off as a widow.[3] The
'burnings' of Froude's *Shadows of the Clouds* in 1847
by his father the Archdeacon and of *The Nemesis of
Faith* in 1849 by the Sub-Rector of Exeter College
seem to have been rather from disapproval of religious heterodoxy than of sexual impropriety. Contemporary reviewers of *Jane Eyre* did not suggest its
unsuitability for young girls. Almost the only attack
on its morality came in the well-known review in the
Quarterly, which appeared over a year after the novel
was published, and was probably designed to coun-
teract the general applause. Even here what was emphasized was less impropriety than an unchristian,

---

[1] 'Advice to an Intending Serialist' (mainly aimed at Dickens, but
presumably not in this respect), in *Blackwood's* (November 1846),
p. 595.

[2] Wilkie Collins's second novel *Basil* (1852), the story of a youth
trapped into a private, unconsummated marriage, was, he reports, 'condemned off-hand by a certain class of readers, as an outrage on their sense
of propriety' (Dedication of revised edition, 1862).

[3] There were more favourable than unfavourable reviews, but one
library withdrew the book from circulation and at least two fathers of
families burnt the last volume. See Mrs. Gaskell's letters as quoted in
E. Haldane, *Elizabeth Gaskell and her Friends* (1931), and the survey
in A. B. Hopkins, *Elizabeth Gaskell: Her Life and Work* (1952), ch. vii.

jacobinical spirit. Of course some situations in the novel were found surprising by many reviewers, but mainly on the grounds of improbability, grounds which the author had provided against. At no period can it have been common for an employer to describe his illicit affairs to an eighteen-year-old governess. But it was meant to be exceptional: Rochester and Jane are drawn as exceptional people, and the author signalizes the unusualness by making Rochester himself observe:

'Strange that you should listen to me quietly, as if it were the most usual thing in the world for a man like me to tell stories of his opera-mistresses to a quaint, inexperienced girl like you!'[1]

There was no general protest[2] against *The Tenant of Wildfell Hall*, where Anne Brontë makes the effect of dipsomania upon married life painfully clear. To those critics who did accuse her of a 'morbid love of the coarse', she replied in the Preface to the second edition;

when we have to do with vice and vicious characters, I maintain it is better to depict them as they really are than as they would wish to appear. . . . Is it better to reveal the snares and pitfalls of life to the young and thoughtless traveller, or to cover them with branches and flowers? . . . When I feel it my duty to speak an unpalatable truth, with the help of God, I *will* speak it.

(Here, in an unexpected quarter, is an echo of

[1] Ch. xv.
[2] The critic who reviewed it in *Fraser's* found it 'powerful' and 'interesting', if unfit for girls, and thought its exposure of evils justified some coarseness (April 1849; pp. 423-4).

Thackeray's manifesto in *Catherine*.) Whether the writer is a man or a woman is immaterial:

> All novels are or should be written for both men and women to read, and I am at a loss to conceive how a man should permit himself to write anything that would be really disgraceful to a woman, or why a woman should be censured for writing anything that would be proper and becoming for a man.[1]

All the Brontë novels were seen as containing coarseness of speech. But objection was mainly to the novelty of Yorkshire speech, noticeable then as now for its bluntness, rather than to its immodesty. In *Wuthering Heights* objection was also raised to the oaths, but these Charlotte Brontë, in her preface to the 1850 edition, declined to modify:

> A large class of readers, likewise, will suffer greatly from the introduction into the pages of this work of words printed with all their letters, which it has become the custom to represent by the initial and final letters only—a blank line filling the interval. I may as well say at once that, for this circumstance, it is out of my power to apologize; deeming it, myself, a rational plan to write words at full length. The practice of hinting by single letters those expletives with which profane and violent people are wont to garnish their discourse, strikes me as a proceeding which, however well meant, is weak and futile. I cannot tell what good it does—what feeling it spares —what horror it conceals.

We have some little evidence that publishers occasionally censored a novel before publication. In 1845 Geraldine Jewsbury had to alter one scene of her first novel, *Zoe*, by arranging—in her own mocking

---

[1] The Preface is dated 22 July 1848.

words—for 'a more liberal distribution of spotted muslin'[1] (the heroine wakes to find her bedroom on fire and is rescued by the hero). She cannot have supplied quite enough of it, since *Zoe* was 'put into a *dark cupboard* in the Manchester Library of that day—because . . . calculated to injure the morals of the *young men*'.[2] But this is the less important, since in the following year in her second novel she can freely publish this sentiment:

> A strong emotion—a real feeling of any kind, is a truth; no matter whether it be compatible or not with received notions of right and wrong.
>
> A married woman, in love with a man not her husband, is a fact worthy of all reprobation . . . when all the anathemas have been expended the fact remains the same; she is under the dominion of a real feeling, deep as life, and overpowering as death. It is a fact, and requires to be exorcised by something as deep, strong, and vital as itself. It will not stir for being called hard names, it does not recognise them.[3]

In 1851 another publisher, John Chapman, insisted that Eliza Lynn (later Mrs. Lynn Linton) should tone down one of the love scenes in her novel *Realities*. He was supported in this view by his wife, his mistress, and Mary Ann Evans ('George Eliot'), for once unanimous. Here are the relevant extracts from his diary:

> Received and read through one of Miss L's 'proofs' of a love scene which is warmly and vividly depicted, with a tone

---

[1] Geraldine Jewsbury, *Letters to Jane Welsh Carlyle*, ed. Mrs. Ireland (1892), pp. 145–6.

[2] Letter quoted by Sadleir, *XIXth Century Fiction*, i. 193.

[3] *The Half Sisters* (1848), ii, ch. xii.

and tendency which I entirely disapprove. Miss Evans concurs with me, and Elisabeth and Susanna are most anxious I
should not publish the work. . . . Went with [Miss Evans] to
call on Miss Lynn in the hope of inducing her to cancel some
objectionable passages, and succeeded to the extent of a few
lines only. I said that such passages were addressed [to] and
excited the sensual nature and were therefore injurious;—and
that as I am the publisher of works notable for the[ir] intellectual freedom it behoves me to be exceedingly careful of the
moral tendency of all I issue.[1]

Other publishers were tried in vain; finally Miss
Lynn consented 'to submit to the censorship of
Thornton Hunt' who agreed with Chapman, and
the novel was eventually published, though at Miss
Lynn's own expense, by Saunders and Ottley.[2] But
even so, the novel made Miss Jewsbury feel 'trailed
in the mud'.[3] Perhaps she feared rivalry.

Nevertheless many novels, daring in situation and
even verbally outspoken, at least by the standards of
the sixties, were published uncensored and often unreproved. Some, like Theodore Hook's *Fathers and
Sons* (1842), must be accounted survivals from the
earlier coarser period of the Regency; but it is a
revolutionary idealism characteristic of the forties
that underlies the audacities of Froude's *Shadows of
the Clouds* and *The Nemesis of Faith*. The obliquities
of narrative method and the philosophical speculations and serious purpose in 'The Lieutenant's

---

[1] Gordon Haight, *George Eliot and John Chapman*, New Haven and
London (1940), pp. 130–1. Chapman's private life may have been another
motive for caution.

[2] Haight, pp. 133–4, 137; and see Geraldine Jewsbury's *Letters*, p. 405.
[3] Ibid.

Daughter' (the second story in *Shadows of the Clouds*, 1847) remove the story from any risk of pornography, but the brothel is not concealed from the reader's view—

And Lord William offers two hundred pounds you said, if it's quite fresh. . . .[1]

Some outspokenness was necessary in the novels which exposed social abuses and pleaded for the emancipation of the oppressed. The exploitation of women and children, the horrors of the mills, the cellar-dwellings, and the open drains, were 'facts'; they could not be handled with kid-gloves, even by novelists. The age that read the Commission reports, the *Morning Chronicle*'s series on 'London Labour and the London Poor' (1848–9) and the *Westminster Review*'s sixty-page article on the causes, extent, and mitigation of prostitution (1850) was not squeamish. It is true that one notorious social abuse, the uncontrolled sale of corrupting literature, worked against the novelist's freedom: for it was imperative that the dividing line between novels and the produce of Holywell Street should be clearly maintained,[2] the more so since family reading of novels was, as we have seen, increasing. With the Victorian underworld what it was, it is hard to see how the innocent tyranny of the Young Person could have been avoided, though

[1] Ch. iv.
[2] *Fraser's* (October 1851) notes the impossibility for an English novelist of the 'topics' of George Sand's *Indiana* and *Lélia*; such a novel 'would sink at once to Holywell Street and contempt' (p. 378). On the extent of pornographic literature before the passing of the Campbell Act in 1857, see *Early Victorian England*, ed. G. M. Young (1934), ii. 68–69.

it might have been attended with less hypocrisy. But its day was not yet.

At all periods, including our own, novelists have known some limitations, but in the eighteen-forties they were not severe, and what is more important, were seldom *felt* to be cramping. With very few exceptions, novelists were contented with such limitations as existed, and moved freely within them, or figure-skated along the edge. There was no fatal discrepancy between what the writer wished to say and what his public was willing to let him say; and it is that discrepancy, not limitation in itself, which is damaging to the novel, as Hardy and Henry James were to find. Twenty or thirty years later, *Jane Eyre* and *Mary Barton*[1] would have met with far more opposition; in the eighteen-forties they startled, but did not disgust. What Charlotte Brontë wished to say in *Jane Eyre* was something indeed new to English readers; but she was allowed to say it. To her as to Geraldine Jewsbury a woman's passion is a fact stronger than social convention; and Jane's flight from Rochester is no concession to such convention, but the submission of passion to a 'something as deep, strong and vital as itself'—the individual's sense of moral and spiritual integrity. Neither verbal reticence nor sentimentalism hampers Mrs. Gaskell in her faithful picture of 'Manchester life':

'Says I, "Esther, I see what you'll end at with your artificials and your fly-away veils . . . you'll be a streetwalker, Esther"'.

[1] *Mary Barton* was too outspoken for the London County Council in 1907, when it was banned from the schools as unfit for children of fourteen to read.

The words stand in the first chapter of *Mary Barton*,[1] which is a kind of prologue; when the main action develops, John Barton's prediction is seen fulfilled. Esther is not one of the main characters, but she does not disappear; she remains on the edge of the story, meeting the main characters at crucial points, and influencing the action. She is a warning, but never the stereotyped 'outcast'; although the author draws out the pathos of her history, she does it with clear as well as compassionate eyes, making plain the relation of prostitution to poverty, and refusing even the alleviation of repentance. When Jem Wilson offers to help Esther to start afresh, she refuses:

'I could not lead a virtuous life if I would. I should only disgrace you. I must have drink.'

Esther may be contrasted with the much more 'literary', even stagey figure of Alice Marwood in *Dombey and Son*. Dickens did not shun the subject of seduction or unlawful passion, but he was on the whole content with the literary convention of his time: that such sin must be expiated in penitence and death, or at least emigration.[2] Even Edith Dombey, who sinned only in appearance, must retire to Italy. But with Edith, Dickens is least conventional, for he shows her as the victim of an evil social

[1] The whole passage is quoted in the *Westminster Review*'s article on prostitution, p. 454.
[2] Little Em'ly in *David Copperfield*, Lady Dedlock in *Bleak House*; and see the fates of the wives, guilty only in intention, in Miss Jewsbury's *The Half-Sisters* (1848) and Miss Mulock's *The Ogilvies* (1849). Mrs. Trollope, in *Jessie Phillips* (1842–3) is nearer to Dickens in her treatment of the seduced girl than to Mrs. Gaskell in *Ruth*. (So, in essentials, is George Eliot in *Adam Bede*.)

system, revenging herself upon it. What at first sight seems like 'gingerly' treatment in the relation of Edith and Carker discloses on examination considerable moral insight, of a kind more often associated with Thackeray. Both Dickens and Thackeray in the novels they wrote in the eighteen-forties illustrate in different ways the comparative unimportance of such limitations as existed. Both were aware of those limitations, and Thackeray often humorously draws attention to them in prefaces and asides;[1] Dickens does so only indirectly, through his hypocritical characters.[2] He accepted the novel as it was, making it say all he wanted, and without guile. He was fortunate in that his own instincts were generally at one with those of his public. In the 1841 Introduction to the third edition of *Oliver Twist*, a novel in which he had descended to 'the very dregs of life', he wrote:

No less consulting my own taste, than the manners of the age, I endeavoured, while I painted it in all its fallen and degraded aspect, to banish from the lips of the lowest character I introduced, any expression that could by possibility offend . . .

But the reticence on which Dickens prides himself is only verbal, although this in itself commits him to some factual reticence, especially in the relation of Bill Sikes and Nancy. The same Introduction says

[1] His fullest and most serious statement is in his review of Fielding's *Works* (*The Times*, 3 September 1840; *Works*, iii); and that is an acceptance of limitation.

[2] Cf. the letter of 1856 cited above, p. 8. Excessive verbal prudery is rarely mocked at in Dickens's early novels; the most memorable instance is Mrs. Hominy, the 'mother of the modern Gracchi', who is horrified by Martin's use of the phrase 'with his naked eye'—and she is a New Englander (*Martin Chuzzlewit*, ch. xxii).

plainly that 'the girl is a prostitute';[1] in the book her trade is only suggested faintly. Yet even this factual reticence is defensible, for by its means Dickens keeps faith with a wide range of readers: the knowledgeable are told enough to make a sure guess, the innocent get the essential outline without perplexing detail—and it would surely be a loss, now as then, if *Oliver Twist* had to be ruled out from children's reading. In comic scenes Dickens can get away with much more: comedy has always enjoyed a wider range of permitted reference to doubtful topics. We have only to think of Mr. Pecksniff, drunk and carried up to bed, but making constant reappearances on the landing in his night-shirt, and trying to preach a sermon on the text 'Observe the human leg'. Or of all the incidental immodesties arising from Mrs. Gamp's profession. Here indeed the modern reader must recognize the greater emancipation of the forties, for in our time midwifery is not regarded as a subject for comic treatment. This is a limitation of our own and appears to us—as one's own taboos are apt to do—as a matter merely of taste and natural refinement. The same is true of Sam Weller's macabre jestings about death, as in the anecdote of the man who made himself into sausages.[2]

[1] The shorter version in the edition of 1867 omits these words among others; and this version alone is given in later editions.

[2] Compare the famous story of Sweeney Todd (of which the first version is Prest's *String of Pearls, c.* 1840). This has required expurgation for modern readers: the making of the murderer's victims into meat pies is removed from the text of 1936 (E. S. Turner, *Boys will be Boys,* 1948, p. 47). The worst horrors of Thackeray's *Catherine* as it appeared in *Fraser's* in 1839–40 were expurgated in the collected edition of 1875, and are therefore still unknown to most modern readers.

The kind of freedom sought by Thackeray and his method of attaining it is different. Bagehot's definition of the difference can be accepted in the main; it has to be remembered that he wrote in 1858, when the awareness of limitations was already growing stronger:

No one can read Mr. Thackeray's writings without feeling that he is perpetually treading as close as he dare to the border-line that separates the world which may be described in books from the world which it is prohibited so to describe. No one knows better than this accomplished artist where that line is, and how curious are its windings and turns. The charge against him is that he knows it but too well; that with an anxious care and a wistful eye he is ever approximating to its edge, and hinting with subtle art how thoroughly he is familiar with, and how interesting he could make the interdicted region on the other side. He never violates a single conventional rule; but at the same time the shadow of the immorality that is not seen is scarcely ever wanting to his delineation of the society that is seen. Everyone may perceive what is passing in his fancy. Mr. Dickens is chargeable with no such defect; he does not seem to feel the temptation. By what we may fairly call an instinctive purity of genius, he not only observes the conventional rules, but makes excursions into topics which no other novelist could safely handle, and, by a felicitous instinct, deprives them of all impropriety. No other writer could have managed the humour of Mrs. Gamp without becoming unendurable.[1]

But does Thackeray feel even the constraint implied by the phrase 'wistful eye'? Does he not rather make play at his readers' expense with his awareness of the winding line, and, ingenious in circumvention, never-

[1] *Literary Studies*, ii. 187–8.

theless say all he needs to? That was at least the view of more than one contemporary: 'his hint', says Charlotte Brontë,

is more vivid than other men's elaborate explanations, and never is his satire whetted to so keen an edge as when with quiet mocking irony he modestly recommends to the approbation of the public his own exemplary discretion and forbearance.[1]

The passage she had in mind is given particular emphasis by its position at the beginning of the concluding double number of *Vanity Fair*: the eye here is surely not 'wistful':

. . . it has been the wish of the present writer, all through this story, deferentially to submit to the fashion at present prevailing, and only to hint at the existence of wickedness in a light, easy, and agreeable manner, so that nobody's fine feelings may be offended. I defy anyone to say that our Becky, who has certainly some vices, has not been presented to the public in a perfectly genteel and inoffensive manner. In describing this syren, singing and smiling, coaxing and cajoling, has he once forgotten the laws of politeness, and showed the monster's hideous tail above water? No! Those who like may peep down under waves that are pretty transparent, and see it writhing and curling, diabolically hideous and slimy, flapping amongst bones, or curling round corpses; but above the water-line, I ask, has not everything been proper, agreeable, and decorous, and has any the most squeamish immoralist in Vanity Fair a right to cry fie? When, however, the syren disappears and dives below, down among the dead men, the water of course grows turbid over her, and it is labour lost to look into it ever so curiously. They look pretty enough when they sit

[1] Letter to W. H. Williams, 14 August 1848; *S.H.B.* ii. 244.

upon a rock, twanging their harps and combing their hair, and sing, and beckon to you to come and hold the looking-glass; but when they sink into their native element, depend upon it those mermaids are about no good, and we had best not examine the fiendish marine cannibals, revelling and feasting on their wretched pickled victims. And so, when Becky is out of the way, be sure that she is not particularly well employed, and that the less that is said about her doings is in fact the better.[1]

By means of this artful imagery, Thackeray makes Becky's goings-on sufficiently clear. The reader who wants further hints may gather them from a considerable number of details scattered over the book, and the uncertainty as to particulars has its own verisimilitude. Thackeray has lost nothing by his half-observance of propriety. A more direct treatment would have put the emphasis wrong. Becky's master-passion is for money and power; what precisely she paid for them is not important— and we know enough of her to be sure that the price would be as low as possible. Thackeray, proceeding by means of suggestions, found it easier to do so because of the period and place in which his action lay (the last years of George IV, the post-war London of the eighteen-twenties), a time associated with licence and one that many of his readers remembered for themselves. No one who reads *Vanity Fair* carefully would dream of calling it a squeamish novel. Thackeray does more than avoid squeamishness on his own part; he exploits it as it exists on the part of many of his readers. It is turned against them-

[1] Ch. lxiv.

selves, and very openly. The passage quoted above continues:

If we were to give a full account of her proceedings during a couple of years that followed after the Curzon Street catastrophe, there might be some reason for people to say this book was improper. The actions of very vain, artless, pleasure-seeking people are very often improper (as are many of yours, my friend with the grave face and spotless reputation;—but that is merely by the way); and what are those of a woman without faith—or love—or character?

But sometimes skill in circumvention was not enough; Thackeray had to challenge his readers' limited pre-conceptions about the novel:

Since the writer of *Tom Jones* was buried, no writer of fiction among us has been permitted to depict to his utmost power a MAN.

Some of the subscribers to *Pendennis*, he says in the Preface, left him because he described a young man 'affected by temptation'; but he had not made concessions to them.

A little more frankness than is customary has been attempted in this story. . . . If truth is not always pleasant, at any rate truth is best.

This passage, which refers of course to the Fanny Bolton episode, has sometimes been misunderstood, as if Thackeray were in fact making concessions by showing Pendennis as in the end resisting temptation. This, however, is in character; Arthur Pendennis is not Tom Jones, but a sentimental well-intentioned young man of the eighteen-thirties. The pressure of the time is seen, if at all, in Thackeray's initial choice of such a hero. And the doubt as to how far he will go, combined with the anxious suspicions of his mother, adds to both narrative suspense and moral interest.

The point at which possessive affection shades into jealousy held a fascination for Thackeray, and here perhaps is found a more insidious undermining of convention. First in Amelia, and then in Helen Pendennis, the sacred emotion of mother-love is tentatively explored, and its seamier side ambiguously indicated; and in his next novel, *Esmond*, Thackeray went far enough to disturb many of his readers. Such words as 'uneasiness' and 'sinister' recur in criticisms of the novel;[1] Charlotte Brontë, Thackeray's ardent admirer, was 'grieved and exasperated' by Lady Castlewood's jealousy;[2] and George Eliot probably voiced a common response when she wrote:

'Esmond' is the most uncomfortable book you can imagine. You remember how you disliked 'François le Champi'. Well, the story of 'Esmond' is just the same. The hero is in love with the daughter all through the book, and marries the mother at the end.[3]

It is 'uncomfortable' because the reader (and this includes the modern reader) is led on in innocence, supposing Lady Castlewood's feelings to be purely maternal when in fact they are otherwise. One could not feel safe with such an author; he held the keys of

[1] See for example *Fraser's* (December 1852), pp. 622–33.
[2] Letter to George Smith, 14 February 1852; *S.H.B.* iii. 314–15.
[3] Letter to the Brays, 22 October 1852; Cross, ch. v.

what Carlyle called 'the Bluebeard Chambers of the heart'.[1]

§ 13

The moral sympathies of the novel-readers of the eighteen-forties were more considerably enlarged in another direction, by the extension of the social frontiers observed in fiction. In the previous decade the area favoured by writers and readers had been restricted. Novels of 'high life'—what contemporaries called the 'silver-fork' school—were still the most popular; the work of Bulwer, Disraeli, Theodore Hook, Lady Blessington, and Mrs. Gore delighted equally (though differently) those within and those without the pale of 'society'.[2] The taste is mocked by Dickens in the superb extract from *The Lady Flabella* which Kate Nickleby reads aloud to Mrs. Wititterly:

'"Cherizette," said the Lady Flabella, inserting her mouse-like feet in the blue satin slippers, which had unwittingly occasioned the half-playful half-angry altercation between herself and the youthful Colonel Befillaire, in the Duke of Mincefenille's *salon de danse* on the previous night. "*Chérizette, ma chere, donnez-moi de l'eau-de-Cologne, s'il vous plait, mon enfant.*"

'"*Mercie*—thank you," said the Lady Flabella, as the lively

[1] Reported by Caroline Fox from 'The Hero as Man of Letters' in her journal for 1840; *Memories of Old Friends* (2 vols., 1882), i. 186. It is not in the published version of *Heroes*.

[2] Michael Sadleir, *Bulwer and his Wife, a Panorama 1803–1836* (1933), p. 118; there is a useful survey of the type in pp. 118–27. See also M. W. Rosa, *The Silver-Fork School: Novels of Fashion preceding Vanity Fair* (New York, 1936).

but devoted Cherizette plentifully besprinkled with the fragrant compound the Lady Flabella's *mouchoir* of finest cambric, edged with richest lace, and emblazoned at the four corners with the Flabella crest, and gorgeous heraldic bearings of that noble family; "*Mercie*—that will do."

'At this instant, while the Lady Flabella yet inhaled that delicious fragrance by holding the *mouchoir* to her exquisite, but thoughtfully-chiselled nose, the door of the *boudoir* (artfully concealed by rich hangings of silken damask, the hue of Italy's firmament) was thrown open, and with noiseless tread two valets-de-chambre, clad in sumptuous liveries of peach-blossom and gold, advanced into the room followed by a page in *bas de soie*—silk stockings—who, while they remained at some distance making the most graceful obeisances, advanced to the feet of his lovely mistress, and dropping on one knee presented, on a golden salver gorgeously chased, a scented *billet*.

'The Lady Flabella, with an agitation she could not repress, hastily tore off the *envelope* and broke the scented seal. It *was* from Befillaire—the young, the slim, the low-voiced—*her own* Befillaire.'

'Oh, charming!' interrupted Kate's patroness, who was sometimes taken literary; 'Poetic, really. Read that description again, Miss Nickleby.'

Kate complied.

'Sweet, indeed!' said Mrs. Wititterly, with a sigh. 'So voluptuous, is it not—so soft?'

'Yes, I think it is,' replied Kate, gently; 'very soft.'

'Close the book, Miss Nickleby,' said Mrs. Wititterly. 'I can hear nothing more to-day. I should be sorry to disturb the impression of that sweet description.'[1]

The passage is a document in the reaction against the predominance of society novels, which was well

[1] *Nicholas Nickleby* (1838–9), ch. xxviii.

under way by 1839, thanks to the gradual effect of
Carlyle's attack on *Pelham* in *Sartor Resartus*, and the
continuous sniping of *Fraser's*.[1] But the first phase of
this reaction in the novels themselves was more apparent than real. Some of the romantic novelists—
Bulwer in *Paul Clifford* and *Eugene Aram*, Ainsworth
in *Rookwood* and *Jack Sheppard*—carried their sentimental views of character into low life,[2] and these
'Newgate novels' provoked a further and more serious
reaction first from Dickens, and then, in a slightly
different direction, from Thackeray.[3] In *Catherine*
Thackeray went further in frank sordidness than
Dickens in *Oliver Twist*, but Dickens's exploration
proved more fruitful; *Catherine*, designed as 'medi-
cine' to produce wholesome nausea, proved merely
destructive, and has more significance in Thackeray's
critical than in his creative writing. Dickens's 1841
Introduction to *Oliver Twist* shows that he well
knew that he was breaking new ground:

I had read of thieves by scores—seductive fellows (amiable
for the most part), faultless in dress, plump in pocket, choice
in horseflesh, bold in bearing, fortunate in gallantry, great at

[1] There were also earlier protests, notably Hazlitt's in 'The Dandy
School' (*Examiner*, 18 November 1827; *Works*, ed. P. P. Howe, xx.
143–9), which gave the school its new label by making fun of Hook's
preoccupation with 'silver forks'. Rosa (op. cit) has shown the relation
of the school to the economics of authorship, and emphasizes the attempts
of both Disraeli and Bulwer to escape from their publishers' demands.

[2] 'These two extremes of novel-writing—the Almack and Jack Sheppard schools—deviate equally from the standard of real excellence . . .
low and humble life are sophisticated just as much as elevated and fashionable' (*Blackwood's*, September 1845, p. 343).

[3] The decline of the 'Newgate novel', even on the lowest level of 'penny
literature', was noted by Charles Knight in 1846 (*The Old Printer and
the Modern Press*, 1854, p. 281).

a song, a bottle, pack of cards or dice-box, and fit companions for the bravest. But I had never met (except in
HOGARTH) with the miserable reality. It appeared to me that to
draw a knot of such associates in crime as really do exist; to
paint them in all their deformity, in all their wretchedness, in
all the squalid poverty of their lives; to show them as they
really are, for ever skulking uneasily, through the dirtiest
paths of life, with the great, black, ghastly gallows closing
up their prospect, turn them where they may; it appeared to
me that to do this, would be to attempt a something which
was greatly needed, and which would be a service to society.
. . . Here are no canterings upon moonlit heaths, no merry-
makings in the snuggest of all possible caverns, none of the
attractions of dress, no embroidery, no lace, no jack-boots, no
crimson coats and ruffles, none of the dash and freedom with
which 'the road' has been, time out of mind, invested. The
cold, wet, shelterless midnight streets of London; the foul
and frowsy dens, where vice is closely packed and lacks the
room to turn; the haunts of hunger and disease, the shabby
rags that scarcely hold together; where are the attractions of
these things?

He sees that his realism may not be welcomed by
those versed in romances:

there are people of so refined and delicate a nature, that they
cannot bear the contemplation of these horrors. Not that they
turn instinctively from crime; but that criminal characters,
to suit them, must be, like their meat, in delicate disguise. . . .
Now, as the stern and plain truth . . . was a part of the purpose
of this book I will not, for these readers, abate one hole in
the Dodger's coat, or one scrap of curl-paper in [Nancy's]
dishevelled hair.

Thackeray felt that even Dickens had made too
many concessions to the sentimental reader, and

charged him as well as Ainsworth with making his rascals too agreeable.[1] The 'Newgate' part of *Oliver Twist* and *Jack Sheppard*, he says,

gives birth to something a great deal worse than bad taste, and familiarizes the public with notions of crime.

The satire of *Jonathan Wild* and the *Beggars' Opera* encloses a moral:

But in the sorrow of Nancy and the exploits of Sheppard, there is no such lurking moral, as far as we have been able to discover; we are asked for downright sympathy in the one case, and are called on in the second to admire the gallantry of a thief. The street-walker may be a very virtuous person, and the robber as brave as Wellington; but it is better to leave them alone, and their qualities, good and bad . . . in the name of common-sense, let us not expend our sympathies on cut-throats, and other such prodigies of evil![2]

He reverts to the danger of 'rose-water novelists . . . whose works from their very charity, become un-trustworthy' in the original version of *Barry Lyndon*; authors, he says,

are bound surely to represent to the best of their power life as it really appears to them to be; not to foist off upon the public figures pretending to be delineations of human nature, —gay and agreeable cut-throats, otto-of-rose murderers . . . that never have or could have existed.[3]

And finally he returns to the charge in the preface to *Pendennis*, where he pretends that he originally meant

---

[1] Dickens's 1841 Introduction should be regarded as partly a reply to this charge.

[2] *Catherine*, 'Another Last Chapter' (*Works*, iii. 186–7).

[3] *Fraser's* (1844), note to ch. xvii and end of ch. xix (*Works*, vi. 252, 310).

to write about a virtuous ruffian in St. Giles's visited constantly by a young lady from Belgravia:

> But I abandoned the idea from want of experience of ruffians. To describe a real rascal, you must make him so horrible that he would be too hideous to show; and unless the painter paints him fairly, I hold that he has no right to show him at all.

The passage also defines his own dilemma. Many readers of *Barry Lyndon* in the pages of *Fraser's* had evidently thought the hero 'too hideous to show', and his long career of prosperity immoral; the way of the anti-sentimentalist is hard.

In other novelists the flight from the romantic novel took other forms. *Oliver Twist* and *Catherine* opened the door to a new kind of novel of low life, but in the work of Disraeli, Kingsley, and Mrs. Gaskell the release was welcomed for other reasons than those of Dickens and Thackeray. *Sybil*, *Yeast*, and *Mary Barton* were more precisely documented and propagandist. They were intended to open people's eyes to certain evils of the time. The ignorance they enlightened was indeed widespread in the novel-reading public. Not only did wealth and poverty exist at this time in extremes, but they were sharply disconnected. Social classes were then stratified, even isolated, not only geographically but within the limits of a single town. Some of the credit for breaking down this isolation must go to Dickens: as Arthur Stanley, the Dean of Westminster, said in his funeral sermon, 'By him that veil was rent asunder which parts the various classes of society.'[1] But it was these

---

[1] *Sermons on Special Occasions* (1882), p. 134.

lesser novelists who were more precisely instructive as to what was revealed when the veil was rent. Their factual detail was what really shocked the novel-readers of the eighteen-forties. We can best gauge this shock by entering into the experiences of the heroes of *Sybil* and *Yeast*. These young men, Egremont and Lancelot Smith, are made to discover respectively some of the horrors of the manufacturing towns and of agricultural districts; and they are shown as explorers coming upon savage tribes.[1] Lancelot, for example, listening to the conversation of the labourers drinking at the fair, found to his astonishment that

> He hardly understood a word of it. It was half articulate, nasal, guttural, made up almost entirely of vowels, like the speech of savages.[2]

What Sybil and Stephen Morley show to Egremont in the towns, what Tregarva shows to Lancelot in the country, is terrible enough, but as terrible is the previous unawareness of both young men that such

---

[1] The review of *Sybil* in *Douglas Jerrold's Shilling Magazine* (June 1845), p. 558 calls the author 'a traveller into new regions of humanity . . . who setting out from the salons of the luxurious, penetrates into the dark and unknown regions of the populace'. Thackeray, writing in *Punch* in 1850, emphasized the ignorance of the upper classes with the same significant metaphor:

> until some poet like Hood wakes and sings that dreadful 'Song of the Shirt'; some prophet like Carlyle rises up and denounces woe; some clear-sighted, energetic man like the writer of the *Chronicle* travels into the poor man's country for us, and comes back with his tale of terror and wonder.

('Waiting at the Station', *Sketches and Travels in London, Punch*, 9 March 1850; collected in *Miscellanies*, ii (1856), and in *Works*, viii. 252–7).

[2] *Yeast*, ch. xiii.

things could exist and that they and their class might have any responsibility for them. '[This is] Manchester life', said a reviewer of *Mary Barton*, 'not ... Indian cholera, famines, or Piedmontese persecutions, or old Norman Conquest butcheries.'[1]

The sub-title of *Sybil*, 'The Two Nations', soon became a household word. It is worth our while to put it back into its context:

Said Egremont . . . 'Say what you like, our Queen reigns over the greatest nation that ever existed.'

'Which nation?' asked the younger stranger, 'for she reigns over two.'

The stranger paused; Egremont was silent, but looked enquiringly.

'Yes,' resumed the younger stranger after a moment's interval. 'Two nations; between whom there is no intercourse and no sympathy; who are as ignorant of each other's habits, thoughts, and feelings, as if they were dwellers in different zones, or inhabitants of different planets; who are formed by a different breeding, are fed by a different food, are ordered by different manners, and are not governed by the same laws.'

'You speak of——' said Egremont, hesitatingly.

'THE RICH AND THE POOR.'[2]

Morley's speech here is not merely novelist's or politician's rhetoric. It represents one of Disraeli's own motives in writing; it repeats his statement in the Advertisement to the first edition:

The general reader whose attention has not been specially drawn to the subject which these volumes aim to illustrate—

---

[1] *Fraser's* (April 1849), p. 430.   [2] Book II, ch. v.

the Condition of the People—might suspect that the Writer had been tempted to some exaggeration in the scenes that he has drawn, and the impressions he has wished to convey. He thinks it therefore due to himself to state that the descriptions, generally, are written from his own observation; but while he hopes he has alleged nothing which is not true, he has found the absolute necessity of suppressing much that is genuine. For so little do we know of the state of our own country, that the air of improbability which the whole truth would inevitably throw over these pages, might deter some from their perusal.

The 'condition of the people', seen in the sharply antithetical terms of the 'two nations', whether simply 'rich and poor' or 'employers and employed'—this theme came more and more to occupy novelists in the forties. Most novel-readers belonged to the other nation; the novelists were scouts who had crossed the frontier (or penetrated the iron curtain) and brought back their reports. Of course the novelists did not act alone; they were often following up the evidence disclosed by Royal Commissions on factory labour, health of towns, and so on; but in some fields the novelist preceded the social investigator—the *Morning Chronicle* articles of 1848–9 were noted as confirming the disclosures of Kingsley.[1] And always, the novelist reached readers unaware of government publications; aware only, perhaps, of a generally menacing cloud—'Slowly comes a hungry people, as a lion, creeping nigher'[2]—and, especially after 1848, of that phenomenon which so noticeably failed to

[1] *Fraser's* (January 1850), p. 3.
[2] 'Locksley Hall', in Tennyson's *Poems* (1842).

observe social barriers—the cholera.[1] The fears, the uneasy conscience, were there for the novelist to play upon and educate. And this receptiveness increased after 1843, not only because of the progress of events, but also because of the influence of that writer and that work which so deeply affected writers and readers at this time—Carlyle and his *Past and Present*. Carlyle's specific influence on the novelists will be suggested later;[2] it is sufficient here to notice that he expressed the idea of the 'two nations' twelve years before Disraeli: 'two Sects will one day part England between them'; 'two contradictory, un-communicating masses'.[3]

The new kind of novel did not fail to encounter resistance. There is evidence of this in the kindly reassurances of some reviews:

Our readers need not be alarmed at the prospect of pene-trating the recesses of Manchester.[4]

And further evidence in the apologetic, or defensive, tone of some novelists. Out of many instances I select one from the beginning of the decade and two from the end. In *Nicholas Nickleby* Dickens headed his four-teenth chapter:

Having the misfortune to treat of none but common people, is necessarily of a mean and vulgar character.

---

[1] In 1853 a nonconformist preacher said that three great social agencies had recently been seen at work: the London City Mission, the cholera, and the novels of Charles Dickens (*Early Victorian England*, 1934, ii. 460).

[2] See below, pp. 152–6.   [3] *Sartor Resartus*, III. x.

[4] *North British Review*, xv (1851), p. 426.

In May 1848 Thackeray headed his sixtieth chapter of *Vanity Fair* with these words, 'Returns to the Genteel World', the second sentence of the chapter running:

> We are glad to get [Amelia] out of that low sphere in which she has been creeping hitherto, and introduce her into a polite circle. . . .

Finally, Charlotte Brontë in *Shirley* headed her eighteenth chapter with these words: 'Which the genteel reader is recommended to skip, low persons being here introduced.' This narrowing of the social area from which art draws its material is a recurrent problem for writers. The very words recall Goldsmith's shabby fellow at the 'Three Jolly Pigeons':

> O damn anything that's low! The genteel thing is the genteel thing at any time, if so be that a gentleman bees in a concatenation accordingly.

But in the forties the social and political implications of the problem were much more acute.

In the thirties the genteel reader, fostered on the fashionable novel, was genteel indeed; he, or more probably she, seems to have looked askance at novels even of ordinary middle-class life. Such at least is the conclusion drawn by Harriet Martineau when she describes in her *Autobiography* the fortunes of her novel *Deerbrook* in 1838. The publisher declined it,

> the scene being laid in middle life. . . . People liked high life in novels, and low life, and ancient life; and life of any rank presented by Dickens, in his peculiar artistic light . . . but it

was not supposed that they would bear a presentment of the familiar life of every day.[1]

Another publisher was found, and *Deerbrook* was a fair success; but some readers expressed disgust, says the author,

that the heroine came from Birmingham, and that the hero was a surgeon. Youths and maidens in those days looked for lords and ladies in every page of a new novel.

And she adds, in her rather pontifical manner,

I believe [the book] to have been useful in overcoming a prejudice against the use of middle-class life in fiction.

One might think such prejudice would have been overcome eight years later; but fashions changed slowly. When in 1846 Charlotte Brontë submitted *The Professor* for publication she met with a somewhat similar resistance and in insuperable form, for this novel was refused by six publishers; part of the background to the rejection is the continued fertility in the forties of such a novelist as Mrs. Gore. (The publishers' resistance to *The Professor* is perhaps not solely a matter of class; it is also the resistance of the 'romantic' to the everyday.) In the 1850 preface the author emphasized her hero's need to earn his living:

I said to myself that my hero should work his way through life as I had seen real living men work theirs—that he should never get a shilling he had not earned—that no sudden turns should lift him in a moment to wealth or high station . . . that he should not even marry a beautiful girl or a lady of rank.

[1] *Autobiography*, iv. 4. There is no contradiction here of my thesis. The novels that people 'liked' are all represented in the work of Bulwer, and 'low life' in this context refers to the novels romanticizing crime.

As Adam's son he should share Adam's doom, and drain throughout his life a mixed and moderate cup of enjoyment.

In the sequel, however, I find that publishers in general scarcely approved of this system, but would have liked something more imaginative and poetical—something more consonant with a highly wrought fancy. . . .[1]

But although novels of high life were still published throughout the eighteen-forties and retained some popularity,[2] the fashion had become vulnerable. Evidence of both the popularity and the critical disesteem is afforded by Thackeray's burlesque of Mrs. Gore in *Punch's Prize Novelists* in June 1847,[3] the title of which runs 'Lords and Liveries, by the Authoress of Dukes and Dejeuners, Hearts and Diamonds, Marchionesses and Milliners, etc. etc. (The title hardly exaggerated the snob-appeal of Mrs. Gore's most recent success, *Peers and Parvenus*.) Here is an excerpt, to put beside Dickens's 'Lady Flabella' of nine years before:

'Corbleu! what a lovely creature that was in the Fitzbattleaxe box to-night', said one of a group of young dandies who were leaning over the velvet-cushioned balconies of the

[1] The Preface was written with the prospect of publication, but a further rejection followed, and *The Professor* did not appear until after her death, in 1856.

[2] There is, however, no fresh name of any note. *D'Horsay, or the Follies of the Day*, By a Man of Fashion [John Mills] (1844) is partly satirical and occasionally anticipates *Vanity Fair*. Mrs. Gore, Lady Blessington, and Lady Charlotte Bury had all begun to write in the twenties; Disraeli and Bulwer Lytton had turned to other if related fields. The latter, with his 'uncanny sense of the literary market' (Rosa, op. cit., p. 86) had made his farewell in *England and the English* (1833).

[3] See also *The Book of Snobs* (1848; first published in *Punch* 1846–7), ch. xvi (*Works*, ix).

'Coventry Club', smoking their full-flavoured Cubas (from Hudson's) after the opera.

Everybody stared at such an exclamation of enthusiasm from the lips of the young Earl of Bagnigge, who was never heard to admire anything except a *coulis de dindonneau a la ste. Ménéhould*, or a *supreme de cochon en torticolis a la Piffarde*; such as Champollion, the *chef* of the Travellers, only knows how to dress; or the *bouquet* of a flask of Médoc, of Carbonell's best quality; or a *goutte* of Marasquin, from the cellars of Briggs and Hobson.

Alured de Pentonville, eighteenth Earl of Bagnigge, Viscount Paon of Islington, Baron Pancras, Kingscross, and a Baronet, was, like too many of our young men of *ton*, utterly *blasé*, although only in his twenty-fourth year. Blest, luckily, with a mother of excellent principles (who had imbued his young mind with the Morality which is so superior to all the vain pomps of the world!) it had not been always the young Earl's lot to wear the coronet for which he now in sooth cared so little.

Perhaps the frequent mention of noted firms is a relic of the practice instituted by Byron; that it had, or came to have, actual commercial value to the author is suggested by a much later burlesque, 'Crinoline and Macassar' in Trollope's *Three Clerks*.[1]

The fashionable novels seem to have taken a lot of killing. At intervals critics surveying the literary scene proclaimed their demise; in 1845 *Blackwood's* asked,

Where now are all the novels portraying fashionable life with which the shops of publishers teemed, and the shelves of circulating libraries groaned, not ten years ago? Buried in the vault of all the Capulets.[2]

[1] Ch. xxii.
[2] 'The Historical Romance' (September 1845), p. 342.

Early in 1849 a reviewer announced that the fashionable novels had at last become

most *un*-fashionable . . . aping the tone of a school and a system of society which really died once and for ever . . . on the 10th of April last.[1]

The date is that of the Chartist petition. The ghost of the aristocratic novel was still walking in the eighteen-fifties; in 1859 David Masson suggested that 'no harm would attend its total and immediate extinction', giving the interesting new reason that its frivolous representation of aristocratic politicians 'is catering for Revolution'.[2] George Eliot, in her 'Silly Novels by Lady Novelists', attacked several examples of what she labelled 'The Mind and Millinery School'. But perhaps the pretence that mind existed alongside millinery itself marks the effort to catch up with a new fashion; in *Tancred*, Lady Constance Rawleigh has read *Vestiges of Creation*.[3]

Meanwhile, as we should expect, the great novelists were using the fashionable novel for their own purposes—purposes ironical, satirical, moral. Charlotte Brontë almost certainly had the fashionable novel as well as her own earlier romances in mind in her picture of what she saw as the high life of the visitors at Mr. Rochester's house party; the daughter's address to her mother 'Baroness Ingram of Ingram Hall' has the very tone of Mrs. Gore (and of 'Lords and Liveries'). Anne Brontë exposed the most unpleasant side of that life as a moral warning in *The Tenant of*

---

[1] *Fraser's* (April 1849), p. 419.
[2] *British Novelists and their Styles*, pp. 229–31.
[3] Book I, ch. ix.

Wildfell Hall. Thackeray was continually occupied
with its seamier side, and penetrated into high life
at its highest in the Gaunt House chapters of *Vanity
Fair.* Dickens, after a crude sketch of villainous and
inane aristocrats, Sir Mulberry Hawk and Lord
Frederick Verisopht in *Nicholas Nickleby,* rose to the
pathetic comedy of the Honourable Mrs. Skewton,
the even more subtle Cousin Feenix,[1] and the glitter-
ing and ghastly tragedy of Sir Leicester and Lady
Dedlock in *Bleak House.*[2] Disraeli, of course, shows
less detachment. His novels, especially *Tancred* (and
the much later *Lothair*) exhibit his skill in making
the best of two worlds: for the first half of the book
the aristocratic hero is shown in fashionable society,
in the second half in flight from it. That at bottom is
the pattern of his novels from *Coningsby* onwards.

§ 14

The widening of the novel's social range carried
with it the widening of its geographical range: inevitably a novel about factory workers must be set in an
industrial town. And the cultivation of both 'low'
and middle-class life as material necessitated more
variety of setting; one Mayfair mansion, or one
country 'place' is very much like another, and each
may exist in a vacuum of locality, almost as indefinite

[1] It was after *Dombey and Son* that a reviewer in *Blackwood's* deplored
Dickens's tendency 'to decry, and bring into contempt as unfeeling, the
higher classes . . . a very vulgar as well as evil taste' (October 1848),
p. 468.

[2] He returns to burlesque of the fashionable novel in the political
chatter of Lord Boodle and Mr. Buffy at Chesney Wold.

as the 'not . . . anywhere in particular . . . up in a mountain, near a castle' of the historical romance.[1] But in the middle-class we may range from Todgers's to Princess's Place, from Gateshead Hall to Thornfield and Marsh End—places distinctive in themselves and felt as part of a larger locality. Then, if the novelist writes with the purpose of revealing one 'nation' to another, he must document his revelations with some exactness; he will otherwise hardly be believed. The kind and variety of setting, the way it is described, its function in the novel, were all changing, and novel-readers in the forties met with many surprises. In *Oliver Twist*, Whitechapel first passed from the police reports to the novel. *Mary Barton* announced its novelty of setting in its subtitle—'a tale of Manchester life'; *Wuthering Heights*, in its very title. The impact of strangeness may be recovered from the reviews and from other recorded comments, such as that of the lady who after reading the Brontë novels felt she would rather visit the Red Indians than trust herself in Leeds.[2] That the Yorkshire of *Wuthering Heights* was an unknown country to novel-readers is clear too from the painstaking description of place in the early chapters of Mrs. Gaskell's *Life of Charlotte Brontë*, and from Charlotte's preface to the second edition of Emily's novel in 1850. This preface, written when she had herself had some experience of the standards of literary

---

[1] This is the scene of the burlesque novelette 'Sir Antony Allan-a-dale' in Trollope's *Three Clerks*, ch. xix.

[2] [W. C. Roscoe], *National Review* (July 1857), p. 131; the review was reprinted in *Poems and Essays*, ii. 309–53.

London, is an apology as well as a defence. She saw
that to those readers for whom Yorkshire and its
people were 'alien and unfamiliar' such a work must
appear 'rude and strange'. As a concession she revised
certain details; she smoothed away the quasi-phonetic
representation of dialect in order to remove superficial obstacles to appreciation:

I am sure Southerns must find [Joseph's speeches] unintelligible; and thus one of the most graphic characters in the
book is lost on them.[1]

Such difficulty was guarded against by Mrs. Gaskell
when, with her husband's help, she provided glos-
sarial footnotes to Lancashire dialect words in the
first edition of *Mary Barton*. The modicum of dialect
in *Jane Eyre* and *Shirley* is skilfully managed: it is
suggestive without being unintelligible.[2] Indeed,
though everyone thinks of *Jane Eyre* as a Yorkshire
novel, no district is specified and the name Yorkshire
never appears. *Shirley* is a much more distinctively
regional novel; it is not surprising that the details
given there were the means by which her local friends
identified Charlotte as the author. This novel is even
defiantly regional, and politically as well as poetically
so: there is a Carlylean challenge in the steadily narrowing definition of locality in this sentence:

A yell followed this demonstration—a rioters' yell—a

[1] *S.H.B.* iii. 165; letter to W. S. Williams, 29 September 1850.
[2] Though Clark said the first volume of *Shirley* would be 'unintelligible to most people, for it is half in French and half in broad Yorkshire' (*Fraser's*, December 1849, p. 693). Even the midland dialect in
Adam Bede was objected to by some (Cross, ch. ix; letter of 23 February
1860).

North-of-England—a Yorkshire—a West-Riding—a West-Riding-clothing-district-of-Yorkshire rioters' yell.[1]

With this extension of geographical range there came, besides a closer localization and a more lively regionalism, a further gain that is as much recovery as discovery. The novel's scene might again lay claim to the spaciousness and beauty of the landscape of the Scottish novels of Scott, or to the intimate settings of the Irish novels of Maria Edgeworth. The 'genius of place' reappears. It presides not only in *Wuthering Heights* and *Jane Eyre* but in *Mary Barton*, with its Greenheys Fields and the scenes remembered by old Alice from her Cumberland childhood; in the Oxford meadows of *Loss and Gain*; in the chapters of *Yeast* where Lancelot goes fishing with Tregarva; on the sea-beaches of Yarmouth and Brighton where David and Paul spend childhood days; and in Camden Town, shatteringly progressive in the railway age.

§ 15

The time of this story is post-Johnsonian, but it is older than its readers; unless, indeed, a chance oldster now and then opens it to see if it is a proper book to have in the house.
William De Morgan, *When Ghost meets Ghost* (1914),
ch. xxv.

There was a further extension of field in the novels of the forties, and one which is little noticed by modern readers. The modern reader tends to assume that any Victorian novel which is not obviously

[1] Ch. xix.

'historical' is intended to be roughly contemporary in setting; but in fact many writers were coming to prefer a setting which was neither historical nor contemporary, but which lay in a period from twenty to sixty years earlier. Reading novels such as *Wives and Daughters* and *Middlemarch* without due recognition of their setting in an England of forty years before the date of writing, the modern reader misses much of their quality.

The story of the rise and popularity of this kind of setting is a long one. A complete survey would need to start at least with *Waverley* (or, *'Tis Sixty Years Since*[1]); and it might conclude with the single modern survivor[2] of a great tradition. It would need also to allow for a variety of motives: the wish to avoid the specific associations of strictly contemporary novels, whether *romans à clef* of fashionable and polite society, or problem and propaganda novels; the desire to escape from the moral constriction of the present;[3] the wish to record change, in its process or by implied contrast; the feeling that the writer's imagination is most readily and valuably

[1] The appeal of this degree of distance is defined in Scott's Introduction. It is reasserted sixty years later by Leslie Stephen in his essay on Scott: 'I often fancy that . . . "'Tis Sixty Years Since" indicates precisely the distance of time at which a romantic novelist should place himself from his creations . . . that period . . . from which the broad glare of the present has departed . . .' (*Hours in a Library*, i. 150; first published in *Cornhill*, September 1871).

[2] Ivy Compton-Burnett; see below, p. 95.

[3] The late eighteenth-century setting of *Barry Lyndon* is used as an excuse for greater frankness of manners (see note to ch. xvii in the original version; *Works*, vi. 252), and probably also in Mrs. Gaskell's *Sylvia's Lovers* (1861) and Reade's *Griffith Gaunt* (1867), written at a date when the novelist had less licence.

stimulated by early memories.[1] There are the special cases of the 'autobiographical' novel and others, including the later family chronicles, which cover a long stretch of time: these 'go back' in order to have room to come forward, but nevertheless usually stop well short of the 'present'.[2] Some novels about the recent past belong to, or encroach upon the category of 'historical novels', because the emphasis is upon public events or 'period' manners; such are *Barnaby Rudge* and *A Tale of Two Cities*, while *Shirley*, *Cranford*, and *Felix Holt*, are in an intermediate category, having obviously a 'historical' colouring absent in *Jane Eyre*, *Villette*, and *The Mill on the Floss*, although their actual distance in time is not greater. Charlotte Brontë consulted old newspaper files about the Luddite riots when she was writing *Shirley*; she consulted nothing but her own early memories (reinforced by the powerful influence of the child's memory of its elders' memories) in writing *Jane Eyre*; while the still more indefinable local memory— villagers' legends, the moors, the old houses—is alone of positive relevance in the early setting of

[1] 'At present my mind works with the most freedom and the keenest sense of poetry in my remotest past' (George Eliot, letter of 1859; Cross, ch. ix).

[2] *Pendennis* (1849–50) moves from the twenties to the edge of the forties, *The Newcomes* (1853) from the seventeen-nineties to the forties. But the life of Jane Eyre in the novel only just overlaps that of Charlotte Brontë. *David Copperfield* (1849–50) is a difficult case. The whole action covers about forty years, corresponding in many ways to Dickens's own life; but there are no railways (the 'Dover coach' is mentioned as late as ch. lix) and the only contemporary matter is the model prison (ch. lxi). There is some deliberate use of 'period' detail, such as the phosphorus box and the Miss Spenlows' three o'clock dinner.

Wuthering Heights. It is the use of the past in novels
of private life which is of particular interest; in its
extent at least it is new in the eighteen-forties, and it
created a new category of novels. The line between
these and the historical novels may not always be
easy to draw; no two readers may quite agree as to
how 'historical' *Vanity Fair* is intended to be; obviously the past here is more definite and documented
than the remoter past of *Jane Eyre*, in which a battle,
even as much offstage as Waterloo, is inconceivable.
Yet Thackeray's main field is surely private life,
although he chooses to borrow for his own purposes
something of the historical novel, something (in Lord
Steyne, for example) of the *roman à clef*, something
even from the 'military novels' which he repudiates.
In his as in Charlotte Brontë's novels, two motives
for choosing the past seem to predominate: that the
past, being past, can be possessed, hovered and
brooded over, with the story-teller's supposed omni-
science; and that the past, being not the present, is
stable, untouchable by the winds and waves which
rock the present. Charlotte Brontë's rejection at the
opening of *Shirley* is explicit:

But not of late years are we about to speak; we are going
back to the beginning of this century: late years—present
years are dusty, sunburnt, hot, arid. . . .[1]

and may recall the great modern novelist whose
twelve novels, all written in the last twenty-five years,

---

[1] Ch. i. Compare Carlyle: 'Why is the past so beautiful ? The element
of *fear* is withdrawn from it for one thing. That is all safe, while the
present and future are all so dangerous' (Journal for 1835; quoted in
Froude, *Carlyle's Life in London*, 2 vols., 1884, i. 20).

are sealed off in a late Victorian past; she has said:

> I do not feel that I have any real or organic knowledge of life later than about 1910. I should not write of later times with enough grasp or confidence. I think this is why many writers tend to write of the past. When an age is ended, you see it as it is.[1]

By turning to the past, the novelist disclaims the responsibility of interpreting contemporary life; Charlotte Brontë wrote to her publisher in 1852:

> You will see that 'Villette' touches on no matter of public interest. I *cannot* write books handling the topics of the day; it is of no use trying.[2]

And so the temporal setting is indicated in an early chapter:

> Fifty miles was then a day's journey; for I speak of a time gone by.

She preferred a past not too closely specified; so, in *Jane Eyre*, in an early chapter, she describes her story as

> now at a distance of—I will not say how many years.

'A time gone by' is perhaps all that the reader is meant to be imaginatively conscious of in *Jane Eyre*, though in the end the data give him, if he is attentive, a definite time-setting—for the main action, 1799 to 1809.[3] That is, not only past, but past beyond

---

[1] Ivy Compton-Burnett, in *Orion, a Miscellany*, ed. R. Lehmann (1945), p. 25.

[2] Letter to George Smith, 20 October 1852; *S.H.B.* iv. 14.

[3] This dating is based on the single precise reference, the mention in ch. xxxiii of *Marmion* (1808) as 'a new publication'. The relative chrono-

personal memory. So in *Wuthering Heights*, where the dating is explicit, and the year 1801 heads the first sentence; here the action runs from 1777 to 1803.[1] In *Vanity Fair*—'While the present century was in its teens'—it is from 1813 to the early eighteen-thirties, and again begins beyond the reach of Thackeray's own memory; Becky and Amelia were grown girls leaving Miss Pinkerton's four years before the author himself went as a small boy to school in Chiswick Mall. It might be fanciful to see a significance in the time-order of these three novels in relation to their novelists' own lives; Thackeray using, but extending, his own remembered experience and observation, Charlotte Brontë disguising or dissociating herself from hers (so that Jane is at Lowood a quarter-century before Charlotte was at Cowan Bridge), and Emily Brontë silently repudiating hers, and escaping from it into the older life of the moors around Haworth. Since all three were precocious readers, the wish to turn back to the period of novels read in childhood may also help to account

logy is clear, and had obviously been carefully worked out by the author. Save for that one date, we should probably place Jane Eyre's childhood in Charlotte Brontë's childhood, for the references to past fashions and tastes ('round curls', 'corsair-songs') and travel (it takes Jane sixteen hours to travel fifty miles) do little more than make the setting *un*-contemporary; and in its context the reference to 'a portrait of George the Third, and another of the Prince of Wales'—in an old-fashioned inn—is ambiguous. But the imaginary 'author' never specifies her age at the time of writing or the distance of the events described, and wishes perhaps simply to give a general impression of writing in middle life. To make Jane Eyre the narrator older than herself (she was about twenty-eight when she wrote) would help to reduce the danger of self-identification.

[1] *Agnes Grey* bears no indication of date; the *Tenant* dates its action in 1821-7.

for the added recession; and for the Brontës the
world in and of which their father[1] had written was
experience at a still lesser remove. But even in
Wuthering Heights the past has some positive point,
and is not only, though it may be mainly, a means
of detemporalizing the action. The eighteenth-century dating gives a certain warrant, in the somewhat
politer eighteen-forties, for the violent behaviour and
speech of the characters; it helps to define Joseph as a
first-generation Methodist; and above all, it increases
the aesthetic distance, underlining the distancing effect
of Mr. Lockwood and Nelly Deans. In *Jane Eyre*
the fashions count for something (the Brocklehurst
daughters, Blanche Ingram) not only in themselves,
but by suggestion; Rochester's Byronic colouring
is heightened in a world where there are ostrich
plumes, turbans, and corsair songs. The isolation of
one village, one set of persons, from another belongs
to the coaching age; the high-society chatter in the
Thornfield house-party (so tediously criticized as unnatural by later readers) is surely an attempt at a
period-piece of manners-painting, legitimately recollected from Charlotte's early reading, through her
own Angrian romances. And Mr. Brocklehurst is
not the less Carus Wilson, the 'black pillar' of her
childhood, if he is also a period figure—an Evangelical clergyman contemporary with Hannah More.[2]
The literary references may not be deliberately
selected, but they, above all, increase the sense of

---

[1] See below, p. 266.

[2] Here and there a later age encroaches; Eliza Reed as a 'Puseyite'
belongs to the eighteen-thirties, as do also Mr. Rochester's cigars.

H

far-stretching vistas of time, and of quiet continuousness; Jane reads Thomson's *Seasons* as quoted by Bewick, Bessie tells her stories from *Pamela*, St. John Rivers gives her the newly published *Marmion*; and Helen Burns reads *Rasselas*. We are aware (as again through Colonel Newcome) of the clear horizon of the eighteen-forties, and of the 'tranquil years' of 'leisure to grow wise' with which Arnold contrasts the present:

> Like children bathing on the shore,
> Buried a wave beneath,
> A second wave succeeds, before
> We have had time to breathe.[1]

From the mild ripples of change represented ten years earlier in Captain Brown's addiction to railway travelling and reading *Pickwick*, Miss Deborah averted her eyes, entrenching herself behind the *Rambler*. Charlotte Brontë, despite the disclaimer of her letter about *Villette*, did not; *Villette* itself is in part a document of the years of the 'Papal aggression'; nor was it quite uncritical of the *Quarterly* reviewer to couple *Jane Eyre* with the Governesses' Benevolent Institution; the waves of feminism and of the conflict of capital and labour sound clearly in *Shirley*. Her novels about the past are still novels for the present, if not, like *Sybil* or *Alton Locke*, tracts for the times. The power of a Charlotte Brontë, as of an Ivy Compton-Burnett, may point the flaw in our current assumption that novels should deal with immediately contemporary life, a flaw not less evident

---

[1] 'Obermann', in *Empedocles on Etna* (1852); written 1849.

because some novelists escape into abstraction or the deeper recesses of the inner life.

The example of Thackeray illustrates other motives, and other rewards, for a novelist's resort to the past. Among its effects are the fuller realization of the narrator's personality, of the characters, and most of all of the irony and pathos which envelop his stories: the sense of flux, of the present as the soon-to-be-past, its fashions faded. Thackeray's own role of reminiscent narrator, looking back down the avenues of memory, is constant; in his confidences to the reader his favourite tone is that of the old man remembering—often of a man older, and remembering more, than is actually possible. 'I have felt the noble passion of love many times these forty years, since I was a boy of twelve', he writes, when he is still under thirty.[1] Seldom is the fictitious arithmetic so explicit; but 'In old-fashioned days, young ladies, and when you were scarcely born'[2] suggests a heavier load of years than thirty-seven; and 'fifty years ago, and when the present writer, being an interesting little boy . . .'[3] assumes it, though here with a playful exaggeration that perhaps expects to be seen through, like the reference to 'my great-grandson Tommy'.[4]

---

[1] 'A Shabby Genteel Story' (1840), ch. viii (*Works*, iii. 358).
[2] *Vanity Fair*, ch. lxvii.   [3] Ch. xli.
[4] *Philip*, ch. xxiv. He mocks this tendency in himself in *Roundabout Papers*: 'When I was presented to the Prince Regent in the uniform of the Hammersmith Hussars', or even 'At the close, let us say, of Queen Anne's reign when I was a boy at a preparatory school'. Compare, 'I am so old, that I might have been at Edial School' (*Philip*, ch. xi). But even these seeming absurdities have a truth of feeling, and suggest the quality that makes his historical novels, *Esmond* and *The Virginians*, also seem novels of memory. It was memory at one remove; through his conversations

With memory goes regret; when Thackeray refers
to some change in manners, he is not content with a
simple 'in those days', but embroiders the mere date
with his own feelings. He has 'a sweet and tender
regret' for the old coaching days: 'Alas! we shall
never hear the horn sing at midnight, or see the pike-
gates fly open any more.'[1]

This is more specific than anything in *Jane Eyre*;
and as a whole, Thackeray's novels are saturated in
the details of a period in the remembered past, yet
without quite becoming novels of manners. The
waltz had just come in, the tide of fashion had not
ebbed from Russell Square, six votes returned a member for Queen's Crawley; such documentation sets
the characters in a context of particulars endeared
by memory; it substantiates them, acts as a kind of
testimony to their actuality, without making them
historical. The glow of recollection, not 'the dark
lantern of Dryasdust' illuminates them. But while
Thackeray may safely specify dates (though in the
later novels at the cost of some discrepancies),[2] and
changes of taste (in houses, furniture, worship, and

with Miss Berry, for example, he 'could travel back sevenscore years of
time' (opening paragraph of *The Four Georges*).

[1] *Vanity Fair*, ch. vii. (Compare the Introduction to *Felix Holt*.)

[2] In *The Newcomes*, ch. xxi, the poems read by Colonel Newcome
include 'Ulysses' (1842), although the date cannot be later than the 1830's.
In *Philip* (1861-2) the original dates of 'A Shabby Genteel Story' com-
mitted the author to a birthdate of 1827 for his hero; but Thackeray is
determined to keep the story clear of the heels of the present—so it is
'twenty years ago', 'in the times of Louis Philippe' (at one point 'before
railways were invented'), even when Philip is grown up and married,
which should be about 1850. In the table in ch. xxxv he pushes Philip's
birth back to 1825; but this is not enough to resolve the inconsistencies.

the arts) and ways of living (coaches and railways)[1] there is one area of change which presents special dangers to the author of an *illustrated* novel—namely, fashions in dress. And it is precisely here that he is driven to define his position, to make it clear that his are not 'costume novels'. As so often, he is teasing his literal-minded readers, but with a serious purpose. In an early number of *Vanity Fair*[2] he took his stand firmly on inconsistency:

It was the author's intention, faithful to history, to depict all the characters of this tale in their proper costumes. . . .But when I remember the appearance of people in those days, and that an officer and a lady were actually habited like this [*a sketch*] I have not the heart to disfigure my heroes and heroines by costumes so hideous; and have, on the contrary, engaged a model of rank dressed according to the present fashion.

Later, in *Philip*, in reply to a 'fair correspondent', he made a fuller defence:

My dear madam, these anachronisms must be, or you would scarcely be able to keep any interest for our characters. What would be a woman without a crinoline petticoat, for example? an object ridiculous, hateful, I suppose hardly proper. . . .[3]

[1] Not always accurately; but he disarms criticism. 'The Eastern Counties did not then boast of a railway (for we beg the reader to understand that we only commit anachronisms when we choose, and when by a daring violation of those natural laws some great ethical truth is advanced)' (*Pendennis*, ch. lii).

[2] No. II, ch. vi; the passage occurs only in the original monthly part and in the first edition of 1848, and is given in the Appendix to *Works*, xi. The *Athenæum* review (1847), p. 785 had cited this as an instance of the author's 'cavalier impertinence'.

[3] Ch. xix (in the original *Cornhill* version; in revision the 'fair correspondent' is removed). Compare Miss Jewsbury's refusal to describe a heroine's court dress 'as the costume of that day is not in accordance with

Not only the concession, but the mockery implied in it, shows where Thackeray stands. Included in the pathos of the 'hideous' or 'ridiculous' fashion of the day before yesterday is that of the present fashion, the past that is to be: as Carlyle had recognized in writing of Scott:

> Consider, brethren, shall not we too one day be antiques, and grow to have as quaint a costume as the rest? The stuffed Dandy, only give him *time*, will become one of the wonderfullest mummies.[1]

Even when he touches the present, Thackeray anticipates the perspective of memory. What Russell Square was, Belgravia will be; the 'simple sleeves and lovely wreaths' will go the way of the '*gigots* and large combs like tortoiseshell shovels'. And this sharpens his moral criticism; the 'manners of the very polite world'[2] change more slowly than its dress, and its nature hardly at all, although the fashions in degree of plain-speaking may obscure the continuity of behaviour. The bonnet may have changed its outline, but it still fits the head.

It is also important that Thackeray's novels exist not in a fixed but in a moving past. His novels cover a long period in time; we see his people ageing (though not changing), their children growing up; we have never seen the last of them, for when one

our present notions of the becoming' (*Zoe*, 1845, ch. xiii). Anachronism in detail may often be necessary for emotional truth of memory; in recollecting episodes of twenty years past we do not visualize the figures precisely in the fashions of the time.

[1] *London and Westminster Review* (1838).
[2] *Vanity Fair*, ch. li.

novel is finished we may yet hear of them again by chance, perhaps on the far edge of a later novel. Both *Pendennis* and *The Newcomes* add to our knowledge of the Crawleys. More powerful in its emphasis upon time is the conscious looking back of the characters themselves. Dobbin looks back, near the end of *Vanity Fair*, to a scene the reader has witnessed, though not through his hoarding eyes:

'I think I loved you from the first minute I saw you. . . . You were but a girl in white, with large ringlets; who came down singing—do you remember?—and we went to Vauxhall.'

But unconsciousness is equally telling; time seen through its effect upon things—Sir Pitt's 'garden-chair...rotting in the outhouse',[1] in George Osborne's room the 'dried inkstand covered with the dust of ten years'.[2] This looking back may also be more widely reflective, dramatizing the author's own sense of change. It is Major Pendennis, not the author, who draws the long regretful contrast between the twenties and the forties:

'The breed is gone—there's no use for 'em; they're replaced by a parcel of damned cotton-spinners and utilitarians, and young sprigs of parsons with their hair combed down their backs. I'm getting old; they're getting past me; they laugh at us old boys', thought old Pendennis.[3]

---

[1] Ch. xliv.   [2] Ch. l.

[3] Ch. lxviii; this is part of a much longer passage. The use made of Colonel Newcome's memory is of course subtler and more pervasive, but is too generally recognized to require emphasis here. Another later instance of a *laudator temporis acti* is Lord Ringwood in *Philip*, ch. xxi.

Compare George Eliot's Mr. Deane, who looked back from the thirties less regretfully; together the Major and the merchant summarize half a century of change:

The world goes on at a smarter pace now than it did when I was a young fellow. Why, sir, forty years ago . . . a man expected to pull between the shafts the best part of his life, before he got the whip in his hand. The looms went slowish, and fashions didn't alter quite so fast: I'd a best suit that lasted me six years. Everything was on a lower scale, sir—in point of expenditure, I mean. It's this steam, you see, that has made the difference; it drives on every wheel double pace, and the wheel of fortune along with 'em. . . . I don't find fault with the change, as some people do. Trade, Sir, opens a man's eyes; and if the population is to get thicker upon the ground, as it's doing, the world must use its wits at inventions of one sort or another.[1]

She is writing ten years after *Pendennis*. The novelists' concern with past time deepened, if anything, in the sixties; but the past has not as it were moved forward with them. It still lies somewhere on the far side of a line drawn about the mid-thirties. For this there may be reasons; and it is a late essay of Thackeray's which helps to make them clear.

The ten years between 1850 and 1860 brought Thackeray himself into the reality of the middle-age he had loved to assume and into the shadow of 'that illness from which one does not convalesce at all'. In the enlarged freedom of the essay, he fixed his eyes more firmly on the golden-glowing past. As it receded, his sense of its distinctness was sharpened and formu-

[1] *The Mill on the Floss*, Book VI, ch. v.

lated. The *Roundabout Papers* hold the key to much in his novels: and in 'De Juventute',[1] he speaks for all the sensitive middle-aged of his time; 'The middle-aged, who have lived through their strongest emotions, but are yet in the time when memory is still half passionate and not merely contemplative.'[2] (The writer of those words is his great admirer George Eliot; and the sixties are the decade of two of the greatest novels about the past, *The Mill on the Floss*[3] and *Wives and Daughters*.[4]) And this is what he says, in a passage with the refrain, 'We who have lived before railways were made, belong to another world':

In how many hours could the Prince of Wales drive from Brighton to London, with a light carriage built expressly, and relays of horses longing to gallop the next stage? Do you remember Sir Somebody, the coachman of the 'Age', who took our half-crown so affably? It was only yesterday; but what a gulf between now and then! *Then* was the old world. Stage-coaches, more or less swift, riding-horses, pack-horses, highwaymen, knights in armour, Norman invaders, Roman legions, Druids, Ancient Britons painted blue, and so forth— all these belong to the old period. I will concede a halt in the midst of it, and allow that gunpowder and printing tended to modernize the world. But your railroad starts the new era,

[1] First published in *Cornhill Magazine* (October 1860).

[2] *The Mill on the Floss*, Book VI, ch. ix.

[3] 1860; the period of the story is from the late eighteen-twenties to the late eighteen-thirties; it is not very exactly specified, but its remoteness is constantly, and often satirically, emphasized.

[4] *Cornhill Magazine* (1864–6); the period is rather earlier than that of *The Mill on the Floss*, as befits Mrs. Gaskell's longer life, but the indications are not consistent. Molly Gibson is twelve when the story begins, 'five-and-forty years ago' (1819), and twenty when it ends (1827), but already 'these new-fangled railways' are being talked of and even experienced (ch. lii), which is unlikely before 1830.

and we of a certain age belong to the new time and the old one.

The flying-machine, when it comes, will be only one more step forward; the old world lies

on the other side of yonder embankments. You young folks have never seen it; and Waterloo is to you no more than Agincourt, and George IV than Sardanapalus. We elderly people have lived in that prærailroad world, which has passed into limbo and vanished from under us. I tell you it was firm under our feet once, and not long ago. They have raised those railroad embankments up, and shut off the old world that was behind them. Climb up that bank on which irons are laid, and look to the other side—it is gone. There *is* no other side. . . .

We who lived before railways, and survive out of the ancient world, are like Father Noah and his family out of the Ark. The children will gather round and say to us patri-archs, 'Tell us, grandpapa, about the old world'. And we shall mumble our old stories; and we shall drop off one by one. . . . We who lived before railways—are antediluvians—we must pass away. We are growing scarcer every day; and old—old—very old relicts of the times when George was still fighting the Dragon.

That railway-embankment is something more than an easily seized symbol for the line between the two worlds. Anyone of middle age, in any period, is likely to be aware of a line dividing the world of his child-hood from that of the present; but what Thackeray says means even more than a writer born about 1900 may feel looking back from 1953 to the summer afternoons before the First World War. The sense of division, of belonging to two ages (not 'wandering between' them) can never have been so strong as for those authors who grew up into the railway age. Cut off abruptly from the stagecoach world in their youth, they prolonged and idealized it in memory. By constantly recreating it, they made good their age's seeming betrayal.

By the eighteen-sixties the wrench is past; the 'ante-diluvians', the 'patriarchs', in a decreasing minority, 'mumble their old stories' of a vanished world—of their Dorlecote Mills and their Hollingfords, and their Dullboroughs. The two worlds are by then at least separate and distinct. In the forties the new was being roughly superimposed on the old. As is well known, the mid-forties, years of 'railway mania' (1846–8), saw hundreds of new lines opened every month.[1] Changes in the landscape of town and country, movements of population, changes in social habits, all were abrupt, disconcerting, immediately evident. Nothing analogous has ever so changed the face and mind of England in so short a span of time; the mere change in speed of travel was a more sudden leap than any subsequent developments have brought—from twelve to fifty miles an hour.[2] To reflect the double social image in terms of its rapid movement—movement almost from month to month

[1] In three years 2,486 miles, making a total of over 5,000 miles by the end of 1848.

[2] It is often forgotten that railway travel a century ago was little less fast than it is now. A journey to Folkestone took Dickens just over two hours in 1851 (see 'A Flight', *Household Words*, iii, and *Reprinted Pieces*). The journey from Euston to Birmingham, described in ch. xx of *Dombey and Son*, could be made in under three hours by the time of publication, though at the date implied in the book (1841) it took nearly five hours.

—demanded a hardihood of which only one novelist, and he in only one novel, was capable.

Night and day the conquering engines rumbled at their distant work, or, advancing smoothly to their journey's end, and gliding like tame dragons into the allotted corners grooved out to the inch for their reception, stood bubbling and trembling there, making the walls quake, as if they were dilating with the secret knowledge of great powers yet unsuspected in them, and strong purposes not yet achieved.

But Staggs's Gardens had been cut up root and branch. Oh woe the day! when "not a rood of English ground"—laid out in Staggs's gardens—is secure![1]

The power that forced itself upon its iron way—its own—defiant of all paths and road, piercing through the heart of every obstacle, and dragging living creatures of all classes, ages, and degrees behind it, was a type of the triumphant monster, Death.[2]

Dombey and Son is Dickens's first novel of contemporary life, and it is so partly by virtue of its sense of the past under the assaults of the present, which is imaged both in the new railway, shearing off pieces of Camden Town[3] in its headlong rush to Birmingham, and in the contiguity of the great rising firm 'wholesale, retail, and for exportation' and the ineffective retail shop of the Wooden Midshipman. Dickens is here on the 'railway embankment', looking into both worlds; in no other novel is the double image

---

[1] *Dombey and Son*, ch. xv. Dickens is adapting a line from Wordsworth's recent sonnet against railways.

[2] Ibid., ch. xx.

[3] Dickens's old school, the Wellington House Academy in Hampstead Road, was cut in half.

so powerful, and none so clearly measures the exactions from which other novelists turned away.

It had taken him twelve years of writing to arrive at this clairvoyance, and he did not sustain it. Both before and after *Dombey* he too was in his strange way a novelist of the past. Like Thackeray and Charlotte Brontë, he drew upon his own early memories. But more surreptitiously than they. He commenced novelist so young that memory had hardly time to mature; moreover his loyalty and repulsion to his own childhood were long unresolved, perhaps never even fully recognized. Besides, Dickens, while exceptionally aware of his past, is exceptionally unaware of his distance from it; all that he sees is equally present to his brilliant observing eye, and to recall is, for him, to annihilate the intervening years. 'I am exactly nineteen when I write their names' is how he recalls friends of his youth; seeing their handwriting, 'three or four and twenty years vanished like a dream'.[1] 'The very queer small boy' that he was seems still to exist and is encountered, not remembered; he can see Rochester then and now, on the same plane.[2] His sense of the past was much less reflective and self-critical than Thackeray's. Add to this immediate, unreflective sense of the past, his vivid sense of some of the 'topics of the day' and his almost dense unresponsiveness to others, and the result is necessarily bewildering.

[1] *Letters*, ii. 392, 625; on Maria Beadnell and her sister. Hence his naïve resentment when she no longer looked 'exactly nineteen'.

[2] 'Travelling Abroad' and 'Dullborough Town', collected in *The Uncommercial Traveller* (1861).

Ordinary readers have not however been bewildered. The reason is that they have simplified.
Misconceptions about the 'contemporariness' of Victorian novelists have been more fixed and more dis-
torting in effect in Dickens's case than others; his
novels are responsible for the entirely inaccurate
image in the popular mind of the world of 1836 to
1870 as brightly crowded with coaches and coaching inns; and at the same time Dickens is accepted
as an up-to-the-minute social reformer, catching
abuses living as they rise. But for this misapprehension there is substantial excuse. Unlike Thackeray
and Charlotte Brontë, Dickens is himself confused.
Hardly any of his novels outside his 'historical' tales
—*Dombey* is perhaps the one exception—bears any
semblance of time-consistency.[1] It is not a matter of
committing occasional anachronisms, in forgetfulness
or fun, nor yet of a calculated *de te fabula*; the relation of Dickens's novels to the past and the present
is complex and contradictory—'extensive and peculiar'. So many clear paths have been cut through this
critical (and sociological) tangle in Mr. Humphry
House's *The Dickens World*[2] that it is almost sufficient to refer the interested reader to this invaluable
book; but one misconception might survive a study
of it.

Dickens is not isolated in showing the stresses of
the claims of past and present on the novelist. What

---

[1] Where they have specific internal dating, it is self-consistent (more
so than Thackeray's); but their colouring is always of more than one
period.

[2] 1941; second and revised edition, 1942 (references are to the latter).

is unusual is that in him they visibly converge and
do battle—indecisively. For any novelist at this
period the drag of the past was natural and strong;
there is no need, with Mr. House, to call in Proust,[1]
or to speak as if Dickens were in this respect exceptional. What was new was the nature of the pull in
the other direction. In the thirties it was normal for
a novel that was not a *roman à clef* and not 'historical'
to be set either in a specified recent past, or in a realm
supposed unchanging. By the forties there was less
and less that could be supposed unchanging; and
there was this new and strong pressure, as attested
by Charlotte Brontë, to write about 'topics of the
day'.[2] The lower-grade novelists made their intention plain in their sub-titles—'a tale of the times'—a
manifesto which is itself evidence that it was not
taken for granted that novels were about immediately
contemporary life. To dissociate themselves from
these (and for their own individual reasons), the
Brontës, and Thackeray, make a partly conscious
choice or at least a conscious rejection. They turn
from the present, emphasizing their choice by a
specified and even increased 'pastness'; their approach
to 'topics of the day' is oblique and incidental. But
Dickens, more completely perhaps a child of his
time, remains uncommitted, subject at once and in
the same novels to the drag of the past and the pull
of the present.

A further tempting simplification would be that he
responded unawares, that he did not think in terms
of this or that time, and did not know what he was

---

[1] House, p. 21.   [2] See below, p. 115.

doing. This might cover *Pickwick* ('the time-strands
in the book are so various that the period they suggest is an imaginary one'[1]) and even *Oliver Twist*,
with its confusion of the old and the new Poor Laws;[2]
but it does not fit *Dombey and Son*, consciously
planned, from its title onwards, as a new departure,
a 'contemporary' novel, and designed for consistency
and unity. Just in the mid-forties, Dickens's time-
sense seems to clear; the next two novels are centred,
Dombey upon the present and *David* upon the past.
Mr. House (approaching the problem, it must be
remembered, rather from the social historian's point
of view) sees a line between the first two 'Christmas
books': *A Christmas Carol* (1843), 'a story of vague
undated benevolence', and *The Chimes* (1844), 'a
topical satire',[3] which is perhaps to overlook their
common basis of fantasy and fairy-tale. He calls
Martin Chuzzlewit 'uncertain ground' and leaves it
undiscussed; I should say rather that it is Dickens's
first tentative and half-successful attempt to centre a

[1] House, p. 27.

[2] This was Harriet Martineau's criticism, which I do not think Mr.
House completely answers. It was not a thing that the author of *Illustrations of Political Economy* was likely to be wrong about; at least her evidence
has the value of a well-informed *contemporary* view, which even a better-
informed historian must respect. A probable source of Dickens's confusion here is that he could not write about any child and avoid the
'period' of his own childhood.

[3] House, p. 136. For Dickens's design and purpose in *The Chimes*, see
Forster, iv. 5, especially the letters of October 1844. Filer and Alderman
Cute are the two most immediately topical characters; Filer, the 'political
economist', was evidently more fully drawn in the original draft, which
also contained 'a Young England gentleman'. Dickens had been annoyed
by the *Westminster Review*'s criticism of Bob Cratchit's turkey as bad
political economy.

novel in the present time. His first; for *Pickwick* and *Nickleby* are mainly backward-looking (Yorkshire schools were an old story, and Dickens's very awareness of them sprang from a childhood recollection). *Oliver Twist* and *The Old Curiosity Shop*, despite the topicality of theme in the former, are rooted in the author's own childhood as well as in timeless fairy-tale; and *Barnaby Rudge* is openly 'historical'. With *Martin Chuzzlewit* (quite apart from the horrid contemporaneity of America) Dickens began to plan. We know certain important things about this novel: that Pecksniff, embodiment of the 'national vice', was Dickens's starting-point, and that (says Forster)

Broadly what he aimed at he would have expressed on the title-page if I had not dissuaded him, by printing there as its motto a verse altered from that prologue of his own composition to which I have formerly referred: 'Your homes the scene, yourselves the actors here!'[1]

The prologue was composed by Dickens for Westland Marston's play *The Patrician's Daughter* in 1842; a prologue whose repeated cry is 'Awake the Present!'[2] Dickens's wish to use this 'motto' is indi-

---

[1] Forster, iv. 2; and cf. iv. 1, where the original line is quoted.

[2] Its sentiment is vague enough:

> Awake the Present! shall no scene display
> The tragic passion of the passing day?

but the general bearing upon *Martin Chuzzlewit* is clear, especially in these lines (later removed):

> And Truth and Falsehood, hand-in-hand, along
> High Places, walk in monster-like embrace,
> The modern Janus with the double Face.

[*Note continued on next page*

cative of a more conscious intention: but it is only intermittent in this novel, being, like much else in the design,[1] obscured and overlaid in the execution. It is in *Dombey* that Dickens's conscious choice of 'the Present' becomes clear and effective.

Equally conscious, on the biographical evidence, is the choice in *David Copperfield*; it is not, as it might seem, entirely a 'return upon himself', for Paul and Florence Dombey awoke specific recollections of his own childhood and led to the writing of the 'chapter of autobiography' in 1847. *David Copperfield* is consistently (much more so than *Great Expectations*) a novel of the past; it is a *Pendennis* confined to private life, lacking its social background and its reminiscent ironic tone. It is perhaps nearer to *Jane Eyre*, from which there may be some influence.[2] In the novels after 1850 Dickens is 'inconsistent' again, but we must assume that by then he knew what he was doing, odd though it was; that

The spectators are exhorted to

> Learn from the lesson of the present day.
> Not light its import, and not poor its mien,
> Yourselves the actors, and your homes the scene.

The prologue was first printed in the *Sunday Times*, 11 December 1842 (not, as Eckel states, in the published editions of the play) and is given in R. H. Shepherd's *Plays and Poems of Charles Dickens*, ii. 218–20, and in revised form in the *Letters* (1880), i. 77–78, and *Poems and Verses of Charles Dickens*, ed. F. G. Kitton, pp. 81–83. I have quoted from the original version.

[1] See below, pp. 159–62.

[2] The sequence of incidents in *Jane Eyre*, chs. i–v, and *David Copperfield*, chs. iv–v, is similar; both children defy their substitute-parents, are physically ill treated by them, half-crazed by solitary confinement, and then sent away to severe and inefficient schools, where they form their first friendships.

Bleak House is deliberately of no time, and several times; that *Little Dorrit* is both a story of thirty years ago, scarred with the Marshalsea of the eighteen-twenties, and as topical to the eighteen-fifties as the Circumlocution Office.[1] Dickens indeed has 'swallowed all formulas' and bestrides all the categories.[2]

§ 16

'I *cannot* write books handling the topics of the day; it is of no use trying', wrote Charlotte Brontë in 1852; that is, she could not, whatever her publishers' pressure,[3] range herself with Mrs. Gaskell, Kingsley, and Disraeli. She spoke not merely in apologetic regret for her personal disability but with an instinctive shrinking from this kind of novel. In 1854 she wrote to Mrs. Gaskell about *North and South*, then appearing in *Household Words*:

The subject seems to me difficult; at first, I groaned over it . . . it is good ground, but still rugged for the step of Fiction; stony—thorny will it prove at times.[4]

Many novelists in the forties and fifties chose the stony and thorny ground of social and religious controversy; many different motives converged to make the 'novel-with-a-purpose' a common type, and as

[1] See House, pp. 28–32.
[2] Even, as may be seen, the informal ones of this study. I do not include his work in the next section, for it could only be cramped by being placed alongside the social novels of such writers as Disraeli and Kingsley; the special contemporary relevance of *Dombey and Son* is considered in Part II below.
[3] *S.H.B.* iv. 14; letter to George Smith, 30 October 1852.
[4] Ibid. iv. 153; letter of 30 September 1854.

vulnerable to mockery as its predecessors. That com-
pendious burlesque, Charley Tudor's 'Sir Anthony
Allan-a-dale', a novel in halfpenny daily numbers,
and a historical romance, is also a novel with a purpose—several purposes:

'The editor says that we must always have a slap at some
of the iniquities of the times. He gave me three or four to
choose from; there was the adulteration of food, and the want
of education for the poor, and street music, and the miscellaneous sale of poisons. . . . Then we have the trial of the
apothecary's boy; that is an excellent episode, and gives me
a grand hit at the absurdity of our criminal code.'

'Why, Charley, it seems to me that you are hitting at
everything.'

'O! ah! right and left, that's the game for us authors. . . .'

. . . 'And what's the end of it, Charley?'

'Why, the end is rather melancholy. Sir Anthony reforms,
leaves off drinking, and takes to going to church every day.
He becomes a Puseyite, puts up a memorial window to the
Baron, and reads the Tracts. At last he goes over to the Pope,
and gives over his estate to Cardinal Wiseman. Then there
are the retainers; they all come to grief, some one way and
some another. I do that for the sake of the Nemesis. . . . The
editor specially insists on a Nemesis.'[1]

Ten years earlier, Thackeray had had his jibe at
Disraeli's political axe-grinding in *Novels by Eminent
Hands*; but he expressed his objection more directly
in the 'Plan for a Prize Novel'.[2]

My dear Snooks, . . . You are bringing, I see, your admirable novel, *The Mysteries of May Fair*, to an end—(by the

[1] Described by Charley to his friend Norman in ch. xix of Trollope's
Three Clerks (1858).

[2] *Punch*, 22 February 1851; *Works*, viii. 175.

way, the scene, in the 200th number, between the Duke, his Grandmother, and the Jesuit Butler, is one of the most harrowing and exciting I ever read)—and, of course, you must turn your real genius to some other channel. . . .

Unless he writes with a purpose, you know, a novelist in our days is good for nothing. This one writes with a Socialist purpose; this with a Conservative purpose: this author or authoress with the most delicate skill insinuates Catholicism into you, and you find yourself all but a Papist in the third volume: another doctors you with Low Church remedies to work inwardly upon you, and which you swallow down unsuspiciously, as children do calomel in jelly. Fiction advocates all sorts of truth and causes. . . .

Novelists who, for one reason or another, avoided the thesis-novel themselves might be regarded as interested critics; but already in 1850 reviewers were complaining of the growing practice of ·

writing political pamphlets, ethical treatises, and social dissertations in the disguise of novels. . . . To open a book under the expectation of deriving from it a certain sort of pleasure, with, perhaps, a few wholesome truths scattered amongst the leaves, and to find ourselves entrapped into an essay upon labour and capital, is by no means agreeable.[1]

This complaint, in its simple form of the cheated anticipation of pleasurable entertainment, often recurred: it is a mistake to suppose that resistance came only with the enlightenment of *l'art pour l'art*. Other

---

[1] *Fraser's* (November 1850), p. 575; the books under review included *Alton Locke*. But some reviewers took a different line, and complained when they found lack of 'purpose'. A writer in *Tait's Edinburgh Magazine* (February 1848), pp. 138–40, was perplexed by *Wuthering Heights*, which did not 'dissect any portion of existing society'. In the end he found a 'moral' in the 'volumes': 'they show what Satan could do with the law of Entail'.

objections may legitimately be made: the work of the novelist who handles the topics of the day may fade as those topics fade, or be read only by social and ecclesiastical historians; even in its own day it may give 'to party what was meant for mankind' (how many low-church or dissenting readers could the tales published by Mr. Burns[1] count on, even in the forties?); by becoming too preoccupied with outward matters, it may lose touch with the other world of imaginative reality; the novelist's 'purpose' may too firmly predestine the individual fates of his characters, destroying both suspense and spontaneity.[2] Yet there are gradations. *Mary Barton* may still be the least read of Mrs. Gaskell's novels, as is *Hard Times* of Dickens's; but most modern readers can get more from these than from *Sybil* or *Yeast*, and more from these again than from *Michael Armstrong, the Factory Boy*[3] or *Helen Fleetwood*,[4] or *Forest and Game Law Tales*.[5] A very little effort will disperse the dust that lies on *Loss and Gain* and *The Nemesis of Faith*, but only a slightly morbid curiosity will ever lead readers again to *Hawkstone*, or *Steepleton*, or *Rest in the Church*.

[1] These included the *Englishman's Library* (1840-1), the *Juvenile Englishman's Library* (1844-9), and the *Fireside Library* (1845), in which tales by the Rev. William Gresley and the Rev. Francis Paget were published.

[2] William Sewell's *Hawkstone* (1845) is an extreme instance; the Evangelical is allowed to repent after many sufferings, but the atheist falls into melted lead and the Jesuit is eaten by rats. (It was Sewell who burnt Froude's *Nemesis of Faith*, and who 'edited' the early novels of his sister Elizabeth Sewell.)

[3] By Frances Trollope, 1839-40.

[4] By 'Charlotte Elizabeth' (Mrs. Tonna), 1839-40, as a serial in *The Christian Lady's Magazine*; in one volume, 1841.

[5] By Harriet Martineau, 1845-6.

Degrees neither of sincerity nor of clear-headedness will account for the difference (or Reade, with his effective graft of the sociological tract on to the sensation novel, would rank higher than he does); and 'the very obvious truth that the deepest quality of a work of art will always be the quality of mind of its producer'[1] does not explain why Mrs. Gaskell could and Charlotte Brontë could not choose the subjects they did. The matter is explored a little farther in a later chapter; here I am content to assume that for the 'stony ground' of 'topics of the day', some novelists (and some readers) are better shod than others.

So much, then, for the present, for the objections and limitations; but certain positive benefits of the 'purpose' or 'problem' novel, to the status of the novel, to its readers, as well as to the 'causes' themselves, cannot be overlooked. (Some, which are peculiar to the religious novel, will be considered later.) Speaking largely, any original effort at the imaginative translation of actuality must increase the interest of the art-form which receives it. The formal ordering of ideas into narrative, the presentation of 'views' through persons, the creating of a world which bore a strangely close relation to the actual contemporary world and was nevertheless newly created— all these were problems which exercised the novelist's art to the utmost; the finer his artistic conscience, the less he could be content to 'think aloud', the more concerned to 'make something'[2] of this new, raw, and recalcitrant material. (That 'making' is not

[1] Henry James, 'The Art of Fiction' (1884).
[2] Arnold objected to 'the modern English habit . . . of using poetry

impossible, *Hard Times* alone may stand to witness.) The novel rather than drama or poetry was the most favoured imaginative medium for 'topics of the day', as a natural consequence of its status as 'dominant form'; Disraeli doubtless speaks for many others when he writes in 1849:

> It was not originally the intention of the writer to adopt the form of fiction as the instrument to scatter his suggestions, but after reflection he resolved to avail himself of a method which, in the temper of the times, offered the best chance of influencing opinion.[1]

(The 'best chance', perhaps, but one with diminishing returns, as *Fraser's* protest shows.) But at all times writers have seen the obvious advantage of 'truth embodied in a tale', of catching the reader off his guard, 'under the expectation of pleasure'. Some writers of this kind of novel have a worthier reason for the deception. In narrative (as also in drama) the writer can be or seem to be relatively uncommitted; if his care is genuinely to think out a problem, if he is concerned to ask questions and not merely to hand out ready-made answers, then he finds the dramatizing, the projecting, of the issues, or the different possible approaches, more useful than direct statement or argument. His novel is then less an advertisement of his universal panacea (Carlyle's 'Morrison's Pill'), than a diagnosis; it puts his questions, and shows his progress towards an answer. The debate,

as a channel for thinking aloud, instead of making something'. *Unpublished Letters of Matthew Arnold*, ed. Arnold Whitridge (New Haven, 1923), p. 17; letter of 1849.
   [1] Preface to fifth edition of *Coningsby*.

whether it is in his own mind or with recognized opponents, takes shape outside him; no doubt he takes sides, but that is less important than that he *shows* sides. His problem may almost coexist with the writing of his novel—Kingsley, it seems, was nearly his own Lancelot Smith, and only after *Yeast*[1] was he ready for *Politics for the People*—or it may be seen in the drier light of retrospection; Newman projected at least some of his own debates of ten years before into the imaginary situation of *Loss and Gain*. The debate is usually only a deeper disguise for the author's actual prejudgement of the 'problem' he presents; but not necessarily; Mrs. Gaskell does not even take sides between John Barton and Job Legh. Even so, there is at least a show of open-mindedness, of distance; a valid distinction, among 'purpose-novels', exists between the 'debate-novel' and the 'Morrison's Pill' novel. And in such novels the appeal is not narrowed to that of the thinly disguised party pamphlet: *Mary Barton* was valued by men of widely differing views on capital and labour; every angle could catch some of the lights from Newman's opal mind in *Loss and Gain*.

For its extension of social (and geographical) range the Victorian novel is partly indebted, as has already been suggested,[2] to the novels on 'topics of the day'. This extension includes not only such settings as the tommy-shop and the factory, such persons as the hand-loom weaver and the poacher, such questions as sanitary reform and church restoration. It also

---

[1] The title of the 1851 edition is *Yeast: a Problem*.
[2] See above, pp. 78–91.

includes new areas of the inner life. At least some of
the characters of these novels are less maimed on the
intellectual side than the heroes and heroines of the
fashionable and romantic novel. The complaint was
often expressed that novels made love and marriage
seem the main business of life; it was Harriet
Martineau's complaint against Charlotte Brontë,
Carlyle's against novels in general.[1] That complaint
could not stand against Disraeli or Mrs. Gaskell or
Kingsley, whose heroes are necessarily thinking,
reading, voting, money-making beings. Indeed, the
problem for Disraeli in *Sybil* and Kingsley in *Yeast*
is rather to make the love-interest, in human terms,
'tell' at all; it is not solved either by the almost allegorical role given to Sybil, or the ruthless disposal of
Argemone Lavington. (The use, by Disraeli, Kingsley
in *Alton Locke*, Mrs. Gaskell, and indeed Dickens, of
the inter-class marriage or love-affair,[2] is perhaps the
most appropriate compromise between romance and
sociology; it is a motif which persists, and is finally
justified, in the novels of Gissing.) One thing the
heroes of these novels have in common: Coningsby,
Egremont, Tancred, John Barton, Lancelot Smith,
Alton Locke, all *think*—perhaps ineffectually, ignor-
antly, fitfully, but in their puzzled or impulsive way

[1] H. Martineau, *Biographical Sketches* (1869), p. 362 (in *Daily News*,
1855); F. Espinasse, *Literary Recollections* (1893), p. 279. Lady Ash-
burton's summary protest—'all about feelings'—is often quoted. (Miss
Hilbery in Virginia Woolf's *Night and Day* is probably intended to
recall it.)

[2] Compare also Reade's *Christie Johnstone* (1853) and Mrs. Craik's
John Halifax, Gentleman (1856). The symbolic value of the situation is
patent in Clough's *Bothie*.

they do think, and about their social rights and responsibilities. The novel has entered upon that career of thoughtfulness which, crude, chaotic, unbalanced as its early stages may be, leads to *Middlemarch*.

Whatever the problems for the novel as an art, there is no doubt that the novel gains something in prestige, is redeemed from mere entertainment, when it reflects the urgent preoccupations of its time. The accuracy and value of this reflection, the particular relevance of the 'topics' of *Sybil*, *Yeast*, and *Mary Barton* to their 'day' of 1845 to 1848 and their immediate influence,[1] are questions too large to be considered here and are perhaps more appropriate to the historian of society or of ideas. To the historian it would also be important to explain why the rapid emergence and multiplication of such novels should belong to the forties and not to the thirties; he might see them as the delayed fruits of Reform, as arising directly from the Commission Reports, as part of the instinctive barricade against revolution; he could perhaps relate them to the impulse towards revelation, exposure, prophecy; to the more articulate or more fearful conscience of the time. The literary historian must be content simply to range them alongside such other works of their decade as *Past and Present*, Elizabeth Barrett's 'The Cry of the Children', and Hood's 'The Song of the Shirt' and 'A spade, a hoe, a bill'; yes, and alongside 'Locksley Hall', *The*

---

[1] This is the approach made by Louis Cazamian in what is still the standard survey of the field, *Le Roman Social en Angleterre, 1830–1850* (Paris, 1904).

Princess, and *The Bothie*—the last two even adopt the method of debate. The altered role of the novel is apparent if one contrasts the forties with that other stormy period, the early eighteen-thirties. At that time there had been a slump in the market for novels (and still more for poetry) because no one could think of anything except public events:

No one talks of literature in these stormy and changeful times . . . no attention is paid to anything but speculations on reform and change of rulers.[1]

Fiction had to be disguised as *Illustrations of Political Economy* to succeed.[2] But in the late eighteen-forties, people read novels more than ever; for the novel was now ready and able to absorb and minister to their 'speculations on reform'. No longer does it belong to the world of indolent languid men on sofas, of Aesthetic Tea; to the 'sect' whose temple was Almack's and whose sacred books were fashionable novels.[3] It belongs to the no-man's-land on the frontier between the two nations: 'the claims of the Future are represented by suffering millions',[4] the millions who 'darken in labour and pain'.[5]

The more I reflected on this unhappy state of things between those so bound to each other by common interests, as the employers and the employed must ever be, the more anxious I became to give some utterance to the agony which,

[1] *Athenæum* (12 May 1832), p. 307.
[2] Cf. Carlyle's *Reminiscences* (1881), where his difficulties in publishing *Sartor* are referred to the Reform Bill.
[3] Carlyle, *Sartor Resartus*, ii. 4, iii. 10, and 'Sir Walter Scott' (1838).
[4] Conclusion of *Sybil*.
[5] Matthew Arnold, 'The Youth of Nature', 1852.

from time to time, convulses this dumb people; the agony of suffering without the sympathy of the happy, or of erroneously believing that such is the case.

Thus does Mrs. Gaskell introduce *Mary Barton*;[1] and similar announcements of purpose occur in other novels. 'In the following pages', writes Kingsley in *Yeast*, 'I have attempted to show what some at least of the young[2] in these days are really thinking and feeling.'

And here as a general reminder is an example of what those who had been young in the eighteen-forties remembered of that thinking and feeling. Froude looks back from the eighties:

It was an era of new ideas, of swift if silent spiritual revolution. . . . All were agreed to have done with compromise and conventionalities. . . . All round us, the intellectual lightships had broken from their moorings. . . . The present generation which has grown up in an open spiritual ocean and has learnt to swim for itself will never know what it was to find the lights all drifting, the compasses all awry, and nothing left to steer by but the stars.[3]

§ 17

In that passage Froude perhaps was thinking less of the social than the religious uncertainties of the

---

[1] Preface to first edition, 1848.

[2] He found his audience there, especially among thoughtful Cambridge undergraduates. Henry Bradshaw sat up till 3 a.m. reading *Yeast*; Hort said that its 'burning words . . . used to make me almost bound from the floor of the Union'; and see Fitzjames Stephen, 'The Relation of Novels to Life', *Cambridge Essays . . . 1855*, pp. 184–5.

[3] J. A. Froude, *Carlyle's Life in London* (1884), i. 289–91.

age, which Dean Church recalled in a more specific form, in the Oxford of 1845–6:

We sat glumly at our breakfasts every morning, and then some one came in with news of something disagreeable— some one gone, some one sure to go . . . the recurring tales, each more sickening than the other . . . stories, often incredible, of the break-up of character for the moment; mixtures of tragic pathos with broad farce, of real self-sacrifice with determined indulgence . . . of blundering trickery and a conscience like a compass which has lost its magnetism, with undoubted and most serious earnestness.[1]

The most 'thorny' of the 'topics of the day' in the eighteen-forties were the controversies in religion, and these are occasionally reflected in most novels of the time, not excepting the historical ones and those concerned with the recent past: the novels of Ainsworth, as later of Kingsley and Reade, have their propagandist slant, while Mrs. Bute Crawley in *Vanity Fair*, Eliza Reed in *Jane Eyre*, the curates in *Shirley*, though all ostensibly pre-1820,[2] gain in definition from their authors' awareness of contemporary circumstances.[3] Dickens restricts his direct reflection of contemporary religion to minor characters, but these may be as distinct, and in their way topical, as the ludicrous Mrs. Mac Stinger and the Reverend Melchizedek Howler in *Dombey and Son* and the

[1] *Life and Letters of R. W. Church* (1894), pp. 321–2; letter of 1886.
[2] In the first chapter of *Shirley* Charlotte Brontë makes her topical reference clear, while hedging over dates.
[3] As do Charles Honeyman, and 'Laud Latimer', in *The Newcomes*. (With Honeyman compare Mr. Hatfield in Anne Brontë's *Agnes Grey*, ch. x.)

gloomy Murdstones in *David Copperfield*.[1] Naturally, novelists concerned about the 'condition-of-England question' take in religious questions: as Disraeli does through Eustace Lyle in *Coningsby*, and through his hero in *Tancred* ('What is Duty, what is Faith? . . . What ought I to believe?');[2] as Kingsley does in *Yeast*, both through Lancelot's correspondence with his curate-cousin Luke who is in process of 'going over', and his opposition to Argemone's proposal to enter a sisterhood; and Mrs. Gaskell, less explicitly but perhaps more effectively, throughout *Mary Barton*. Earlier than any of these, that diligent and fervent Evangelical writer 'Charlotte Elizabeth' had written, in *Helen Fleetwood*,[3] a vivid and authentic tale of factory life in which the main impetus is horror at its heathenism; but her social and doctrinal purposes occasionally blunt each other. Borderline cases are Paget's *Luke Sharp* (1845), and Gresley's *Colton Green: a Tale of the Black Country* (1846); both are set in colliery towns, but the emphasis is upon the miners' need for religious teaching and church-building respectively. These two authors, whose Tractarianism issued in a flow of tract-like tales, were acknowledged as 'the fathers' of the 'church novel'.

[1] And later, in Mrs. Pardiggle of *Bleak House* (Dickens's notion of a Puseyite mother) and Mr. Crisparkle in *Edwin Drood* (a 'muscular Christian').

[2] And see the satirical sketch of the Bishop in ii. 4. Effective satire of a broader kind is found in the account of the monastic experiment in Marmion Savage's *The Falcon Family* (1845) and of the Rev. Bat Owlet in his *The Bachelor of the Albany* (1848); and, outside novels, in Thackeray's *Our Street*.

[3] See above, p. 118, n. 4; this novel, which was admired by Mrs. Stowe, has been curiously neglected, except by Cazamian (op. cit., pp. 430–4).

For there is in the forties a mass of novels and tales, bearing on controversial religious questions; they were regarded as a distinct type of the 'purpose-novel', and had received their labels.[1] 'We are weary of pro- and anti-Pusey novels', wrote an *Athenæum* reviewer in 1847;[2] and if this defines the commonest party-division (in novels at least), there are also novels and tales pro- and anti-Evangelicalism, Dissent, Rationalism, even novels mainly concerned with some specific issue such as church-restoration.[3] And others again (usually the most interesting) which are suffused by the general ethos of a party. Some only expect to evoke in their own time an extra-critical response of approval, rage, or impatience; some (not always the same ones) must now be seen only as straws in the wind of great movements of opinion. But others are lifted beyond their purpose and occasion, are the products of minds distinguished in other fields, or the work of true novelists. They are far more numerous than the social novels, and their range is even more considerable. It runs from *The Rector in Search of a Curate*[4] to *The Nemesis of Faith*, from that to *Loss and Gain*. Many indicate their 'party' in their titles, whether blatantly, like *From*

[1] The fullest contemporary treatments are 'Low-Church Novels' in the *Christian Remembrancer* (November 1843), pp. 518–38; 'Religious Stories', *Fraser's* (August 1848), pp. 150–66; 'The Hard Church Novel' in *National Review* (July 1856), pp. 127–46. A fairly comprehensive modern study is Joseph Ellis Baker, *The Novel and the Oxford Movement* (1932), to which I am sometimes indebted.

[2] In 1848 this periodical hoped that *Loss and Gain* might be 'the last of its silly and sickly family' (18 March, p. 292).

[3] F. E. Paget, *St. Antholin's* (1841).

[4] 'By a Churchman', 1843.

Oxford to Rome,[1] or more allusively, like *Amy Herbert* and *Margaret Percival*.[2] Newman mocked at them in the bookshop scene of *Loss and Gain*;[3] the clergyman's bride has forgotten what she has come to buy:

'Is it "the Catholic Parsonage?"' he asked again; '. . . or "Confessions of a Pervert?" or, "Eustace Beville?" or, "Modified Celibacy"?'

The *Christian Remembrancer* of 1848, while welcoming the prevalence of a better influence than Lytton's in fiction, paused to hint at dangers:

Whether another and a more fatal humbug may not succeed, and whether a certain phase of the religious novel may not prove that humbug, remains yet to be seen.[4]

The possibilities of 'humbug' may be seen even in innocent examples; in *Margaret Percival* the battle for the heroine's faith between the rival influences of the clergyman uncle and the charming Italian Countess is handled with earnestness and simplicity, but nevertheless suggests the popular (and quite unreligious) appeal of the suspended-conversion motif. Other writers were more frankly sentimental and sensational, exploiting the obvious possibilities of confession, celibacy, and (especially in later novels) the husband–wife–priest triangle;[5] these need not

---

[1] 'By a Companion Traveller', 1847. The author was Elizabeth F. S. Harris, who also wrote *Rest in the Church*, 1848.

[2] Both by Elizabeth Sewell.

[3] Part III, ch. ii. There is also effective mockery, from another point of view, in George Eliot's *Janet's Repentance*, ch. iii (*Scenes of Clerical Life*, 1856).   [4] April 1848, p. 408; and see April 1847, pp. 540–2.

[5] And, as at all periods, the sensation-novelist is quick to seize the scandalous possibilities of convent life. 'Rosa Matilda' (Charlotte Dacre, author of *Confessions of a Nun*, 1805) had a long ancestry and a consider-

detain us. Rather more serious are stories in which a
painful chapter of personal experience (such as are
hinted in Church's summary) is combined with
romantic imaginings; *From Oxford to Rome* and *The
Nemesis of Faith* measure the extremes of this class—
both falling short of art, and distinguished from each
other chiefly by the intellectual (and educational)
equipment of the authors. And each was condemned
by the very writer who might have been supposed,
on a rough view of the book's content, to have
approved its general religious direction. Carlyle
described Froude's novel as

a wretched mortal's vomiting up all his interior crudities,
dubitations, and spiritual, agonising bellyaches into the view
of the public, and howling tragically, 'See!'[1]

From Oxford to Rome was the novel sent to Newman
in Rome in 1847; he found it 'wantonly and pre-
posterously fanciful', but it stirred him to

the production of a second tale; drawn up with a stricter regard
to truth and probability . . . showing, as in a specimen, that
those who were smitten with love of the Catholic Church,
were nevertheless as able to write common-sense prose as
other men.[2]

—a claim triumphantly vindicated in *Loss and Gain*.

able progeny. Her name was long used as a label for certain brands of
fiction and religious polemic. The translation of Diderot's *Nun* was reprinted (with expurgations) in a popular series of 1851; and the notorious *Maria Monk* (1836) was wittily exposed by Newman in *The Present
Position of Catholics* (1851).

[1] *New Letters of Thomas Carlyle* (1904), ii. 59; letter to John Forster,
spring 1848. Froude disclaimed autobiography in the Preface to the
second edition (1849).

[2] 'Advertisement to the 6th edition', 1874. Newman does not name the

Nevertheless these three contrasted novels, and the class they represent, have something in common other than their value[1] as documents in the history of thought. Religious novels enforced, and perhaps even initiated, the growing tendency to introspection in the novel.[2] They are not a backwater, but a tributary of the main stream. I have said that the heroes of novels-with-a-purpose do at least think; the heroes and heroines of the religious novels think in a special way—they analyse their own states of mind.

Introspection as a 'note' of the thirties and forties has never been duly recognized; yet contemporaries regarded the 'diseased habit of analysis', the 'ingenious invention of labyrinth meandering into the mazes of the mind', or in nobler phrase, 'the dialogue of the mind with itself'[3] as characteristic of the times.[4]

novel, but the identification was guessed, and is confirmed by Henry Tristram in 'On Reading Newman' (*Newman Centenary Essays*, 1945); see also Charlotte E. Crawford in *M.L.N.* lxv. 6 (June 1950), pp. 414–18.

[1] That of the *Nemesis* is considerable. The hero's simultaneous admiration for Carlyle and Newman ('Confessions of a Sceptic') suggests comparison with Arnold and Clough. As a study of 'doubt' the novel had many successors, and one predecessor in Geraldine Jewsbury's *Zoe* (1845).

[2] How completely it had 'arrived' by the fifties is seen by a letter from Emily Winkworth (b. 1822) to her sister; she had been reading *Westward Ho!* but found it 'had too little of the inward' to suit 'one's modern taste', although the 'inward' might sometimes be 'morbid' (*Memorials of Two Sisters*, 1908, pp. 127–8). By that time the general change of emphasis had been finally assured by the Brontë novels; a point clearly made in the *North British Review* (August 1851), pp. 422–3.

[3] *Fraser's* (March 1848), p. 329; *Blackwood's* (April 1846), p. 413; Matthew Arnold, Preface to *Poems* (1853).

[4] *Sartor Resartus*, ii. 2. 'These autobiographical times of ours' is

Sartor Resartus, Dipsychus, In Memoriam, and *Empe-docles on Etna* exhibit this 'dialogue' in other forms; but, despite the precedent of *Caleb Williams,*[1] it was slower to establish itself in the novel, partly because it was obstructed in different ways by the dominance of Scott, of the 'silver-fork' novels, and of Dickens. Its most obvious non-literary manifestation is the habit (not confined to Evangelicals) of careful self-examina-tion, as seen in such published journals as Hurrell Froude's, and many more published only long after;[2] it is therefore not surprising to find it first develop-ing in a simple but not necessarily crude form in tales about young people—Harriett Mozley's, Elizabeth Sewell's, and Charlotte Yonge's.[3] Introspectiveness in miniature is exquisitely traced in the moral dilemma of ten-year-old Grace of *The Fairy Bower*; and here, as not in many large-scale instances, the heroine's conflict of conscience is perfectly integrated with the narrative. Like Mr. Harding's in *The Warden,* it arises from and modifies an interesting and convincing human situation. (The contempo-rary critic who attempted a general review of

---

Carlyle's comment on the thirties; cf. Harriet Martineau, of herself in 1831—'I had now plunged fairly into the spirit of my time—self-analysis . . .' (*Autobiography,* iii. 3).

[1] *Blackwood's* (loc. cit.) regarded Godwin's tale as the only one 'in which this style of descriptive searchings into the feelings is altogether justifiable'.

[2] Such as Macready's, Henry Taylor's, Mark Pattison's, Anne Clough's, Lord Amberley's—to name only the most accessible.

[3] Harriett Mozley (Newman's sister) wrote *The Fairy Bower* in 1839 and published it in 1841. It was followed by a sequel, *The Lost Brooch* (1841) and by one novel, *Louisa* (1842). Elizabeth Sewell's *Amy Herbert* and Charlotte Yonge's *Abbeychurch* were published in 1844.

'religious stories'[1] praised its 'skill and delicacy'; he also recognized some 'Newmanly over-subtlety'.) In *Loss and Gain* the situation is more stereotyped, as befits its deliberate intention of substituting sense for nonsense; but the same subtlety prevails. Here the 'dialogue of the mind with itself' might seem at first too 'inward' for the novel form, yet the external debates, with their wit and high spirits,[2] their clash of young mind upon mind, and the subtle inter-twining of Charles's progress towards decision with the academic and idyllic Oxford setting give that dialogue a firm embodiment and also a typical and timeless truth.[3] As so often with Newman's work, there is no need to make historical and doctrinal allowances: 'cor ad cor loquitur'.

The analysis of motives and states of mind makes the stories of the two Newmans more interesting simply as narratives. But in inferior artists such analysis often conflicts with the narrative interest, and its dangers are patent in the tales of Froude and Miss Harris. The Newmans have a respect for the formality and continuity of narrative art; they are 'making', not merely 'thinking aloud', and have be-sides a fine sense of comedy.[4] But without such

---

[1] *Fraser's* (August 1848), p. 151.

[2] One can see why a friend found him 'frequently laughing' over his manuscript in 1847 (Wilfrid Ward, *Life*, i. 191); and why the *Athenæum* review called it 'flippant and farcical' (18 March 1848).

[3] The description of the state of mind of young men who have not yet formed their 'views' is a good example (Part I, ch. iii).

[4] This distinguishes them also from such a writer as Gresley, whom Harriett Mozley reports as saying that 'he would give up writing if his stories were found amusing' (unpublished letter).

respect, and with an unbroken solemnity in the characters' 'interior dubitations', introspectiveness can sink a novel.[1] Further, its display, as Carlyle saw, can be indelicate. Indelicacy is not a concomitant of religious scepticism; Miss Harris is also guilty of it (and Emily Brontë is not). But at least Tractarian principles were heavily on the side of 'reserve' and reticence in religious discussion, and the maturer and more disciplined Tractarian novelists accepted and applied this tenet of the party, to their benefit as novelists. This at once distinguishes them from novelists of the Evangelical school;[2] it was of Evangelical writers that Newman was thinking when he spoke out against 'certain religious novels' in a lecture of 1843:

that they sometimes do good, I am far from denying;—but they do more harm than good. They do harm on the whole; they lead men to cultivate the religious affections separate from religious practice.

Charlotte Yonge remembered Keble's warning 'against too much talk and discussion of Church matters, especially doctrine'—remembered it in her novels, as well as in her life.

If doctrines were not to be discussed, there remained 'three-fourths of life'—the sphere of conduct, the novelist's true sphere. The best 'religious stories'

[1] The narrative in the *Nemesis* is clogged by letters and even has an incorporated essay, the hero's 'Confessions of a Sceptic'. *From Oxford to Rome* has a sixty-page selection from the hero's writings (ch. vi) and *Rest in the Church* is largely soliloquy.

[2] The distinction is made particularly clear in *The Fairy Bower*, ch. ii, where the Evangelical's wish to inquire into the state of a child's beliefs is gently but firmly put in its place as unwarrantable interference.

of the time occupy the ground of everyday domestic and social behaviour, with doctrines and beliefs but discreetly suggested and implied. Their text might be Keble's verse about 'the trivial round, the common task'; or the lines from the *Excursion*:

> Turn to private life
> And social neighbourhood; look we to ourselves;
> A light of duty shines on every day
> For all.[1]

All repeatedly emphasize by example that '*home* is the element and trial of a Christian'.[2] Nor are the issues 'dated' by the particular standards of the time; perennially interesting, whatever the scales chosen, is the weighing of the claims of self-development and submissiveness, of virtue and expediency, sincerity and good manners. 'Home is the element and trial': that is, family life, parents and children,[3] brothers and sisters, in a secure and specified setting. In the forties it was re-establishing itself in the novel, after a long exile;[4] and to this, the religious novels notably contributed.[5]

[1] v. 381–4; used as a title-page motto in Miss Sewell's *Gertrude* (1846); J. E. Baker, op. cit., ch. x, has emphasized its significance. *The Fairy Bower* has a verse from the 'Ode to Duty' on the title-page; *The Lost Brooch* has *Excursion*, iv. 66–73.

[2] *The Fairy Bower*, ch. xlvi. Cf. Miss Harris's chapter-heading, 'The Warfare of Daily Life'.

[3] The emphasis is generally here rather than on courtship and marriage.

[4] Reviewers were generous with comparisons to Jane Austen; and undiscriminating though these are, they show how scarce the novel about an 'ordinary family' had become.

[5] The dates of Charlotte Yonge's early works, and her stated indebtedness to Harriett Mozley and Elizabeth Sewell (Preface to *Scenes and Characters*, 1886 edition) invalidate the conclusions of Ernest Baker, who says she 'took domestic fiction as it had been shaped by . . .

The danger here is insipidity; the 'trivial round' left as trivial, or merely said and not shown to be a road to eternal life. But where the religious impetus is strong and not narrowly operative, there is at least the promise, the potentiality, of that telling contrast of scale which is the novelist's peculiar opportunity:

> In the dim background there was the burning mount and the tables of the law; in the foreground there was Lady Debarry privately gossiping about her, and Lady Wyvern finally deciding not to send her invitations to dinner.[1]

My argument is that the 'religious novels' of the forties assisted in important changes of emphasis in the novel as a whole. Without making exaggerated claims for individual writers, it is possible to discern a vital connexion between their work and that of later and greater novelists. For this, it is no disqualification that some of their work would now be classed as 'juvenile'. These tales were read by adults in their own time, and were surveyed in serious reviews, as different in religious complexion as *Fraser's* and the *Christian Remembrancer*.[2] They resisted rigid categories then, and still do.[3] Obviously, any narrative

Charlotte and Anne Brontë, and Mrs. Gaskell' (*History of the English Novel*, viii, 1937, p. 103).

[1] *Felix Holt*, ch. xl. Compare *Sartor Resartus*, i. 4: 'a whole immensity of Brussels carpets, and pier-glasses, and or-molu . . . cannot hide from me that such Drawing-room is simply a section of Infinite Space, where so many God-created Souls do for the time meet together'.

[2] See also Charlotte Yonge's 'Class Literature of the last thirty years', in *Macmillan's Magazine* (September 1869), pp. 448–56.

[3] Harriett Mozley modestly feared that her work was 'too deep for children, too shallow for grown-ups—just the unhappy medium' (unpublished letter). In the event her appeal was, and could be again, to both.

whose main characters have the age-range typical of a long Victorian family may look either way for its readers; or may prefer not to choose. And if, as often happens, it looks especially towards readers of sixteen to twenty-one, it has to compete with full-grown novels.

It may be necessary to agree with Henry James that many of them are 'semi-developed' novels; but we must also admit his qualification:

Occasionally . . . they almost legitimate themselves by the force of genius. But this is only when a first-rate mind takes the matter in hand.[1]

The scale of his praise suggests George Eliot; but his chosen instance is *The Heir of Redclyffe*.[2] It is a judgement well supported in its time, and defensible even today.

§ 18

The change that had come within his own generation is summed up by Walter Bagehot—writing on the Waverley novels in 1858, and conceding that Scott 'omits . . . the delineation of the soul' and 'the abstract unworldly intellect':

Above all minds, his had the Baconian propensity to work upon 'stuff'. At first sight, it would not seem that this was a defect likely to be very hurtful to the works of a novelist.

[1] From a review of 1865, collected in *Notes and Reviews* (1921), pp. 77 ff.
[2] Written in 1850–2, and published in 1853.

The labours of the searching and introspective intellect, however needful, absorbing, and in some degree delicious, to the
seeker himself, are not in general very delightful to those who
are not seeking. . . . The theological novel, which was a few
years ago so popular, and which is likely to have a recurring
influence in times when men's belief is unsettled, and persons
who cannot or will not read large treatises have thoughts in
their minds and inquiries in their hearts, suggests to those who
are accustomed to it the absence elsewhere of what is necessarily one of its most distinctive and prominent subjects. The
desire to attain a belief, which has become one of the most
familiar sentiments of heroes and heroines, would have seemed
utterly incongruous to the plain sagacity of Scott, and also
to his old-fashioned art. Creeds are *data* in his novels; people
have different creeds, but each keeps his own. Some persons
will think that this is not altogether amiss; nor do we particularly wish to take up the defence of the dogmatic novel.
Nevertheless, it will strike those who are accustomed to the
youthful generation of a cultivated time, that the passion of
intellectual inquiry is one of the strongest impulses in many of
them, and one of those which give the predominant colouring
to the conversation and exterior mind of many more. And a
novelist will not exercise the most potent influence over those
subject to that passion if he entirely omit the delineation
of it.[1]

After the eighteen-forties, accordingly, people in
novels (even if 'Birmingham people') may have souls,
and may be animated by 'the passion of intellectual
inquiry'. How far this was compatible with the novel's
function of entertainment was (as already implied by
Bagehot) a continuing matter for debate. Later in the
century the debate centred in the leading case of

---

[1] *Literary Studies*, ii. 154–5, 160–1.

George Eliot; and Leslie Stephen's dry defence in his obituary article[1] may stand:

> I confess that, for my part, I am rather glad to find ideas anywhere. They are not very common; and there are a vast number of excellent fictions which these sensitive critics may study without the least danger of a shock to their artistic sensibilities by anything of the kind.

§ 19

So far I have made no attempt to relate the novels of the forties to earlier novels, except by noting certain reactions against novel-fashions of the preceding decade; for I see the novelists of the forties as initiating rather than continuing, and am more aware of their legacy to succeeding novels than of their own inheritance from the novel's past. In a sense every novelist starts afresh; yet it is not quite true that novelists 'completely forget their grandfathers',[2] if only because they know that novel-readers will not and cannot do so. Matthew Arnold paused in his admiration of *Esmond* to contrast it with 'the *heaven-born* character of *Waverley*';[3] Trollope recalled that as a youth of nineteen

> I had already made up my mind that *Pride and Prejudice* was the best novel in the English language,—a palm which I only partially withdrew after a second reading of *Ivanhoe*,

---

[1] *Hours in a Library* (1909), iii. 196; *Cornhill Magazine* (February 1881).

[2] Virginia Woolf, reviewing E. M. Forster's *Aspects of the Novel*, 1927; see *The Moment and Other Essays* (1947), p. 89.

[3] *Letters of Matthew Arnold to Arthur Hugh Clough*, ed. H. F. Lowry (1932), p. 133; letter of 1853.

and did not completely bestow elsewhere till *Esmond* was written.[1]

Such were the standards that novelists of the forties had to rise to meet; Scott, and Jane Austen, and, to a less degree, the 'classics' of the eighteenth century.

Readers and writers alike had grown up alongside the Waverley novels; many[2] could have echoed Thackeray's tribute ('the friend whom we recall as the constant benefactor of our youth')[3] or even Charlotte Brontë's, in the youthful dogmatism of her advice to a friend[4] ('For fiction—read Scott alone; all novels after his are worthless'). His death in 1832 was felt as the closing of an epoch, and the unquestioned greatness of his achievement was of a kind almost to preclude direct influence or imitation. Those who most obviously tried to imitate him, the historical novelists, are perhaps the least influenced. That genial improvisation from stores of long-held knowledge of the past, imaginatively grasped, was not to be counterfeited by a deliberate reading-up of sources; still less was Scott's unique conviction of the value of heroic sentiment, the seriousness and truth of 'romance'—if indeed it was ever understood. Not only inferior art, but impure motives, brought the 'historical novel', as produced by Bulwer Lytton, Harrison Ainsworth, and G. P. R. James, into critical

[1] *Autobiography*, ch. iii.

[2] A few examples are Ruskin (*Praeterita*, ch. ii, § 45, and *Fiction Fair and Foul*, i), Newman (Wilfrid Ward, *Life*, ii. 355), and George Eliot (Cross, ch. i, and letter of 9 August 1871, in ch. xvi).

[3] *Roundabout Papers*, 'De Juventute'; op. cit., 'On a Peal of Bells'.

[4] Letter to Ellen Nussey, 1834; *S.H.B.* i. 122.

disrepute;[1] Ainsworth in particular is obviously a
sensation-seeker, exploring the past for grosser stimu-
lants, bloodier horrors, and more violent crime. There
are signs that by the late forties the old type of historical novel was regarded as played out. Lytton, infallible reflector of changes in taste, turns from it
after *Harold*; young writers starting with historical
novels—Eliza Lynn, Wilkie Collins—quickly desist;
and by 1857 Trollope, whose *La Vendée* (1850) had
been among the failures, was greeted at a publisher's
office with, 'I hope it's not historical, Mr. Trollope?
Whatever you do, don't be historical; your historical
novel is not worth a damn.'[2]

About the same time Kingsley, Reade, and Newman were enlisting the historical novel in the service
of special interests; the sub-title of *Hypatia*—'New
Foes with Old Faces'—could be more generally
applied. This helped to revitalize the languishing
form; and so, probably, did the honest simplification of the historical romance into a tale deliberately
written for children. The best works in this humble
but valuable kind are Charlotte Yonge's, which are
mostly later;[3] but Marryat's *Children of the New*

[1] Its lowered status is made clear by G. H. Lewes ('Historical Romance',
Westminster Review, March 1846, pp. 34–55). Its readers, he says, are
'either very good-natured, or very ignorant; or both'; in this kind of
novel alone is 'mediocrity at its ease'. But see the plea for its revival in
Blackwood's (September 1845), pp. 341–56.

[2] *Autobiography*, ch. vi. The speaker was the foreman of Hurst and
Blackett, who had succeeded Colburn (publishers of *La Vendée*), and to
whom Trollope offered *The Three Clerks*. Trollope's burlesque in that
novel is an amusing comment (see above, p. 116).

[3] She began with *Kenneth* (written before 1850) and *The Lances of
Lynwood* (serialized 1851–2).

Forest (1847) is an outstanding example in the forties. More characteristic of this decade, however, is a critical amusement or impatience with historical novels, as may be seen (the more significantly as coming from Scott's great admirer) in Thackeray's *Legend of the Rhine, Rebecca and Rowena,* and *Barbazure.* But the reaction against the debased historical novels, insipid or sensational, should not be allowed to disguise the extent and permanence of Scott's larger legacy to the Victorian novel. This may be suggested, though not fully comprised, under such heads as the use of a remembered past, and a spacious landscape; 'regionalism' in speech, customs, manners;[1] and the new perception of the dignity of character in humble life. This last, perhaps, is the most far-reaching influence, reinforcing that of Wordsworth's poetry; and perhaps it is responsible for the distinction between the 'low-life' characters of eighteenth-century novels and those of Dickens, Mrs. Gaskell, George Eliot, and Thomas Hardy. Diverse as these writers seem, Toodles and Peggotty, John Barton and Alice Wilson, Dolly Winthrop, Marty South would all be more at home in the Waverley novels than in the novels of Fielding and Smollett.

The modern reader, putting more emphasis on the 'art' of the novel, as shown in economy of structure and nice calculation of detail, has a more lively awareness of the value of Jane Austen, and is inclined to think less of the Victorian novelists because of their

---

[1] The effects of this are seen first and most fully in Scottish and Irish novels, but are also present in the work of Charlotte and Emily Brontë, and of Mrs. Gaskell.

apparent inability to learn from her. (George Moore
thought that hers were rare among English novels,
in tending 'towards the vase rather than the wash-
tub'.[1]) But she was not neglected in this generation,[2]
not even generally underrated (Lewes refers to 'an
universal note of praise');[3] her name figures not only
in such informal records as letters and memoirs[4] but
in formal criticism.[5] But more than Scott's, her novels
seemed to 'date', because of their concern with the
minutiae of manners (masking a deeper concern with
unchanging human nature); standards of the class
about and for whom she wrote had become steadily
more refined in the half-century following her death.[6]
In the thirties her work may have suffered from the
discredit which had fallen upon the middle-class
domestic novel; the novel which attempted against
odds to recover this social territory—Harriet Martineau's *Deerbrook*—was written by one of her

[1] *Avowals* (1924 ed.), p. 35.

[2] See R. W. Chapman, *Jane Austen* (1948), p. 160, on editions between
1833 and 1850.

[3] 'The Lady Novelists', *Westminster Review* (July 1852), p. 135.

[4] The enthusiasm of Macaulay and Tennyson is well-known; there is
further evidence in W. Ward, *W. G. Ward and the Oxford Movement*
(1889), p. 36; Mrs. Russell Barrington, *Life of Walter Bagehot* (1915),
p. 264; F. H. Doyle, *Reminiscences*, pp. 353–7.

[5] Dr. Chapman thinks that her work, although read and enjoyed, was
not used 'as a critical touchstone' (op. cit., p. 149). But Lewes's article
and numerous other novel-reviews in the forties suggest that it was
occasionally so used. For example, the *North British Review* (May–
August 1847, p. 121) draws a distinction unfavourable to *Vanity Fair*—
'She never wrote a "novel without a hero".'

[6] Evidence is to be found, for example, in the *British Critic* (1841),
p. 187, and in private letters (for Lady Knatchbull's, *c.* 1860, see G. B.
Stern, *Benefits Forgot*, 1949, p. 173; for Kate Stanley's, in 1858, *The
Amberley Papers*, ed. B. and P. Russell, 1937, i. 53–54).

steadiest admirers.[1] None of the great novelists (except Trollope)[2] speaks of having read her, as they read Scott, in impressionable youth. Thackeray was reading her in 1859,[3] Charlotte Brontë in 1848, under pressure from G. H. Lewes, who wanted her to see what her own work lacked;[4] we do not know that Dickens[5] and Mrs. Gaskell read her at all. There is some specific influence (as in *Deerbrook* and Harriett Mozley's *Louisa*) though perhaps not so much as some readers imagined.[6] In Lady Georgiana Fullerton's *Grantley Manor*[7] there is really no more than the rough parallel of situation with *Emma*—a heroine mistaken in her reading of behaviour because she is unaware of a secret marriage. More interesting are what must, on the evidence, be rather affinities than influence: *Mansfield Park* and *Jane Eyre* open with the same (perhaps 'archetypal') situation, of the little girl adopted into a household of rich and arrogant

---

[2] *Autobiography* ('Memorials'), journals of 1838.

[2] See above, pp. 139–40.   [3] *Letters*, iv. 155.

[4] *S.H.B.* ii. 178–81; letters of 12 and 18 January 1848 (Gaskell, ch. xvi). But the name 'Northangerland' in the Angrian cycle may suggest that she knew at least something of *Northanger Abbey*.

[5] 'I told him, on reading the first dialogue of Mrs. Nickleby and Miss Knag, that he had been lately reading Miss Bates in *Emma*, but I found that he had not at that time made the acquaintance of that fine writer' (Forster, ii. 4).

[6] By 1853, comparisons were so common and undiscriminating as to arouse the *Christian Remembrancer* to protest:

'A writer of the school of Miss Austen' is a much-abused phrase, applied now-a-days by critics who, it is charitable to suppose, have never read Miss Austen's works, to any female writer who composes dull stories without incident, full of level conversation, and concerned with characters of middle life (July 1853, p. 33).

[7] The parallel is drawn in some detail in a review in the *Athenæum* (3 July 1847, p. 695), and is at least a testimony to the fame of *Emma*.

cousins; the speculations of Jane Eyre at Thornfield and Catherine Morland at Northanger confront similarly mysterious situations, and Catherine's fancy about General Tilney's wife is curiously paralleled by what proves for Jane to be fact. Becky Sharp has a possible prototype in Mary Crawford, and the running contrast and parallel between the fortunes and feeling of Becky and Amelia sometimes recalls the second half of *Mansfield Park*. This too may be archetypal—the fairy-tale contrast of bad girl and good girl.[1]

Few novelists have paid such homage to their 'grandfathers' as Dickens and Thackeray. It will be sufficient here, without attempting to define all the affinities and the differences, to recall Dickens's admiration (and emulation) of Smollett, and Thackeray's of Fielding. In the list of Dickens's books beloved at nine years old (drawn up in the chapter of autobiography written in 1847 and incorporated into *David Copperfield* two years later)[2] the first three of the eight books named are *Roderick Random*, *Peregrine Pickle*, and *Humphrey Clinker*. And although the list also includes *Tom Jones*, *The Vicar of Wakefield*,[3] and *Robinson Crusoe*, it is from Smollett that Dickens inherits most; sometimes recalling specific situations or comic devices,[4] resembling him in comic breadth

---

[1] Cf. p. 234 below.

[2] Forster, i. 1; *David Copperfield*, ch. iv.

[3] He also read *The Bee* and *The Citizen of the World*; and the influence of Goldsmith may be traced in the Christmas books (he planned the *Carol* to be 'about the length of *The Vicar of Wakefield*') and in the tone of some of his descriptions of humble domestic happiness.

[4] As in Sam Weller's following Mr. Pickwick to prison (Forster,

and buoyancy and the fearless exposure of social evils; and, what is more important, in all his earlier novels using Smollett's pattern of loosely linked adventures of a hero (sometimes accompanied by a comic 'squire') through a series of contemporary scenes. This plan supplied the natural and easy transition (especially useful for a serial writer) from unstrung sketches of contemporary life to deliberately constructed novels; Dickens's gradual advance towards a more complex and calculated unity in his novels after 1842 may be seen in terms of an emancipation from the Smollett tradition.[1] Less has been made of this relation by later critics[2] than of Thackeray's to Fielding. But the latter is of another order, and can hardly be accounted an influence. In two respects Thackeray perhaps consciously made Fielding his standard. As early as 1840 he noted that Fielding does not '[fall] in a passion with [his] bad characters' but 'treats [them] with a philosophic calmness';[3] and that he strives after unity and design

ii. 1). Fanny Squeers's letter in *Nicholas Nickleby* resembles Winifred Jenkins's, as E. A. Baker, *History of the English Novel* (vii. 258), has noted.

[1] See John Butt, 'Dickens at Work', *Durham University Journal*, N.S., ix. 3 (June 1948).

[2] Perhaps because Smollett's own rank has been depressed; Scott had regarded Fielding and Smollett as of 'equal rank' and 'far above any of their successors' (Preface to *Novelist's Library*, 1821). Many contemporary reviews noted the resemblance: e.g. *North British Review*, xv. (1851), p. 423. Leslie Stephen, writing in 1877, says that the 'double parallel has often been pointed out' (*Hours in a Library*, ii. 164).

[3] From his review of Fielding's *Works* in *The Times*, 2 September 1840; *Works*, iii. 383–93. Compare his criticism of Charlotte Brontë: 'Novel writers should not be in a passion with their characters . . . but describe them, good or bad, with a like calm' (*Letters*, iii. 67).

in his novels. Developing the latter theme, Thackeray contrasts Fielding with Smollett:

Let any man examine [*Tom Jones*] as a work of art merely, and it must strike him as the most astonishing production of human ingenuity. There is not an incident ever so trifling but advances the story, grows out of former incidents, and is connected with the whole. Such a literary *providence*, if we may use such a word, is not to be seen in any other work of fiction. You might cut out half of *Don Quixote*, or add, transpose, or alter any given romance of Walter Scott, and neither would suffer. Roderick Random and heroes of that sort run through a series of adventures, at the end of which the fiddles are brought, and there is a marriage. But the history of Tom Jones connects the very first page with the very last, and it is marvellous to think how the author could have built and carried all the structure in his brain, as he must have done, before he began to put it on paper.

Apart from this, Thackeray's preference throws little light on his own novels, which suggest no real dependence; their decisive stimulus is not imitation of Fielding but reaction from contemporary novel-conventions, the desire to substitute the true for the sham; and it is coincidence only that this was one of Fielding's motives in *Joseph Andrews*. The sense in which Thackeray is called 'the Fielding of the nineteenth century' (already almost a critical cliché in his own time) is rather one of correspondence than derivation. Deliberate emulation is probably confined to *Jonathan Wild* (in *Barry Lyndon*). The difference between *Pendennis* and *Tom Jones* is even wider than the difference between the two societies they reflect. The difference in moral attitude may be illustrated by Thackeray's letter of 1848, considering criticisms of the harshness of *Vanity Fair*:

> Forster says. . . . After a scene with Blifil, the air is cleared by a laugh of Tom Jones—Why Tom Jones in my holding is as big a rogue as Blifil. Before God he is—I mean the man is selfish according to his nature as Blifil according to his.[1]

His admiration for Fielding is often expressed, in all phases of his career;[2] but as a writer he diverged increasingly from him. He does not dissociate himself from Colonel Newcome's strictures on *Tom Jones*.[3] (The literary models he acknowledged for Colonel Newcome were Don Quixote and Sir Roger de Coverley.) Thackeray's true distance from Fielding is suggested by Charlotte Brontë's admiration for his novels, and the vigour, if not the terms, of her fierce repudiation of the comparison: 'he resembles Fielding as an eagle does a vulture'.[4]

Charlotte Brontë's own revulsion from Fielding, and the convergence of various 'romanticisms' (German as well as English) in her novels and those of her sisters might suggest that the break with the eighteenth-century novel would there be complete. But the early reading of one who wrote in 1834, 'adhere to standard authors, and don't run after

[1] *Letters*, ii. 424; Thackeray expanded the criticism in his lecture on Fielding delivered in 1851.

[2] See ibid., i. 107 n., ii. 416; the review cited above; Preface to *Pendennis*; 'Charity and Humour', 1852 (*Works*, x. 615, 622); *Lectures on the English Humourists*, 1853.

[3] Ch. iv.

[4] Dedication to second edition of *Jane Eyre*, 1848; see also *S.H.B.* ii. 166, iii. 322. Bagehot also protested, contrasting Fielding's 'joyful energy' with Thackeray's 'musing fancifulness' and 'irritable sensibility' (*Literary Studies*, ii. 127–8).

novelty'[1] could not be rejected. Jane Eyre was consoled by the nursemaid's story-telling of 'passages of
love and adventure . . . from the pages of *Pamela*'.
At a deep and probably unconscious level *Jane Eyre*
looks back to Richardson; the Thornfield chapters
are haunted by the situation of Pamela, Mr. B. (and
Mrs. Jervis). But perhaps more important than the
specific parallels[2] is that nightmare-like impression,
so strong in both *Pamela* and *Clarissa Harlowe*, and
recurring in most of the Brontë novels, of a closed-
in world with the heroine as captive or in frantic
flight. The intense concentration on the heroine in
Jane Eyre and *Villette*, her protracted inner debates,
her sense of the other characters as mysterious and
alien, are also found in Richardson. Although it has
been less often canvassed by critics than Charlotte
Brontë's other and more superficial literary reminiscences of novelists of the past,[3] this alone seems of
importance in her mature work; other influences may
be discovered when the 'Angrian' cycle and her other
early work have been more fully and critically
explored.[4]

The one major novelist of the eighteenth century

---

[1] *S.H.B.* i. 122.

[2] See Janet Spens, 'Charlotte Brontë', *Essays and Studies by members
of the English Association* (1929), xiv. 56–57. (The emphasis on social
difference, and the episode of the gipsy, appear to me to clinch the argument.) Miss Spens's is the fullest examination of the likeness glanced at
by the *Quarterly Review* (December 1848) and developed by Helen
Shipton in the *Monthly Packet*, xcii, No. 549 (November 1896).

[3] Such as Mrs. Radcliffe, whose *Italian* she certainly read; perhaps also
The Sicilian Romance, which has a concealed mad wife.

[4] The minor 'Gothic' novels, and the periodicals the Brontës read as
children, would probably reward investigation.

who seems to lack Victorian 'grandchildren' is Sterne; Lytton, in his search for novelty, mimicked some of the devices of *Tristram Shandy* in *The Caxtons* (1849), but without real understanding. If there is any relationship it is with Thackeray;[1] but as a genuine stimulus to a novelist Sterne appears only in our own time—in the work of the very writer who said that novelists 'completely forget their grandfathers'.

§ 20

Although the novel of the forties makes no clear break with the past, anyone reading the major novelists in chronological order would be more struck by change than continuity. One reason for this impression (a reason I have already implied,[2] though not yet explicitly distinguished) is the operation of an influence not from the past, but the present: the influence of Carlyle. All serious novelists were affected by it in some degree, both in ways common to all and individually modified; and it is an influence not merely upon the content but upon the mode and temper of the novel.

That Carlyle was generally felt as a dominant force in the forties, both at the time and in retrospect, hardly needs illustration.

In and from 1840 [his] name was running like wildfire through the British Islands and through English-speaking America; there was the utmost avidity for his books . . . especially among the young men; phrases from them were in

---

[1] See Bagehot's 'Sterne and Thackeray' (1864), in *Literary Studies*, ii.
[2] See p. 82 above.

all young men's mouths and were affecting the public speech. . . .[1]

The numerous witnesses differ only about whose name, if any, to put beside his; Harriet Martineau[2] coupled Carlyle and Wordsworth; Froude,[3] on different occasions, Carlyle and Tennyson, Carlyle and Newman. The immediate influence of his current pronouncements was perhaps at its strongest in this decade; the reputation established by the *French Revolution* in 1837 had led to the republication of *Sartor Resartus* in 1838 and to the collection of earlier articles in *Critical and Miscellaneous Essays* in 1839, which now reached a far wider public than before;[4] and the *réclame* of the courses of public lectures[5] was consolidated and extended by *Chartism* (1840), *Past and Present* (1843) and *Cromwell* (1845). This contemporary response to Carlyle included an eager acceptance of his ideas; he had 'knocked out his window from the blind wall of his century',[6] and the

---

[1] David Masson, *Carlyle Personally and in his Writings* (1885), p. 67.

[2] *Autobiography*, iv. 2.

[3] *Carlyle's Life in London* (1884), i. 291, and 'The Oxford Counter-Reformation' (*Short Studies on Great Subjects*, fourth series, Letter II). With the latter compare 'Confessions of a Sceptic' in the *Nemesis of Faith* (1849); this testimony would have been supported by others of this Oxford generation, such as Clough, the Arnolds, and Thomas Hughes, who recalls the undergraduate response to *Past and Present* in *Tom Brown at Oxford* (1861), ch. xxv. See also Swinburne's sonnets, 'Two Leaders' (Carlyle and Newman), first published in 1876 and collected in *Poems and Ballads, second series* (1878).

[4] 'A nobler [book] does not live in our language I am sure, and one that will have such an effect on our ways of thought and prejudices' (Thackeray in a letter of 1–2 December 1839; *Letters*, i. 396).

[5] On literature (1837–8) and on *Heroes and Hero-Worship* (1840).

[6] R. H. Horne, *A New Spirit of the Age* (1844), ii. 256.

direction and quality of his vision could be shared, even where not all its horizons were equally discerned.

Such men affect the very roots and foundations of our being, reinvigorate the total frame.[1]

Accordingly, even when such acceptance was shaken by *Latter-Day Pamphlets* at the end of the decade, Carlyle's power over men's minds did not wane. Partly because the earlier writings stood, and gained in relevance; still more because the visionary, the 'radio-active force',[2] the 'true, pathetic eloquence',[3] was felt to be greater than his doctrines.[4] He might be Trollope's 'Mr Pessimus Anticant',[5] but he remained 'Our dear old English Homer—Homer in prose' whose nods must be forgiven.[6] Only towards the close of the century[7] did it become usual to measure Carlyle by the content of his teaching, and especially by its potential dangers and distortions; a misapprehension which remains an impediment[8] to the understanding not only of him but of the literature of a whole age.

The novelists' response to Carlyle is in part that

[1] Masson, op. cit., p. 104.

[2] Dr. Warren, 'Fitzgerald, Carlyle, and others', in *Tennyson and his Friends*, ed. Hallam Tennyson (1911), p. 132.

[3] Matthew Arnold, 'Emerson', in *Discourses in America* (1885).

[4] 'How noble Carlyle continues in spite of some nonsense!' (*Life and Letters of Fenton John Anthony Hort*, 2 vols., 1896, i. 151; letter of 1850).

[5] *The Warden* (1855), chs. xiv–xv.

[6] Manuscript Introduction to his projected 'History of Fiction' (M. Sadleir, *Trollope, a Commentary*, 1927, p. 421).

[7] The recession of Carlyle's fame is conveniently marked by Saintsbury's defence in *Corrected Impressions* (1895).

[8] At least in England; the work of French and American scholars (e.g. Cazamian, Bonnerot, Emery Neff) shows a clearer view.

of all thinking men, heightened by individual pre-
dilections. Here too the evidence is overwhelming;
for Dickens, Thackeray, and Kingsley alone there
is material for a full-length study. Dickens, for
example, considered it 'indispensable' to try out *The
Chimes* on Carlyle before publication, dedicated *Hard
Times* to him, and long before he wrote the *Tale of
Two Cities* was reading 'that wonderful book', *The
French Revolution*, 'for the 500th time';[1] and such
open acknowledgements (like Thackeray's *Times*
review)[2] are no more than pointers to a deeper indebtedness. And Kingsley's propagation and cita-
tion of Carlyle's views in *Yeast* and *Alton Locke*
(partly by means of two Carlylean personalities, Tregarva and Sandy Mackaye) are less significant than
the way *Mary Barton* is built on the assumptions of
Chartism and *Past and Present*: John Barton is the very
type invoked in *Sartor*: 'Thou wert our Conscript,
on whom the lot fell, and fighting our battles wert so
marred.'[3] What is more imaginatively significant,
however, than the 'condition-of-England question'
in itself is the way that this and other crises for the
community and the individual are seen as converging

---

[1] *Letters*, ii. 335 (letter of 1851). Even if the two noughts are discounted
as rhetoric, this is a notable tribute for a writer not remarkable for his
study of contemporary literature. In 1854 Dickens writes to Carlyle 'no
man knows your books better than I' (ibid., ii. 567).

[2] 3 August 1837; *Works*, i. 67–79. To Thackeray the work 'possesses
genius, if any book ever did'; he praises especially the lofty impartiality,
the absence of cant, and (notwithstanding some doubts about the style),
the 'gloomy rough Rembrandt kind of reality'. Alton Locke called it
'that great prose poem, the single epic of modern days' (ch. ix); even the
hero of Newman's *Loss and Gain* quotes from it.

[3] iii. 4.

points of eternal forces—not just for particular
novels or kinds of novel, 'social' or 'introspective',[1]
but for the novel in general. After Carlyle, the poetic,
prophetic, and visionary possibilities of the novel are
fully awakened. Through symbols, said Teufels-
dröckh, 'Fantasy with her mystic wonderland plays
into the small prose domain of Sense, and becomes
incorporated therewith';[2] the reader of Dickens and
Thackeray, still more of Charlotte and Emily Brontë,
becomes aware of an aura of symbolism (in Dickens,
even of allegory) that is absent from earlier English
novels.[3] And there are glimpses too of the fulfilment
of Carlyle's prophecy about style:

what a result, should this piebald, entangled, hypermeta-
phorical style of writing, not to say of thinking, become
general among our Literary men! As it might so easily do.[4]

The reader of Thackeray is also often reminded of
Carlyle's use of *personae* and self-projections, even of
his device of 'editing' with its deliberate complica-
tion of the distance between introspection and communication.

Carlyle's known views on novels also affected
novelists. His harsh judgement on the Waverley
novels may have left Scott standing unscathed; but
he had shown that imitation of Scott was a dead end.[5]

---

[1] To Carlyle's influence E. A. Baker partly attributes Charlotte
Brontë's emphasis on 'the individual soul, rather than the social being'
(*History of the English Novel*, viii. 22–23). But she seems to have known
little of his work at first hand before 1848; see *S.H.B.* ii. 222, 322, 326.

[2] *Sartor Resartus*, iii. 3.

[3] With the possible exception of *Tristram Shandy*, which Carlyle often
recalls in *Sartor*.   [4] *Sartor Resartus*, iii. 12.

[5] 'Sir Walter Scott', first published 1838.

His mockery of Bulwer's *Pelham*[1] drove the author himself to revision, besides giving a new impulse to the campaign against fashionable novels, continued by the precept and example of Thackeray. Carlyle seldom encouraged a novelist; it was wryly observed, and with justice, that he 'was ever admonishing poets to write in prose, and novelists to write history and biography'.[2] On another occasion, in 1833, he wrote that he thought it

reasonable to prophesy that this exceeding great multitude of Novel-writers and suchlike, must, in a new generation, gradually do one of two things: either retire into nurseries, and work for children, minors and semifatuous persons of both sexes; or else, what were far better, sweep their Novel-fabric into the dust-cart, and betake them with such faculty as they have to understand and record what is *true*,—of which, surely, there is, and will forever be, a whole Infinitude unknown to us, of infinite importance to us! Poetry, it will more and more come to be understood, is nothing but higher Knowledge; and the only genuine Romance (for grown persons) Reality.[3]

The novelists knew better than to accept such advice and threats; but they were put on their mettle. And there was another challenge, but with ironical encouragement:

Of no given Book, not even of a Fashionable Novel, can you predicate with certainty that its vacuity is absolute; that there are not other vacuities which shall partially replenish

---

[1] *Sartor Resartus*, iii. 10.
[2] F. Espinasse, *Literary Recollections* (1893), p. 212.
[3] 'Diderot', in the *Foreign Quarterly Review* (1833); collected in *Critical and Miscellaneous Essays*, 1839.

themselves therefrom, and esteem it a *plenum*. How knowest thou, may the distressed Novelwright exclaim, that I, here where I sit, am the Foolishest of existing mortals; that this my Long-ear of a Fictitious Biography shall not find one and the other, into whose still longer ears it may be the means, under Providence, of instilling somewhat? We answer, None knows, none can certainly know: therefore, write on, worthy Brother, even as thou canst, even as it has been given thee.[1]

Mrs. Gaskell used the second and third sentences as the title-page motto of *Mary Barton*; Thackeray recalled the passage, with other Carlylean phrases, in his manifesto in *Vanity Fair*:

And while the moralist . . . professes to wear neither gown nor bands, but only the very same long-eared livery in which his congregation is arrayed: yet, look you, one is bound to speak the truth as far as one knows it, whether one mounts a cap and bells or a shovel-hat; and a deal of disagreeable matter must come out in the course of such an undertaking.[2]

I have said that these novelists rose to the challenge; they did not discard the long-eared livery, but they claimed that it concealed a 'week-day preacher', one who 'lifts his voice and cries his sermon'. After Carlyle, the rift between the 'prophetic' and the merely entertaining novel widens. There were, and have continued to be, innumerable novels produced by his two arch-foes Dilettantism and Mammonism; but the 'novel proper' as distinct from the novel as the product of an 'amusement-industry' was helped by Carlyle to a status in literature and life which it has hardly yet lost.

[1] 'Biography', first published in *Fraser's* (April 1832), pp. 253–60; collected in *Critical and Miscellaneous Essays*, 1839.

[2] Ch. viii.

∿∿

DOMBEY AND SON

§ 1

*D*OMBEY AND SON stands out from among Dickens's novels as the earliest example of responsible and successful planning; it has unity not only of action, but of design and feeling. It is also the first in which a pervasive uneasiness about contemporary society takes the place of an intermittent concern with specific social wrongs. These are the main reasons why this novel rather than *Martin Chuzzlewit* or *David Copperfield* is here chosen to represent Dickens in the eighteen-forties; and these form the main headings—of unequal, but related importance—under which it will now be considered.

It is Dickens's seventh novel, and the fourth of those written in this decade. A gap unusually long for Dickens divides it from its predecessor; *Martin Chuzzlewit* was completed in July 1844, and the writing of *Dombey* was not begun until 27 June 1846.[1] The interval had been fully occupied in travel, theatri-

[1] Forster, v. 2; but it had been in his mind at least since the beginning of March (vi. 2) and probably earlier (v. 1).

cals, writing 'Christmas books', founding and for a
short time editing the *Daily News*; at the end of May
came what Forster calls the 'retreat to Switzerland',
and it was at Geneva, Lausanne, and Paris that the
first six numbers were written.[1] The writing was attended with many difficulties ('You can hardly
imagine what infinite pains I take, or what extraordinary difficulty I find in getting on FAST'). He
suffered from 'the absence of streets and number of
figures'—required not as material, but as stimulus—
and from the new problem of beginning a novel and
writing a 'Christmas book' in the same months; but

> Invention, thank God, seems the easiest thing in the world;
> and I seem to have such a preposterous sense of the ridiculous
> after this long rest as to be constantly requiring to restrain
> myself from launching into extravagances in the height of my
> enjoyment.[2]

It was necessary for his illustrator to co-operate in
avoiding 'extravagances' ('enormous care' is required
with Dombey and Miss Tox, and 'the Toodle Family
should not be too much caricatured, because of
Polly').[3] He wrote the christening scene with 'the
drag on', to avoid satire—'malice in christening
points of faith'.[4] There is evidence that he restrained
himself especially in comic dialogue. When he had
'over-written' a number, it was the non-functional

[1] As a result of his absence from England the early stages of *Dombey*
are fairly fully documented in letters to Forster; quotations from these
are scattered through v. 2–7, vi. 1–2.

[2] Forster, v. 5, letter of 30 August, written while at work on the second
number.

[3] Forster, v. 3, letter of 18 July 1846; and *Letters*, i. 768.

[4] Forster, vi. 2.

comic dialogue (between Miss Tox and Mrs. Chick)
that was cut, as the original proofs show.

I have avoided unnecessary dialogue so far, to avoid over-
writing; and all I *have* written is point.[1]

This deliberate control of comic exaggeration and
inventiveness marks one of the differences between
Dombey and its predecessors; the comedy is in lower
relief and is subordinated to the design of the whole.[2]
The overflowing comic inventiveness is here kept
within bounds; Dickens was setting himself new
standards. His was the genius that 'progresses and
evolves and does not spin upon itself'; it would have
been easy (and remunerative) for him to repeat the
happy improvisation of his early novels—but this no
longer contented him. With *Dombey* he began to
write novels founded on a theme, embodied in a relation between characters. This more conscious technique (contrast 'I thought of Mr. Pickwick') and the
particular theme chosen, with its gravity, and its
subtle and various relevance to his own time, give
Dombey and Son a peculiar interest.

§ 2

Despite the gap, there is a significant relation
between *Dombey and Son* and its predecessor. In
Martin Chuzzlewit, says Dickens,

I have endeavoured to resist the temptation of the current

[1] Forster, vi. 2, letter of 6 December 1846, written while at work on
the fourth number.
[2] On this, see Chesterton's Introduction to the Everyman edition of the
novel, especially his remarks on Mrs. Skewton.

Monthly Number, and to keep a steadier eye upon the general purpose and design. With this object in view I put a strong constraint upon myself.[1]

What was new was little more than the endeavour; the temptations were not always resisted nor the constraint effective. The origin of the book, we learn from Forster, lay in Pecksniff;

the notion of taking Pecksniff for a type of character was really the origin of the book; the design being to show, more or less by every person introduced, the number and variety of humours and vices that have their root in selfishness.[2]

This is a very general 'purpose and design', leaving much room for improvisation and modification. There was no narrative plan, no dynamic view of the interaction of characters, such as we find in the long letter to Forster outlining the design of *Dombey*;[3] evidence of foresight and design is found only after the writing, even the publication, is well under way. The plot of old Martin was drawn up when the third number was being written; Forster's comment on this bears upon *Dombey*:

the difficulties he encountered in departing from other portions of his scheme were such as to render him, in his subsequent stories, more bent on constructive care at the outset, and on adherence as far as might be to any design he had formed.

In *Dombey* he again had a 'general purpose and design', which is explicitly compared to that of *Chuzzlewit*; it is 'to do with Pride what its predeces-

[1] Preface to first edition.   [2] Forster, iv. 1.
[3] Appendix II, pp. 316–17 below.

sor had done with Selfishness'.[1] Rather, what he had *meant* its predecessor to do; he would learn from its stumbling endeavour and work out the design of *Dombey* more precisely. This novel, even without its numerous surrounding documents—number-plans, letters to Forster and Browne, corrected manuscript and proofs—is eloquent of his far greater success. To say this is not to belittle *Chuzzlewit*; but it is doubtful there whether a reader lacking preface or biography would recognize that Selfishness, or even Hypocrisy (it is never quite clear which Dickens means) was its theme. Circumstances worked against him; sales of early numbers were disappointing, and 'America' was resorted to as an expedient to stimulate them. Although it is made relative to the theme (exposing Martin's selfishness, and magnificently illustrating the unconscious self-deception of another national character, which might be judged a kind of hypocrisy) it remains an expedient and an episode; 'a place Martin Chuzzlewit happens to go to'.[2] And throughout this novel the details mask the 'general purpose and design'; it is largely remembered and valued for single scenes and characters, either loosely attached to the theme or too expansively illustrative of it. Whereas *Dombey* has its firm centre, of theme, character, and scene, Pecksniff and Martin divide the centre, the one static, but giving out vitality, the other progressing, but uninteresting. There is no scenic centre, and no coherent impression of period; no one would select *Chuzzlewit* as especially representative or reflective of the early eighteen-forties.

[1] Forster, vi. 2.   [2] Chesterton, loc. cit.

We cannot mistake the earnestness of Dickens's moral and social concern to expose in Pecksniff a peculiarly English and contemporary vice,[1] as distinct from remediable and specific abuses. But for various reasons the exposure is not complete—far less so than in the smaller scale figures of Chadband and Podsnap. Dickens had not grasped the difficulty of having a hypocrite bearing the weight of a main character—he can hardly stand the strain if he is only to be exhibited, never analysed. We need to know, at least to suspect, how he appears to himself; we are told that Pecksniff had solitary thoughts by the fireside, but never what they were.[2] Pecksniff exists mainly in the limelight of a series of superb scenes (and also as refracted in the contrasted natures of Tom and Martin); but under this continued exhibition, with its extravagantly comic dialogue, he becomes less not more repulsive. Dickens's comic inventiveness is still overflowing, neither subordinated to the general purpose nor fully contained by moral and social criticism. The resulting ambiguity is clearer still with Mrs. Gamp, who is almost extraneous to the plot. We are less aware of the horrors of her ministrations than of the private world she blissfully inhabits, 'as light as any gash balloon', and which Dickens makes it seem a privilege to share. Contrast the continued yet unstrained harnessing of the comedy to the 'general purpose and design' in *Dombey*, where the absurd is on the side of the angels. Toots and Susan Nipper and Captain Cuttle and

---

[1] See above, p. 113; and cf. Dickens's Preface, and Forster, iv. 2.

[2] Ch. ix (which concludes Number III).

Miss Tox, all, by their natures and their share in the action, supply continuous moral comment on the evil represented in Mr. Dombey; and they do so naturally and implicitly, without the copybook pointedness of Mark Tapley. So, from the other side, does Major Bagstock, whose function Dickens defined when he called him 'a kind of comic Mephistophelean power'[1] (with Mr. Dombey as Faust?)·

Not only the comedy, but all the characters and all the action are subordinated to Mr. Dombey. This is the first novel of Dickens to be dominated by a leading idea, embodied in a single character. He is the origin, centre, and continuum of the novel, as no previous character of Dickens's had been. Before this is demonstrated in relation to the structural unity of the book it will be necessary to look into this idea and character, and the other character upon whom they chiefly act.

§ 3

That the origin of the book lay in Mr. Dombey is not indeed clearly attested by direct external evidence, as it is with Pickwick and Pecksniff; but everything even outside the novel itself points that way. Forster's report that as first conceived 'it was to do with Pride what its predecessor had done with Selfishness';[2] Dickens's anxiety for secrecy—'The very name getting out, would be ruinous';[3] the 'outline of [his]

---

[1] Letter to Browne, 10 March 1847; *Letters,* ii. 17.

[2] vi. 2; Forster is referring to what Dickens told him before he left England in May.   [3] v. 3; 18 July 1846.

immediate intentions' in the letter to Forster with the manuscript of Number I;[1] his 'nervous dread of caricature in the face of his merchant-hero'[2]—all these agree in their emphasis. It is safe to assume that the originating idea took the form of a 'merchant-hero', in whom business and family pride are twisted into a single hard knot; the continued interplay between the affairs of the firm and the family is emphasized by the early chapter-titles[3] and 'shadowed forth' in the semi-allegorical cover design; although in the working-out less is made of the firm than Dickens seems to have intended. The title is its epitome (there is no record of hesitation over this title as with most others); and is also deliberately misleading—serving to keep the secret of Paul's early death, and to point the irony of the book's true subject—which is, of course, Dombey and Daughter.[4] The relation between Mr. Dombey and Florence is the backbone of the whole book; structurally, the relation between him and Paul, and that between Florence and Paul, are only means of exposing and developing it.

[1] vi. 2; 25 July 1846. (See Appendix II, pp. 316–17 below.)

[2] vi. 2; August 1846. To prevent caricature, Dickens asked for a sheet of sketches from which to select; this is reproduced by Forster.

[3] See chs. iii, xiii, xxii.

[4] In the original edition, and in all editions up to 1858, the 'turn' is emphasized by the closing words of No. V, chorically delivered by Miss Tox: 'To think . . . Dombey and Son should be a Daughter after all!' (cf. letter to Forster, 25 July; vi. 2, and Appendix II below). When Dickens removed this sentence in 1859 (perhaps because it then seemed to him to mar the pathos of the conclusion) he forgot that it was echoed in ch. lix:

'And so Dombey and Son, as I observed upon a certain sad occasion . . . is indeed a daughter, Polly, after all.' See above, p. 45, n. 1.

From that time [Paul's death], I purpose changing his feelings of indifference and uneasiness towards his daughter into a positive hatred. . . . At the same time I shall change *her* feeling towards *him* for one of a greater desire to love him, and to be loved by him; engendered in her compassion for his loss, and her love for the dead boy whom, in his way, he loved so well too. So I mean to carry the story on, through all the branches and off-shoots and meanderings that come up; and through the decay and downfall of the house, and the bank-ruptcy of Dombey, and all the rest of it; when his only staff and treasure, and his unknown Good Genius always, will be this rejected daughter, who will come out better than any son at last, and whose love for him, when discovered and under-stood, will be his bitterest reproach.[1]

Through this changing relation works Mr. Dombey's pride, the master-motive of the novel, the mainspring of all its events. Much then depends upon the ade-quacy of these two characters, Mr. Dombey and Florence, to sustain this central interest, and especi-ally upon Dickens's power—not hitherto manifested—to draw a character undergoing inner conflict.

This continued inner conflict was also a part of the original intention; the letter just quoted continues:

For the struggle with himself, which goes on in all such obstinate natures, will have ended then; and the sense of his injustice, which you may be sure has never quitted him, will have at last a gentler office than that of only making him more harshly unjust.[2]

The last point alone shows Dickens's psychological insight; and it is repeated in the new Preface added

[1] Letter of 25 July 1846; see Appendix II, pp. 316–17 below.

[2] Cf. ch. lix: 'obstinate and sullen natures . . . struggle hard to be such. Ground long undermined, will often fall down in a moment.'

by the author twelve years later—apparently in reply to criticism of the supposed 'violent change' in the hero.[1]

> The two commonest mistakes in judgment . . . are the confounding of shyness with arrogance . . . and the not understanding that an obstinate nature exists in a perpetual struggle with itself.
>
> Mr. Dombey undergoes no violent change, either in this book, or in real life. A sense of his injustice is within him, all along. The more he represses it, the more unjust he necessarily is. Internal shame and external circumstances may bring the contest to a close in a week, or a day; but, it has been a contest for years, and is only fought out after a long balance of victory.[2]

The moment in the novel when the contest is nearest to the surface is in chapter xxxv, where Mr. Dombey watches Florence, who believes him asleep.

> There are yielding moments in the lives of the sternest and harshest men, though such men often keep their secret well.

So begins the long paragraph in which his brief relenting is traced, and its hidden sources suggested. It ends with a dramatic turn; Edith enters, and, still unobserved, he witnesses her gentle and loving conversation with Florence—a double blow to his pride, and the stimulus to double revenge upon them.

---

[1] See Forster, vi. 2 (opening paragraph), and p. 171, n. 1 below.

[2] The Preface was added in the edition of 1858, and revised for the collected 'Charles Dickens' edition of 1867. I quote from the latter; in the passage quoted, the only differences are that 1858–62 read 'no violent internal change . . . or in life'; 'bring the contest to the surface'; and 'is only fought out then'. The Preface of 1848 is quite distinct—a brief farewell to readers, originally printed at the end of the concluding number.

'Such men often keep their secret well'; "'Dombey'", said the Major . . . "don't be thoughtful. . . . You are too great a man, Dombey, to be thoughtful".'[1] The difficulty, especially to a writer more practised in exhibition than analysis, is to suggest the secret self-doubting of 'stiff-necked sullen arrogance'. Such suggestion is conveyed sometimes by the use of carefully timed silent pauses in the narrative, moments sharply presented to the sight and impressing the imagination: as when Mr. Dombey watches Florence carrying Paul up 'the great, wide, vacant staircase' in the moonlight, and singing to him.[2] Or by a revealing but unannotated gesture: as when Mrs. Chick, promoting the Brighton scheme, hesitantly submits that Florence must accompany Paul:

'It's quite an infatuation with him. He's very young, you know, and has his fancies.'

Mr. Dombey turned his head away, and going slowly to the bookcase, and unlocking it, brought back a book to read.[3]

In Mr. Dombey Dickens achieves the remarkable feat of making us aware of the hidden depths of a character, while keeping them largely hidden; his method respects Mr. Dombey's own proud reserve. The only times his thoughts are unrolled at length before us it is through the phantasmagoria of the railway journey,[4] where Dickens can 'analyse' as it were panoramically, with something of the picturesque freedoms of dream or allegory; and similarly

---

[1] Ch. xx.

[2] Ch. viii. The moment is openly recalled at the end of ch. xviii, and again at the end of ch. xxxvi.

[3] Ch. viii. [4] Ch. xx. See also p. 188 below.

again through the memories and visions called up when he roams through the silent house.[1] Mr. Dombey has 'lonely thoughts, bred late at night in the sullen despondency and gloom of his retirement',[2] but the reader is seldom admitted to them; yet he is often reminded, both by oblique reference and momentary pictures of that silent brooding presence, the shadow behind the figure which Mr. Dombey presents to the world, 'self-important, unbending, formal, austere'.[3] What makes him interesting is the moral suspense: although Florence may serve partly as an externalized conscience, a troublesome and even hated reminder of the whole world of feeling that his pride has forsworn, she does so because something within him responds to her. Before Paul's birth, he had been merely indifferent; afterwards this indifference turns to uneasiness and resentment,[4] which increase after Paul's death.[5] But in this resentment there is an unadmitted sense of guilt, and even the seeds of repentance. His love for his son, involved though it is in 'a partial scheme of parental interest and ambition', is yet also the rift in the ice. We are aware of it even in the cruellest moment in which he repulses Florence's affection, and even aware of it as his justification for doing so: he watches her, silently and hopelessly ascending the stairs.

The last time he had watched her, from the same place, winding up those stairs, she had had her brother in her arms. It did not move his heart towards her now, it steeled it: but

[1] Ch. lix.
[2] Ch. xx.
[3] Ch. xxvii.
[4] Ch. iii.
[5] Chs. xviii, xx; and the reference to 'hatred' in ch. xl.

he went into his room, and locked his door, and sat down in his chair, and cried for his lost boy.[1]

In his momentary relenting towards her (so abruptly terminated by a new jealousy)

She became blended with the child he had loved, and he could hardly separate the two.[2]

Such evidence keeps before us the 'contest [of] years, only fought out after a long balance of victory'; we can accept its bringing to a close, through 'internal shame and external circumstances', in a single chapter of the closing number.[3] We may feel that for 'internal shame' to reach the purpose of self-murder, and for 'external circumstances' to bring Florence home in the nick of time, savours overmuch of the theatre; we may feel that the year's lapse between the last two numbers[4] has cheated us, or spared us, too much of the slow undermining of Mr. Dombey's obstinate pride. But in the account of his days and nights of restless wandering through the desolate house, Dickens prevents us from feeling that the reconciliation is cheaply purchased. In a passage of no more than four pages he condenses Mr. Dombey's

[1] Ch. xviii.   [2] Ch. xxxv.
[3] Ch. lix.
[4] i.e. before ch. lviii, 'After a lapse'. 'The year was out, and the great House was down.' In the first part of this chapter (balancing ch. lix) is concentrated much of the effect on Mr. Dombey of the business failure, although he does not himself appear; and the better side of his pride is recognized by the unimpeachable Mr. Morfin:

'He is a gentleman of high honour and integrity . . . resolved on payment to the last farthing of his means. . . . Ah, Miss Harriet, it would do us no harm to remember oftener than we do, that vices are sometimes only virtues carried to excess! His pride shows well in this.'

history and his present state. And he does it, as always, by a combination of picture and analysis. The deserted rooms, the staircase (that recurring symbol) with its remembered footsteps, carry us backward in time. In Mr. Dombey's thoughts, the whole of the original design of the novel is retraced. It is not a static view; the contest still continues. He has passed beyond Paul's death, the wreck of his marriage, his fallen fortunes:

> That which was his own work, that which he could so easily have wrought into a blessing, and had set himself so steadily for years to form into a curse: that was the sharp grief of his soul. . . .
>
> And yet—so proud he was in his ruin . . . that if he could have heard her voice in an adjoining room, he would not have gone to her. . . . He chiefly thought of what might have been, and what was not. What was, was all summed up in this: that she was lost, and he bowed down with sorrow and remorse.

Inevitably, the passage is introduced by a reiteration of the earlier prophecy: 'Let him remember it in that room, years to come.'[1] But the heavily emphasized pattern of sin, curse, retribution is not the 'figure in the carpet' of *Dombey and Son*. Dickens's impulse towards the cruder simplifications should not obscure from us that his hero is a character of tragic stature. Not seldom, towards the close of the novel, we think of another unbending but vulnerable man of affairs, who wished to stand 'as if a man were author of himself'; or of another proud father and banished daughter, Lear and Cordelia. And no more than

[1] Chs. xviii, lix.

there is the forgiveness a sentimental concession; the famous criticism that Mr. Dombey 'becomes the best of fathers, and spoils a fine novel',[1] is wide of the mark. It might have been ill judged if he were fully shown as 'the best of fathers'; but after this climax we see him only in the moral convalescence of physical illness, and in the afterglow of the epilogue.

§ 4

The contest for Mr. Dombey's soul requires no more of Florence than a perfect goodness and persistent affection; in the words of a chapter-heading, 'The Study of a Loving Heart'. But the balance of the novel requires her to be prominent, and she is not completely absent from the scene for more than a single number.[2] A character conceived in terms of pure feeling, passive, innocent to the point of being almost 'incapable of her own distress', can hardly sustain this prominence. The dilemma, though it is doubtful if Dickens saw it as such, is clear. Conflict within her, introspection, or initiative, would mitigate the pathos of her situation; unmitigated, the pathos risks monotony, if not self-defeat. (It may even raise the more serious criticism that if her state of mind is not morbid, it is improbable;[3] and it is

---

[1] Taine, *History of English Literature* (Paris, 1863–4; trans. H. Van Laun, 1871), Book V, ch. i, § 3. ii. Compare *Blackwood's* (October 1848), p. 469: 'The entire change of character in Dombey is out of all nature.'

[2] No. XVII (chs. lii–liv).

[3] So more than one reviewer thought; e.g. *Blackwood's*, October 1848:

not within Dickens's range in *this* novel to regard it as morbid.)[1]

She has to be entirely lovable, in order to leave us in no doubt of the guilt of Mr. Dombey (and his own sense of it); for the same reason, she has to be, with that noticeable exception, universally loved. The love according to their lights of almost all the other characters carries conviction, and at times Florence gains some reflected vitality from Susan Nipper, Mr. Toots, and Captain Cuttle; even Mrs. Chick was on one occasion struck into silence and 'lost . . . her presence of mind' at the sight of Florence grieving for Paul. But on the whole the effect is still of a space where Florence's character ought to be, with our attention drawn from the vacuum by the ring of admirers. Dickens's difficulties are not peculiar to him,[2] or to this novel; besides the timeless problem of making perfect virtue, and especially the passive virtues, attractive, he has his age's problem of vitalizing a heroine in a period of limiting ideals for girlhood.[3] Yet let the Victorian novel itself dictate our standards, and we see what is lacking in Florence as a heroine attracting the reader; that endearing solidity, even of appearance, that touch of individualizing charm, which Trollope was able to give to all the

'nor does the extraordinary affection of the daughter spring from any known principle of humanity' (p. 469).

[1] Not that the emotional stresses of adolescent girlhood lay altogether outside Dickens's range; witness Tattycoram, also hungry for affection.

[2] Though perhaps accentuated for him by the pressure of his idealized memory of Mary Hogarth, who died at sixteen.

[3] 'Heroines are a sadly featureless class of well-intentioned young women in these days' (*Blackwood's*, April 1855, pp. 464–5).

fifty or so of his young heroines;[1] and which Dickens was to find for his less perfect ones—Dora, Pet, Bella, and Rosa.

This is not to say that Florence fails; only that one must approach her differently from Mr. Dombey, and see her as a character drawn wholly within the bounds of her situation; to an extent that she, and the pathos of that situation, are one and the same. Two approaches have at least the merit of being included in Dickens's own. First, by beginning with Florence as a child of six years old, he is able to sustain our pity and tenderness for her as a child, even after she grows to be seventeen. Because we have seen her 'pressing her small hands hard together'[2] as she timidly enters her father's room, or ragged and lost in the City streets, or clinging crying to Polly's skirts; because we have seen her through Paul's eyes, and Walter Gay's, we continue to think of her, when she is thirteen, fifteen, seventeen, as a child still. Her fear of Carker is of the same colouring as her fear of Good Mrs. Brown; Walter is her 'brother'; flying from her home, she is once again the lost child. Not with the Esthers and Agneses or the child-wives, but with the children of Dickens's novels—Nell, and Oliver—should Florence be classed. There is one qualification. Though her feeling for Edith may begin as childish—the 'new mama'—it becomes more mature. When Florence, now sixteen, is drawn into the orbit of the unhappy domestic situation, Dickens

---

[1] 'It is a wonder how finely he discriminates them' (Henry James, 'Anthony Trollope', in *Partial Portraits*, 1888).

[2] Ch. iii.

does not leave her wholly innocent and bewildered. He attempts to suggest a transition from childhood;[1] which is indeed necessary if he is to lead up to her flight from home—the sole occasion on which she is to act as well as suffer. But in the Dombey–Carker– Edith situation she is chiefly a pawn in the game; and the idiom in which it is conducted makes her less and not more alive.

The other approach is by way of the mysterious simplicities of fairy-tale, never far away in Dickens's work. Walter Gay, before ever he has seen Florence, is compared by his romantic uncle to Dick Whitting- ton, who married his master's daughter;[2] when he finds her as a lost child in the City streets, he feels like Cinderella's prince, and also

not to say like Richard Whittington—that is a tame com- parison—but like Saint George of England, with the dragon lying dead before him.[3]

The 'great dreary house' where Florence lives alone is like a 'magic dwelling-place in magic story, shut up in the heart of a thick wood', with the ironwork of the doorway instead of 'two dragon sentries'; but she 'bloomed there, like the king's fair daughter in the story'.[4] When she has taken refuge with Captain Cuttle, they are compared to 'a wandering princess and a good monster in a story-book'.[5] With these as

---

[1] Chs. xliii, xlvii. 'Florence's reflections', which open the former chapter, formulate the only doubt, the only complexity of feeling, which is ever attributed to her.

[2] Ch. iv.   [3] Ch. vi.

[4] Ch. xxiii.   [5] Ch. xlix.

pointers,[1] we can discern other, unstated, analogues: the recurring witch-figure (Good Mrs. Brown, and Mrs. Pipchin, who has a black cat), the helpful animal (Diogenes attacking Carker), and the comic knight and squire of the anti-masque (Toots and the Game Chicken). The 'adult' characters, Mr. Dombey, Edith, and Carker, are clear of this tincture of romance, but the children (and the fools) not wholly so. It affects us more than we are aware; and it relates *Dombey* to the world of the earlier novels—*Oliver Twist, Nicholas Nickleby,* and *The Old Curiosity Shop.* If we can see Florence as the princess under a spell, or the unrecognized child of royal birth from whom a strange light shines, or even as Spenser's Una, we may come nearer Dickens's own intention. The presence of different modes in a narrative is something we must accept in his novels, as in poetic drama.

§ 5

Two other major characters, Carker and Edith, belong to a different mode again, and one which is nowadays less readily accepted in serious novels. Of the second marriage and the machinations of the Manager[2] the 'design' shows no prevision; but they

---

[1] And others; Paul is compared to a changeling, Mrs. Pipchin's establishment to an ogress's castle.

[2] The cover design proves that they were thought of early: but not necessarily that they were part of the main design. (That was too 'secret' to be given away with the first number, and it is noticeable that Paul's death is not even 'shadowed forth'.) Perhaps Forster omitted some reference to this part of the plot when he quoted the early letter; his concern is to defend Dickens's design as it affects Mr. Dombey and his children—and there are marks of omission.

cannot be reckoned among the 'off-shoots and meanderings'. Both structurally and thematically this part
of the plot is justified, as I shall show. Nevertheless,
in introducing a mode that is neither tragedy nor
fairy-tale romance, though allied to both—in fact,
what is commonly called melodrama—it leads to
some disturbance of tone. As part of the plot, it has
both necessity and unity: it serves as counterplot—
the means by which Mr. Dombey's downfall is
brought about—and it is unified by the single but
branching motive of revenge, in both Carker and
Edith. The irony is emphasized by there being two
of them, and by their revenge being partly directed
against Mr. Dombey, partly against each other.
Carker was the necessary active villain, slowly undermining Mr. Dombey's security, both in firm and
family.[1] But his juxtaposition to Mr. Dombey is
valuable in other ways. His unalloyed evil makes
clearer by contrast the mixed nature of Mr. Dombey
(compare the effect of the cruder Jonas Chuzzlewit
as against old Martin). His pride, concealed in false
servility but militant and climbing, is contrasted
with Mr. Dombey's, self-evident, but dangerously
complacent. This reveals other ironies in the situation: Mr. Dombey is vulnerable, because in his
pride he underrates others, believes them content
in subservience; he is far too proud to be clever

---

[1] He rises to prominence only after Paul's death (his position and
character having been sufficiently expounded in ch. xiii, where his
designs against Walter Gay are already suggested), and his initial plan
is to take the place of the lost son—as son-in-law. When the marriage to
Edith seems to frustrate him there, he schemes against her, now using
Florence as a tool.

about people. Here is both motive and opening for the revenge-plot. Carker schemes revenge against Mr. Dombey, for keeping him down and treating him as a tool; against Walter, for fear he should supplant him; against Edith, for despising him. This is the sum of his motivation, at least on the level of character. It is simple, but adequate for its purpose. Crafty and cat-like, his function is to scheme and be sinister; he requires no redeeming feature, no capacity for remorse. He might be, and is often taken for, an entirely 'flat' character, a mere stage villain—a black-hearted monster with a set of flashing white teeth attached—or a mere machine of the plot. But two things give him depth: Dickens's unquestioning assumption that humanity can produce characters wholly evil, which cannot be reformed, but must be wiped out; and his firm hold on his social theme—Carker the 'new man', the 'forerunner of the managerial revolution'.[1]

Melodrama is Carker's native air; but it is not Edith's. Perhaps the single flaw in this novel is that Dickens, having conceived a character so complex as hers—behaving so consistently with her nature and situation and yet producing such exciting turns of the action—allows her to be drawn into a sphere which distorts her effect. Her share in Mr. Dombey's downfall springs from motives subtly compounded of passionate resentment and self-immolation. She, not Carker, is really Mr. Dombey's 'mighty opposite'; not only because her pride, equal to his in strength but warm blooded where his is cold, is a cry against

---

[1] I cannot now trace this quotation.

corruption; but because she is potentially his equal in stature and depth.

Daughter who has been put through her paces, before countless marrying men, like a horse for sale—Proud and weary of her degradation, but going on, for it's too late now, to turn back.

That is her first appearance in Dickens's notes for the novel;[1] it is the promising basis of a character which never ceases to interest and surprise, and the starting-point for a complicated narrative pattern. From the impact of such a character on the existent characters and situations one could predict the serious conflict of tragic passions; or, almost equally, the high comedy of manners. (One spark of *wit* in her defiant awareness of her predicament, and Edith could have been a recognizable relative of Ethel Newcome.) The chapters in which she first appears do not falsify our hopes; but she is shown only in company, and the revelation of her own view of Mr. Dombey's courtship is delayed. Mr. Dombey has asked to call on her next day, evidently to propose; she is alone with her mother, who has schemed for the marriage.

'Why don't you tell me . . . that he is coming here to-morrow by appointment?'
'Because you know it,' returned Edith, 'Mother.'
The mocking emphasis she laid on that one word!
'You know he has bought me,' she resumed. 'Or that he will, to-morrow. He has considered of his bargain; he has

---

[1] Manuscript of number-plan, No. VII.

shown it to his friend; he is even rather proud of it; he thinks
that it will suit him, and may be had sufficiently cheap; and
he will buy to-morrow. God, that I have lived for this, and
that I feel it!'

Compress into one handsome face the conscious self-
abasement, and the burning indignation of a hundred women,
strong in passion and in pride; and there it hid itself with two
white shuddering arms.

'What do you mean?' returned the angry mother. 'Haven't
you from a child—'

'A child!' said Edith, looking at her. 'When was I a child?
What childhood did you ever leave to me? I was a woman—
artful, designing, mercenary, laying snares for men—before
I knew myself, or you, or even understood the base and
wretched aim of every new display I learnt. You gave birth
to a woman. Look upon her. She is in her pride to-night.'

And as she spoke, she struck her hand upon her beautiful
bosom, as though she would have beaten down herself.

. . . 'There is no slave in a market: there is no horse in a
fair: so shown and offered and examined and paraded, Mother,
as I have been, for ten shameful years,' cried Edith, with a
burning brow, and the same bitter emphasis on the one
word.

Edith's 'tone' is established, and is maintained to the
end. Not a tragic heroine, but a tragedy queen. The
curling lip, the flashing eyes, the burning brow, and
the throbbing bosom monotonously recur with the
phraseology that attaches to them; chapters in which
she appears fall naturally into 'scenes', with all the
stage directions supplied. This mode of treatment is
perhaps rather wasteful than damaging. It does not
distort the other characters by contact. Mr. Dombey's
own style is little affected—

'I beg that Mrs. Granger's very different experiences may now come to the instruction of Mrs. Dombey'—[1]

and there are many moments when the truth of feeling breaks through the theatrical convention, and we lose sight of the too obtrusive hand of the producer. But that convention needs to be consciously disengaged before the seriousness of the design can be appreciated; no doubt many readers have been misled, and have missed Dickens's 'insight' because 'he chooses to speak in a circle of stage fire'.[2]

For this two excuses, though not a justification, may be tentatively offered. From the start Dickens had evidently planned to implicate Edith with Carker; he may have thought of them together, without distinguishing the melodramatic mode appropriate to Carker from the naturalistic mode which Edith really requires. And he thought of her as becoming—even while hating him—the mistress of Carker. His known change of plan here, resulting in the most effective 'scene'—the repudiation of Carker at Dijon —was made at a late stage.[3] Up to and including her departure from Mr. Dombey's roof, Edith is designed to end as an adulteress (and consequently, in death); though not to alienate the reader's sympathy. This role lent itself to the idiom and attitudes of melodrama. Moreover, that may have been the only way in which Dickens felt he could make the situation acceptable to the 'family reader'. The borrowed

[1] Ch. xl.

[2] Ruskin's comment on *Hard Times* in *Unto this Last* (quoted by Forster, vii. 1).

[3] Forster, vi. 2; letter of 21 December 1847—that is, after ch. xlvii had gone to press

colouring of the contemporary theatre may have been a kind of necessary gloss upon such 'domestic relations'[1] as Dickens has to hint at in the Dombey household. This is not to say that he was writing against the grain; 'tremendous scenes' were thoroughly congenial to him. And finally one must admit that they were more congenial to his age than ours; nor necessarily an impediment to the serious treatment of passion.

Carker and Edith are the last of their kind in Dickens's novels;[2] and though no hint of doubt or self-criticism emerges in his comments on the writing of *Dombey*,[3] there is some evidence of it ten years later, in his criticism of another author's heroine:

She is too convulsive from beginning to end. Pray reconsider, from this point of view, her brow, and her eyes, and her drawing herself up to her full height . . . also her asking people how they dare, and the like, on small provocation. . . . I am an impatient and impulsive person myself, but . . . it has been for many years the constant effort of my life to practise at my desk what I preach to you.[4]

---

[1] There are signs of anxiety over the number that included the chapter with this title (ch. xl): it 'requires to be so carefully done' (Forster, vi. 1; letter of 12 September 1847). The manuscript shows that ch. xlvii, 'The Thunderbolt', also caused difficulty.

[2] As may be seen if we contrast Carker with Mr. Tulkinghorn, Edith with Lady Dedlock.

[3] Some deliberate restraint over Carker may be suggested in the memorandum, 'Be patient with Carker. Get him on very slowly, without incident' (No. XII, chs. xxxv–xxxviii), but on the whole the notes suggest satisfaction. Dickens was delighted with the way Phiz depicted Edith in the illustrations, and these emphasize her staginess.

[4] Letter to Miss Jolly, rejecting a story submitted to *Household Words* (*Letters*, ii. 850).

§ 6

The 'minor' characters radiate from the centre of the novel, both in action and in theme. Each one is related, at not more than one remove, to the Dombey household or firm, or both; each one makes its comment, on pride and wealth. The novel could be broken up like a book of the *Faerie Queene*: family pride illustrated variously in Mrs. Chick, the Toodle parents, Mrs. Skewton, Cousin Feenix, and Good Mrs. Brown (even Mr. Perch and Mrs. Mac Stinger contribute their mite); attitudes to wealth and property also in the two 'toadies', honest and dishonest (Miss Tox and Major Bagstock), in Captain Cuttle, and in Mr. Toots. Their comments are dramatic rather than didactic; they could best be illustrated, along with the integration of structure, by the selection of single brief stages of the narrative. For just as there are no inactive characters in *Dombey*, none that are decorative marginal flourishes,[1] there is no episode which fails to advance the 'general purpose and design' and illustrate the theme both in its broadly human and its social implications. I shall

---

[1] Apparent exceptions among the very minor characters are there to give solidity and definition to others: the Game Chicken to Toots, the Reverend Melchizedek Howler to Mrs. Mac Stinger, and she to Captain Cuttle.

The thematic relevance of the characters is not necessarily always an advantage. With Alice Marwood, especially when she is revealed as Edith's 'natural' cousin, the diagram shows too starkly through the pattern. But at the climax, the doubling of the revenge-motif (Alice setting Mr. Dombey in pursuit of Carker) contributes to narrative economy as well as poetic justice.

take two separate chapters, one full of incident and one apparently discursive, as examples.

In the sixth chapter, 'Paul's Second Deprivation', we follow some members of the household into a new scene: Polly Toodle is the bridge between the grandiose gloom of Mr. Dombey's house and the boisterous affection of the humble home in Staggs's Gardens, set in the confusion and poverty of a district hacked up by the railway. Other scenes and representatives of other groups of characters are linked together. Florence is lost in the back streets of Camden Town, captured and stripped by Good Mrs. Brown, turned loose in rags to wander towards the Dombey firm in the City, to be rescued and brought home by Walter Gay, after a brief meeting with Carker the Junior and Sol Gills. With all its richness of detail, its variety of character and dialogue and its pointed social illustration of the contrasted 'two nations', this chapter is firmly tied at both ends to Mr. Dombey's pride, though his appearance in person is brief. Polly has been forbidden to visit her own family, but her anxious affection has been made frantic by Mr. Dombey's interference in enrolling her eldest son as a Charitable Grinder. Her intervention to protect the hapless Rob from his tormentors is the occasion of Florence's loss. Good Mrs. Brown is at hand not entirely by chance, nor does she strip Florence of her clothes in simple acquisitiveness; as we learn much later,[1] she has deliberately 'hung about a family',

---

[1] Ch. xxxiv, in which this incident is recalled. It is Alice's cloak that she puts on to Florence; she spares her hair because it reminds her of Alice's.

watching the Dombey household, and Carker, her
daughter's seducer; she remembers that daughter
and her action is a symbolic vengeance. (Already
it is hinted that she knows the name and the home of
Dombey.) Walter's rescue of Florence initiates his
relation to her, already forecast,[1] and sharpens Mr.
Dombey's irrational hostility to him by putting him
under an obligation which leads directly to his
banishment (in the almost too aptly named 'Son and
Heir'). The most far-reaching and ironical result of
the incident is set down in the title; the infant Paul
is deprived of his wet-nurse, and Mr. Dombey's
parental ambition begins its long course of self-
defeat. At all points the social moral is pressed home:
here first is clearly emphasized the interdependence
of the classes, the relation beyond the cash nexus.
Polly has feelings that wealth cannot buy; the heir
of Dombey and Son has needs which his father's
pride rejects at his peril. None of these links are insisted on; all are vital in the design. (Even the new
scene of Camden Town is not just any poor district;
it is deliberately chosen for its connexion with the
coming railway, to be developed in later chapters.)[2]
It is also an essential part of that design that the
single figure who never disappears from view in this
busily changing chapter is Florence: passively lost,
and found, and little noticed in the concluding
scene.

The entrance of the lost child made a slight sensation,

[1] In ch. iv.
[2] Chs. xv, xx. Its association with Dickens's own childhood is an additional motive.

but not much. Mr. Dombey, who had never found her, kissed
her once upon the forehead. . . .

§ 7

My second instance of this integration is from a
chapter which is particularly important as a transition between two large phases of the action; and
which is also interesting because Dickens's notes
show that he here felt the need for restraint.[1]

In the twentieth chapter, which opens the seventh
number, 'Mr. Dombey goes upon a Journey'. The devoting of a whole chapter to a journey marks the transition; and in its course the inevitability of coming
events is built up, a new relation is defined and the
moral centres of the novel are clearly exposed. The
main concern of the whole number is the visit to
Leamington,[2] and the setting in motion of Mr. Dombey's second marriage, to Edith Granger; of this
event no hint has yet appeared, and none is given in
this chapter. Mr. Dombey has been in shadow since
Paul's death, the only exhibited event being his
repulse of Florence. The second marriage apparently
arises from a chance visit, undertaken as an escape
from sorrow. But we are to assume that it belongs to
his nature as well as to circumstance. Bluntly, he has
lost one son, and must seek another.[3] But deliberate
action would be as inconsistent with his pride as with

---

[1] The manuscript number-plan has 'Take care of the Major'.

[2] The first and fullest note concerns this, and the chapter-heads show
that Dickens first planned to reach Leamington in the first chapter. Then
comes the inspiration 'The Railroad Ride'.

[3] Edith is a widow; he is careful to ascertain that she has borne a child.

his grief. There must be an intermediary. Already a possible (but improbable) second marriage has been prepared for, the instigator Mrs. Chick, and the candidate Miss Tox. Against this issue Miss Tox's neighbour is already scheming; the contrast of the unsuccessful and the successful sycophant, juxtaposed in the desperate gentility of Princess's Place, is carried further at the opening of this chapter. It is comic, but also serious. The grounds of the Major's triumph over Miss Tox are soon to be made clear; in addition to the advantages of his masculinity, in coarseness and heartlessness, he has something besides flattery to sell. By the standards of the time, the retired Indian Army Major (Sandhurst, blue face, curry and clubs complete) is at least on the edge of a class a cut above the wealthy City merchant; his friendship marks an advance in Mr. Dombey's dignified upward climb, whereas Miss Tox owed her temporary elevation only to her insignificance.[1] One of the functions of this chapter is to plant the Major firmly in the picture as the coming instigator of the second marriage; to groom him for the part of go-between in the common exchange of wealth for 'blood'. His status and his outlook are further defined in his treatment of the Native, his anecdotes, his views on the education of the poor; another variety of pride is set beside Mr. Dombey's, supporting and encouraging it, but differentiated. The Major's qualities, so freely exhibited in this chapter, show why 'Mr. Dombey was disposed to regard him as a choice spirit who shone in society . . . a creditable

[1] Ch. v.

companion . . . having an air of gentlemanly ease about him that mixed well enough with his own City character, and did not compete with it at all'.[1] In his growing influence on his friend the Major is already adumbrated as a 'comic Mephistophelean power', and the ease of this influence also makes plain Mr. Dombey's unworldliness. The subsequent chapters are to show the great merchant as easy prey for the unscrupulous; one of the ways in which he gains upon our sympathy is by appearing as a lamb among wolves, hunted down almost without effort by the Major and Mrs. Skewton, and always the dupe of Carker. Such unawareness, whatever its cause, has its own pathos.

The chapter includes a further breach in Mr. Dombey's isolation, but one which he recognizes and resents. At the station he is accosted by the fireman of the engine, who is Mr. Toodle; in him is concentrated Mr. Dombey's recollection of his loss, and the humiliating knowledge that others are aware of it. A common human sympathy is offered, and repulsed; doubly repulsed, for Toodle's sad report of Rob the Grinder, 'gone wrong' after his charitable education, is greeted with a cynical generalization, 'The usual return!'

But the sight of the piece of crape on Toodle's cap rankles in Mr. Dombey's mind.

So! from high to low, at home or abroad, from Florence in his great house to the coarse churl who was feeding the

---

[1] Ch. **xx**. The whole paragraph in which these words occur is an interesting analysis of their relationship.

fire then smoking before them, everyone set up some claim
or other to a share in his dead boy, and was a bidder against him!

The inner stage of his mind is now set for the rush-
ing reverie that accompanies the violent motion of
the train and the race of the passing landscape. The
express train becomes on the one hand 'a type of
the triumphant monster, Death'; on the other, of the
oneness of society. As the train slows down among the
black battered slums of an industrial city, the double
allegory becomes clear:

it is never in his thoughts that the monster who has brought
him there has let the light of day in on these things: not made
or caused them.

The 'monster', railway or death, merely revealed the
social and spiritual desolation that was already there.
Not grief, but guilt, is the cause of the storm in Mr.
Dombey's thoughts;

he knew full well, in his own breast . . . that life had quite as
much to do with his complainings as death.

The haunting image of Florence deepens the gloom:

More than once upon this journey, and now again as he
stood pondering at this journey's end, tracing figures in the
dust with his stick, the thought came into his mind, what was
there he could interpose between himself and it?

The Major, who had been blowing and panting all the
way down. . . .

The chapter is nearly at its end, and we are now prepared for the second marriage; it is thus linked, from
the outset, with Florence. It is one day only since he
turned her from him; on the next day he meets Edith.

§ 8

These two chapters have also illustrated Dickens's use of the railway, both as topical colouring[1] and as symbol, underlining the contemporary intention of the novel and its offered social commentary. (He must be one of the earliest Victorian writers to seize the railways imaginatively.) There are other recurrent symbols, and one, more obviously 'poetic' in itself and in intention, emphasizes rather the values of the 'other world'—not material progress or menace, but the mystery surrounding human life.

Through the whole novel echoes the sea; from the close of the first chapter, at the death of Mrs. Dombey with Florence in her arms—

Thus, clinging fast to that slight spar within her arms, the mother drifted out upon the dark and unknown sea that rolls round all the world—

to the very end, when 'autumn days are shining, and on the sea-beach' Florence and Mr. Dombey walk together, with another Florence and Paul. In all its recurrences the sea is charged with its inevitable associations of separation and reunion, death and eternal life. Seen in their full context, the mysterious voice of the waves and the 'invisible country far away' of Paul's fancy are not a passing effect produced to intensify pathos; they are part of a larger design. In the Brighton chapters at least two further passages[2] prepare for the 'waves' and the 'river that

[1] Cf. ch. xv (disappearance of Staggs's Gardens) and ch. lv (death of Carker). The railway references supply the chronological limits, and define them as about 1835 to 1845.　　　　　　　　[2] Chs. xii, xiii.

is always running on' of his dying hours; a much later chapter recalls them, not too explicitly—the last illness, death, and burial of Mrs. Skewton at Brighton.[1] The day-dreams of Solomon Gills, the supposed drowning of Walter Gay, the wedding voyage of Walter and Florence, all reinforce this covering symbol. Even though its verbal patterns are too pronounced for modern taste, they are at least based upon a perception of something profoundly natural, not factitious.

> And see the Children sport upon the shore,
> And hear the mighty waters rolling evermore.

This was a calculated means of unity; the sea—beyond what the actual incidents call for—is part of the semi-allegorical cover-design, and dominates the wholly allegorical frontispiece; the key phrases are often noted ahead in the notes for coming chapters. But it is a unity that includes much variety of tone. The shop of the Wooden Midshipman, that landlocked harbour past which 'the human tide is still rolling westward', is picturesque embroidery; Master Bitherstone's schemes for reaching Bengal are more absurd than pathetic; and in one of Paul's 'old-fashioned' colloquies his sickly fancy is boldly juxtaposed to comedy. Paul is gazing out of his window at Dr. Blimber's:

'I say!' cried Toots, speaking the moment he entered the room, lest he should forget it; 'what do you think about?'

'Oh! I think about a great many things,' replied Paul.

'Do you, though?' said Toots, appearing to consider that fact in itself surprising.

[1] Ch. xli.

'If you had to die,' said Paul, looking up into his face—
Mr. Toots started, and seemed much disturbed.

'— Don't you think you would rather die on a moonlight night, when the sky was quite clear, and the wind blowing, as it did last night?'

Mr. Toots said, looking doubtfully at Paul, and shaking his head, that he didn't know about that.

'Not blowing, at least,' said Paul, 'but sounding in the air like the sea sounds in the shells. . . . I got up and looked out. There was a boat over there, in the full light of the moon; a boat with a sail.'

The child looked at him so steadfastly, and spoke so earnestly, that Mr. Toots, feeling himself called upon to say something about this boat, said 'Smugglers'. But with an impartial remembrance of there being two sides to every question, he added 'or Preventive'.

'A boat with a sail,' repeated Paul, 'in the full light of the moon. The sail like an arm, all silver. It went away into the distance, and what do you think it seemed to do as it moved with the waves?'

'Pitch,' said Mr. Toots.

'It seemed to beckon,' said the child 'to beckon me to come!'[1]

The boldness is justified. Toots's literalness serves to 'distance' Paul's fancies, suggesting a degree of detachment in the author (though insufficient for the modern reader). It also emphasizes the irrational bond between these two uncommunicative personalities, and this queer association starts Toots off on his eccentric but firm career through the narrative. He owes his very relation to the action to Paul's death, and is continuously faithful to its memory, but never-

[1] Ch. xii.

theless 'sinks into the Silent Tomb with a gleam of joy'. Toots alone would justify Dickens's new technique in comedy; always subordinated to the main design, he yet gives ample elbow-room for Dickens's 'preposterous sense of the ridiculous' . . . 'And all I have written is point'. Speech after speech of Toots could be selected for its ludicrous but unerring penetration to the heart of a situation; 'children and fools speak the truth'. His schooldays remain his touchstone for experience—'I never saw such a world. It's a great deal worse than Blimber's.' He carries their innocence through the novel, as well as their scars.

The child's view of the world is also a source of unity in this novel; it is more important than in *Oliver Twist* and *The Old Curiosity Shop*, though the children there are hero and heroine, and do not grow up. But the children now affect the adults more deeply; the childhood love of Paul and Florence haunts Mr. Dombey, from the first chapter to the last. And their glance is more piercing. After *Dombey*, or even while writing it, Dickens was ready to write *David Copperfield*. The fourteenth chapter, 'Paul . . . goes home for the holidays', is almost in the first person; the single point of view is held throughout, with the child's lucid confusion. And since, for all his mystified intimations of mortality, he is still a normal child enjoying a party and being the centre of attention, it carries more conviction than the death-bed scene. The one has the mark of recovered experience on it; Dickens, after all, had never died. The essence of his childhood experience is of course already, in

Oliver and Nell—the hapless, exploited child, tossed from place to place and from person to person. But in *Dombey* he began to use specific experience, and even to use it closely. Actual places and persons now appear, hardly disguised; Camden Town, and at least one of its denizens.

I hope you will like Mrs. Pipchin's establishment. It is from the life, and I was there—I don't suppose I was eight years old; but I remember it all as well, and certainly understood it as well, as I do now. We should be devilish sharp in what we do to children.[1]

The child's-eye view, bewildered, yet implacable, is impressed upon the Brighton chapters, and especially on Mrs. Pipchin and her household. Perhaps some plausibility is here sacrificed; at least it needed a little manipulation to adjust this particular personal reminiscence to the much more prosperous Dombey family. The landlady takes a few steps up the social scale; her establishment is not in Camden Town, she has seen the better days which Susan Nipper pitied for having seen her, and no unpaid-for natural children[2] are mentioned among her boarders. The rest is evidently 'from the life'; hence Dickens's bitter disappointment over the illustration.[3] Mrs. Roylance-Pipchin was the acknowledged breach in the wall

---

[1] Forster, vi. 2; cf. i. 2, where Mrs. Roylance is described as 'a reduced old lady, long known to our family, in Little-College-street, Camden Town, who took children in to board, and had once done so at Brighton . . .'. Charles was lodged there while working at the blacking factory; later, on leaving the Marshalsea, the whole family went to live there for a time.   [2] i. 2.

[3] vi. 2; letter of November 1846.

that Dickens had built between himself and the darkest days of his childhood—a wall that is apt to crumble as middle age approaches, especially for a parent.[1] In the very letter which identifies Mrs. Pipchin, he first broaches the notion of writing the story of his childhood; he wrote it in 1848, and then wove it into *David Copperfield*. There were other events to awaken recollections; in 1846–7 Dickens's beloved elder sister Fanny had entered her last illness;[2] (the 'Child's Dream of a Star',[3] avowedly written with her in mind, has its parallel in the relation of Paul and Florence). And he had as 'a very young child' fancied the moonlight on the water as the pathway to heaven.[4]

Dombey and Son is also a plea for children; generally, for their right to be treated as individuals, instead of appendages and hindrances to parental ambition, and particularly, against the wrongs done to them in the name of education. It is a measure of this novel's largeness of scope that it is not often thought of as an exposure of misconceived schooling; but it is not less so than *Nicholas Nickleby* and penetrates into more

[1] By 1846 Dickens had two daughters and four sons. Two of his sons were at a school where the master's daughter was 'a thorough classical scholar and assisted him', which 'suggested the Blimber notion' (Introduction by Charles Dickens Jr. to edition of 1892).

[2] Forster, v. 7. She was the wife of Henry Burnett, and had two sons, one of whom, an invalid, is said to have been Paul's original. (The earliest evidence of this tradition seems to be in the recollections of a Manchester minister who had known them well: James Griffin, *Memories of the Past*, 1883, p. 209.)

[3] In the first number of *Household Words*, 30 March 1850. Forster links it with Fanny (vi. 4, last paragraph).

[4] *American Notes* (1842), ch. xvi.

protected places.[1] While forwarding the general
design Dickens has shown, incidentally and half-
humorously but unmistakably, what is wrong with
Dr. Blimber's academy; what the plight of the
cherished rich man's child[2] has in common with that
of the foundling parish boy. Mr. Dombey's other
educational mistake[3] is more briefly but more angrily[4]
exposed: the committing of Robin Toodle to the
mercies of the Charitable Grinders. And here he can
venture to admit the twisting of a character by mis-
education;[5] if not beyond repair, since, restored to his
parent and Miss Tox at the close, Rob is beginning
to reform.

But Dickens is not here concerned to attack specific
abuses. He is not so optimistic. In so far as *Dombey
and Son* is a 'social' novel, its prevailing mood is one
of deep disquiet about contemporary values, a suggestion that more is amiss with them than mere exposure

---

[1] This was recognized by several contemporary reviewers (e.g., *Westminster Review*, xlvii, April 1847) and by Edward Fitzgerald in a letter
to Thackeray: 'a very fine account of the overcramming educational
system, worth whole volumes of essays on the subject. . . . The boy who
talks Greek in his sleep seems to me as terrible as Macbeth' (Thackeray's
Letters, ii. 226).

[2] He defines the limits of Mr. Dombey's obtuseness, however, by
explicitly avoiding the public school; and has indicated his view of Sandhurst through Major Bagstock's grisly reminiscences (ch. x).

[3] Another novelist might have made something of the complete
neglect of Florence's education!

[4] Ch. vi, and ch. xx; and especially the last paragraph of ch. xxxviii,
given salience by being placed at the end of a number. Gissing calls Rob
'one of the most important of Dickens's social studies' (*Charles Dickens*,
1898, p. 208).

[5] Dickens was growing interested in gradual moral deterioration. His
first design was to show Walter Gay going wrong; counselled against it
by Forster, he remembered it in Richard Carstone, and Pip.

and reform can hope to touch. Dickens had formerly presented the wealthy man as a benevolent fairy god-mother or Father Christmas, in Mr. Brownlow, Abel Garland, or the Cheeryble brothers. There would be no place for such characters here. *Dombey and Son* suggests the gloom of wealth (more strongly even than Thackeray was to do) and its capacity to petrify or poison human relations, in the family and in society. 'Papa, what's money? . . . It isn't cruel, is it?' Wealth is an evil, corrupting the heart; prosperity a house built on sand. The moral of the 'valuelessness in themselves of the greatest earthly possessions' commended by one critic[1] and patent to all readers, is inwoven with the main design. The potential cruelty, the emptiness, the cold isolation of a Mammonist society is repeatedly emphasized: but rarely in a didactic way. Dickens is not writing a tract for the times, even at the distance of allegory. There is no overt social reference in his draft of his general design, in his working notes, or his Preface; but in a letter written when he was halfway through he said:

There is a great deal to do—one or two things among the rest that society will not be the worse, I hope, for thinking about a little.[2]

As we have seen, these 'one or two things' become a natural part of the narrative; still more effectively, they become part of the picture. House and firm

---

[1] *English Review* (December 1848), p. 271; and cf. *Christian Remembrancer* (December 1847), p. 347.
[2] Letter to Dr. Hodgson, 4 June 1847; *Letters*, ii. 28.

together dominate the story, and the house, scenically central,[1] is also an emblem of the social theme.

The social intentions of the novel are pointed by the title, and the status of the hero. He is Palmerston's 'princely merchant in his counting house'; a character 'which could only be produced in a country whose commerce embraces the globe, whose merchants are potentates'.[2] Such a merchant-prince no longer, of course, lived in the City, nor even, like Mr. Osborne and Mr. Sedley, near its borders in Russell Square. He has followed the tide of fashion to 'the shady side of a tall, dark, dreadfully genteel street in the region between Portland-place and Bryanstone-square. . . .[3] 'a house of dismal state'. We come to know all its appurtenances: the lustres, chandeliers, and marble floors, its statuary, its bookcase which 'repudiated all familiarities', 'glazed and locked'. The changing state of the house marks the movement of the narrative; we see its dreary magnificence abandoned to neglect in the months of Florence's solitude,[4] then garishly revived in preparation for the second marriage,[5] stripped by the auc-

---

[1] Although there is much variety (Brighton, Leamington, Dijon outside London; Leadenhall St., Princess's Place, Brig Place, Brook St., Staggs's Gardens, and the Carker suburb within London), over a third of the chapters are set or partly set in the Dombey house, and these are among the 'high-lights' of the novel, such as chs. iii, xviii, xxiii, xxviii, xxxvi, xl, xliii, xlvii–xlviii, li, and lix.

[2] Taine, *History of English Literature* (Paris, 1863–4), trans. H. Van Laun, 1871, ed. 2; Book V, ch. i, § 3. ii.

[3] And therefore well within the purview of Devonshire Terrace (opposite York Gate), which was Dickens's home when in London from 1839 to 1850.

[4] Ch. xxiii.   [5] Ch. xxviii.

tioneers—'the house is a ruin, and the rats fly from it',[1] and lastly

frowning like a dark mute on the street; baulking any nearer inquiries with the staring announcement that the lease of this desirable Family Mansion was to be disposed of.[1]

The dreadful spectacle of that sad House of Pride.[2]

Compared with this distinctness and load of significance, the firm of 'Dombey and Son', 'wholesale, retail, and for exportation' is dimly treated;[3] it is the off-stage source of wealth, rather than the hub of activity, and its export trade is distinguished only by the dispatch of Walter Gay. It lives rather through the characters it involves. Firm and household are used skilfully to define the social pyramid, from the loftiest to the lowest, from Mr. Carker the Manager down to Mr. Perch the messenger, while the servants are 'carried through'—Dickens's own phrase—from beginning to end.[4] Every family event has its reverberations in the humming chorus of the servants' hall—'misfortune in the family without feasting in these lower regions couldn't be'; below Susan, and Polly, and (later) Mrs. Pipchin, is ranged the household hierarchy, from the lugubrious Towlinson to the young kitchenmaid in black stockings whose single recorded contribution marks the completeness of the collapse—'Supposing the wages shouldn't

---

[1] Ch. lix.   [2] *The Faerie Queene*, I. v. 53.

[3] The 'exposition' in ch. iv (through Walter Gay) and the description in ch. xiii stand almost alone; in the office scenes the details are never either sharply visual or symbolic.

[4] Note in plan of No. X; cf. ch. xxxi. But this had begun much earlier; see the openings of chs. iii and xviii.

be paid!'[1] More faintly indicated, the clerks' chorus is set in apposition to the servants' chorus in the closing act.[2] Other houses, and one other business, contribute their variations on the theme; one, the town house of Cousin Feenix, confirms the dreariness and heartlessness of wealth with its 'black hatchments of pictures', its 'dark-brown dining-room, which no confectioner can brighten up, let him garnish the exhausted negroes with as many flowers and love-knots as he will';[3] others (the Toodles', the Wooden Midshipman) mark a contrast, with their cosy contrivances of ingenious frugality. Of these, the Wooden Midshipman is used with a twofold purpose of contrast: it is shown not only as a humble source of loyalty and affection, but as an outmoded retail concern representing a superseded past. No customers come to it—as Sol Gills laments, in almost too pointed exposition, 'Competition, competition—new invention, new invention . . . the world's gone past me'. (So much for the England of thirty years before—'when that uniform was worn. . . . fortunes were to be made'.)[4] This pocket of the past, in 'the immediate vicinity' of the offices of Dombey and Son, serves to emphasize the modernity and prosperity of the firm. (At the close, when the firm has fallen, 'Mr. Gills's old investments are coming out wonderfully' and he was after all not 'behind the time' but 'a little before it';[5] a consummation perhaps wisely left vague.) One other recurrent 'place' deepens the contemporary picture. Four phases of

---

[1] Ch. lix.
[2] Chs. li, lviii, lix.
[3] Ch. xxxi.
[4] Ch. iv.
[5] Ch. lxii.

the narrative are punctuated by scenes in the same church: Paul's christening, his funeral, Edith's wedding, and Florence's visit to Paul's grave before her own wedding.[1] In three of these the physical atmosphere is defined, in terms of chill and dust and wheeziness, with choric commentary from the two dried-up professional ministrants, Mr. Sownds and Mrs. Miff. Dickens spares nothing in his suggestion of a soulless society; he seems to point at house, firm, and church as three hollow shells of the established order.

Across the social picture are ruled the ruthless lines of the new order, symbolized in the railway. It links high and low, devastates Camden Town, uproots Staggs's Gardens, provides employment for Mr. Toodle, bears Mr. Dombey from grim past to grimmer future, and finally obliterates Carker. Its appearance on each of the four carefully spaced and placed occasions[2] is emphasized by a volcanic upsurge in the style, by description much overflowing its narrative function. In these descriptions may be discerned the fascination of the new as well as the horror of the strange; but the tone is mainly that of dread. Twice the railway is used to highlight the darker thoughts of hero and villain, thoughts of fear and hate and death.[3] The train is seen only as destructive, ruthless, an 'impetuous monster', a 'fiery devil'. There is no suggestion of hope, of social progress. This colouring of gloom and horror may derive from

[1] Chs. v, xviii (very briefly touched), xxxi, and lvii.
[2] Chs. vi, xv, xx, and lv.
[3] Chs. xx and lv.

the over-riding mood of the novel; it may be a picturesque reflection of contemporary doubts; but more probably, from the evidence of the later novels, it represents a persistent shade in Dickens's own social view, which contains at least as much pessimism as optimism, and always more of the visionary than of the reformer.

The social criticism in *Dombey and Son* cannot be abstracted from the novel, and even such disengaging as is attempted here perhaps distorts it. It is pervasive, unformulated; not documentary in origin or usefulness; no purposeful journeys or reading of newspaper reports lie behind it, and it is not a convenient source for social historians. Partly for this reason, that it is inseparable, it assists instead of disturbing the firm unity of the design. It is part of the 'Idea of the world' which protects Dickens from being 'prevailed over by the world's multitudinousness'.[1]

[1] *Letters of Matthew Arnold to Arthur Hugh Clough*, ed. H. F. Lowry (1932), p. 97; letter of 1848.

MARY BARTON

MARY BARTON, though a distinguished and memorable novel, is hardly of the scale or the quality of the other three novels here selected. It is chosen both because it is the outstanding example—outstanding in merit as in contemporary fame—of a kind of novel which first clearly disengaged itself in the forties: the novel directly concerned with a social problem, and especially with the 'condition-of-England question'; and because it transcends that kind; alike in motive and effect, it is far more than a 'tract for the times'. The same social conditions, and something of the same anxiety about them, inspired *Sybil* and *Yeast* and *Alton Locke*; but Mrs. Gaskell differs from Disraeli and Kingsley in having no axe to grind. A wider impartiality, a tenderer humanity, and it may be a greater artistic integrity, raise this novel beyond the conditions and problems that give rise to it.

I know nothing of Political Economy, or the theories of trade. I have tried to write truthfully. . . .[1]

In the fifteenth chapter, after a tentative and unwonted excursion on the possible causes of the strike, she concludes with relief, 'So much for generalities. Let us now return to individuals'. It is partly because it is a novel which starts from 'individuals'

---

[1] Preface to first edition, 1848.

that *Mary Barton* stands out from the run of 'novels with a purpose'. It is not less truthful than others of its kind, nor less passionate; but it is also, as befits a woman's novel, more purely compassionate; 'the poetry is in the pity'. But there is no patronage or condescension towards suffering. The denizens of the 'other nation' are neither harrowing victims nor heroic martyrs; they are shown in their natural human dignity, as Wordsworth might have shown them had he fulfilled his promise to make 'authentic comment' on 'sorrow barricadoed evermore within the walls of cities'.

It was that sorrow which effectively awoke the writer in the Unitarian minister's wife. That is not to say that we directly owe to it her later master-pieces, such as *Cousin Phillis* and *Wives and Daughters*; but *Mary Barton* was the novel she felt compelled to write, whose instant popularity smoothed her whole subsequent literary career, and the work which set free her powers. Not itself a great novel, it is the first novel of a great novelist; and the progress is an under-standable one, if we agree with the young Henry James that we have here to deal with a novelist whose 'genius' was 'so obviously the offspring of her affec-tions, her feelings, her associations . . . so little of an intellectual matter . . . little else than a peculiar play of her personal character'.[1]

Mary Barton was like *Vanity Fair* in bringing its author her first fame in early middle age; unlike it, in being the work of a comparatively unpractised

[1] Review of *Wives and Daughters* in *The Nation* (22 February 1866), collected in *Notes and Reviews* (Cambridge, Mass., 1921), pp. 154-5.

writer. The author's three stories in *Howitt's Journal*, 1847–8,[1] preceded it in publication, but probably not in composition; the much earlier verses 'Sketches among the Poor',[2] written with her husband, were intended to inaugurate a series 'in the manner of Crabbe . . . but in a more seeing-beauty spirit'; they were not followed up, though the germ of Alice Wilson may be found there. Her self-discovery as a writer is part of her personal life. She was 'cradled into' novel-writing 'by wrong', and learnt in suffering; first her own suffering in the loss of a child, which sharpened her fellow feeling with the sufferings of the Manchester poor. She had known her material for twelve years, ever since her marriage brought her from the country to the industrial city; her novel 'grew up . . . as imperceptibly as a seed germinates in the earth'.[3] When the millworker answered her attempts at comfort with 'Have you ever seen a child clemm'd to death?' the words struck home. She had seen her only son die of scarlet fever; in the grief that followed she had turned to thoughts of the country and the past and had begun to write 'a tale . . . of . . . more than a century ago . . .

[1] 'Libbie Marsh's Three Eras', 'The Sexton's Hero', and 'Christmas Storms and Sunshine', published in that order in vols. i–iii, under the pseudonym 'Cotton Mather Mills'. The Howitts had been her friends for some years, and it was William Howitt who after seeing the first volume of her novel in manuscript urged her to continue.

[2] *Blackwood's Magazine* (January 1837), pp. 48–50; the heading is 'Sketches among the Poor, No. I', but no further instalment followed. The authorship was first pointed out by John Mortimer, 'A Lancashire Novelist', *Manchester Quarterly*, xxi (1902), 205.

[3] Draft of letter to Mrs. Greg, published in A. W. Ward's Introduction to *Mary Barton* (Knutsford edition, vol. i, 1906, pp. lxii–lxiv).

on the borders of Yorkshire'.[1] But now she put it aside:

I bethought me how deep might be the romance in the lives of some of those who elbowed me daily in the busy streets of the town in which I resided. . . .

She wrote in order

to give utterance to the agony which, from time to time, convulses the dumb people; the agony of suffering without the sympathy of the happy, or of erroneously believing that such is the case.

The prevailing thought in my mind when the tale was silently forming itself . . . was the seeming injustice of the inequalities of fortune.[2]

The year was 1845,[3] when the events of the years 1839–42, in which the story is set, were still painfully near in memory. Whether from uncertainty or domestic distraction,[4] she seems not to have finished it until 1847; at the close of that year, after other publishers had rejected it, John Forster read it for Chapman and Hall and recommended publication. In 1848 its substance had a renewed topicality;[5] Mrs. Gaskell, who always combined something of the ser-

[1] Preface to *Mary Barton*, first edition. This does not seem to have survived, though it is possible that it has some relation to *Sylvia's Lovers*.

[2] Letter to Mrs. Greg.

[3] William, the only son, died at the age of ten months in August 1845; and the Preface to *Mary Barton* (dated October 1848) speaks of 'three years ago'. Some writers, following A. W. Ward, have given the year wrongly as 1844; the point is set right by G. D. Sanders, *Elizabeth Gaskell* (Cornell Studies in English, 1929).

[4] Her sixth child and fifth daughter was born in September 1846.

[5] Not only because of the European revolutions, but also because of the closing of many Lancashire mills owing to the failure of the American cotton crop, and the Chartist meeting in April. The novel was published on 14 October.

pent's wisdom with the dove's innocence, insinuates
this timeliness throughout her preface, and concludes by remarking that her impression 'has received
some confirmation from the events which have so
recently occurred among a similar class on the Continent'. The reviews caught the hint, and the anonymous 'tale of Manchester life', by one who knew
'nothing of Political Economy', became required
reading for all thoughtful persons. It was reviewed
less as a novel than as a document; its truth and justice,
its social moral were emphasized:

> It embodies the dominant feeling of our times—that the
> ignorance, destitution and vice which pervade and corrupt
> our society must be got rid of. The ability to point out how
> they are to be got rid of, is not the characteristic of this age.
> That will be the characteristic of the age that is coming.[1]

The reviewer is not ironical. The necessary step was
the tearing of the iron curtain between the two
Nations; and this step was within the power, perhaps
even was peculiarly the role, of the novelist—as the
construction of blueprints for reform was not. The
first step was for those who knew the other nation to
build up pictures in the comfortable reader's mind, to
haunt his imagination and harry the social conscience. This was, indeed, only incidental to Mrs.
Gaskell's desire to promote understanding; but it was
the main effect. The lesson was rhetorically rammed
home by the reviewer in *Fraser's*:[2]

[1] *Westminster Review* (1849), p. 48.
[2] April 1849, pp. 429–32. Other interesting reviews are in the *Athenæum* (21 October 1848), the *Prospective Review*, v (1849), 36–57; and
the *North British Review* (August 1851).

[This is] the life-in-death—life worse than many deaths, which now besets thousands, and tens of thousands of our own countrymen . . . when people on Turkey carpets, with their three meat meals a day, are wondering, forsooth, why working men turn Chartists and Communists.

Do they want to know why? Then let them read *Mary Barton*. Do they want to know why poor men . . . learn to hate law and order, Queen, Lords and Commons, country-party and corn-law leaguer, all alike—to hate the rich, in short? Then let them read *Mary Barton*. Do they want to know what can madden brave, honest, industrious North-country hearts, into self-imposed suicidal strikes, into conspiracy, vitriol-throwing, and midnight murder? Then let them read *Mary Barton*. . . . Do they want to get a detailed insight into the whole science of starving . . .? Let them read *Mary Barton*. . . .

The occasional adverse criticism, of the 'Unfair to Mill-owners' order (as in the *Manchester Guardian* and the review by William Rathbone Greg)[1] is itself a tribute to the novel's power; and though she disclaimed a knowledge of political economy, she aroused the political economists to approach her as an apt pupil.[2] Many shades of opinion are represented in the letters she received,[3] from Samuel Bamford, the veteran Radical (testifying to the novel's truth from his own experience—'of John Bartons I have known hundreds'), from Ashley Cooper (later Lord

[1] Greg, author of *The Creed of Christendom* (1851), was himself a mill-owner until 1850. He reviewed *Mary Barton* in the *Edinburgh Review* (April 1849), and reprinted his article in *Mistaken Aims and attainable ideals of the artizan class* (1876).

[2] See *Westminster Review* (April 1849).

[3] *Letters addressed to Mrs. Gaskell by Celebrated Contemporaries . . .*, ed. R. D. Waller (Manchester, 1935).

Shaftesbury), Lord Brougham, Cobden, Bright, Lord Lansdowne, Sydney Herbert, and Edwin Chadwick; from Dickens, Maria Edgeworth, and Carlyle. William Delafield Arnold wrote to say that it was being widely read in India, where its lessons were needed; and that it was a work of which his father would have approved.

Sybil, three years earlier, had met no such wide and warmhearted response, although its great phrase, 'the two nations', had run through the country and had perhaps prepared the ground; Disraeli's reputation both as society novelist and ambitious politician may have blunted his social message; and though he is more than either of these in *Sybil*, his motive and approach are still limiting. A modern reader turning to these two novels as sociological documents may be struck by the way their evidence confirms and supplements each other—like the Prologues of Chaucer and Langland; but the evidence reaches us differently. The centre of Disraeli's novel is Egremont, the theme is his enlightenment as to the 'condition of England'; he is the discoverer of the 'other nation', and a projection of the author. Mrs. Gaskell's novel need contain no projection of herself; she was not a discoverer, but was writing of what had long been sadly familiar. As one of her most thoughtful critics[1] has said, Disraeli knew his material 'as a traveller knows the botany of a strange country', she 'as an ardent naturalist knows the flora of his own neighbourhood'. More, he was a traveller who travelled

---

[1] William Minto, *Fortnightly Review* (1 September 1878), pp. 353–69.

deliberately in order to write; and something calcu-
lating, almost inhuman, at least journalistic, clings
to his report. It does not satisfy Charlotte Brontë's
standards:

> To manage these great matters rightly they must be long
> and practically studied—their bearings known intimately,
> and their evils felt genuinely; they must not be taken up as
> a business matter and a trading speculation.[1]

Take Devilsdust, the child who defied in infancy
'starvation and poison', and even the usual baby-farm
expedient of sending him 'out in the street to "play"',
in order to be run over'; who slept at night 'with a
dungheap at his head and a cesspool at his feet', and
at the age of five, when all his companions were
corpses, graduated into a factory.[2] A terrible story,
but its force is lessened by its not being concerned
with a character in whom we are asked to take any
human interest, and by being narrated, not shown.
It could equally be a case-history—and an extreme,
not a representative, case, selected with a manifestly
propagandist purpose. The grimmest episode in
Mary Barton, John Barton's visit to the Davenport
family, dying of fever in their cellar dwelling, could
easily have been merely documentary and detachable;[3] instead it is made an essential stage in Barton's
experience, part of the warp of the novel. As often
with Mrs. Gaskell's descriptions, it makes its effect
by slow persistent accumulation; the reader is en-

[1] Letter of 30 October 1852; *S.H.B.* iv. 14.
[2] *Sybil,* Book II, ch. x.
[3] Ch. vi. It is in fact so little detachable that it would not 'tell' in
selective quotation or summary.

meshed in its detail before he is aware, and engaged as a complete human being, not a politician or philanthropist. The reader's response to Devilsdust and to the tommy-shop is simple and immediate: these conditions are wrong and should be altered by legislation. No one would belittle the value of such stimulus; but the only reason why it should be made through a novel is that it will reach a wider audience. The sufferings of the characters in *Mary Barton* evoke this response and something more. The Davenports could have a better drained and ventilated dwelling and law or charity should see that they do not starve because the mill is closed: but with John Barton we are left aware of

> how small, of all that human hearts endure,
> That part which laws or kings can cause or cure.

Not small indeed, but not all; beneath this is the hard core of irremediable suffering 'permanent, obscure, and dark', in John Barton's sense of the mysterious injustice of man's time-bound existence. To counter-act this there must also be a reconciling power; the sense that 'we have all of us one human heart'. *Mary Barton* is a tale of Manchester life, of the Manchester that Engels saw, in whose poorer quarters the infant mortality was sixty per cent; it was also the Man-chester of the opening chapters of *Past and Present*—

> sooty Manchester, it too is built upon the infinite abysses!

'It too'; 'Birmingham people have souls'. Manchester life is the life of men and women stirred by the primary human affections, and made in the divine image. On this simple intuition the novel is built.

§ 2

It has therefore a more complex unity than that of social purpose, a unity rather of theme and tone. But first of all, it has the unity of a single character; the character of the title as originally planned[1]— *John Barton*. He is central both to the mere narrative, and to the theme of class antagonism; both reaching their climax in the eighteenth and exactly half-way chapter, 'Murder'. But he is also bigger than the events, even than the clashing social forces which they represent; rebelling against more than society; marked with the same tragic irrationality as Michael Henchard, Mayor of Casterbridge. Emphatically he is not put forward as a type of the working classes —Mrs. Gaskell herself protested against such critics as Greg; nor is his story simply (as some reviewers thought) a moral fable showing why working men turn Chartists and assassins; it is the timeless history of how a man full of human kindness is hardened into (and by) hatred and violence. This defines the rising curve of the story; one point,[2] for instance, is clearly plotted in the third chapter, when on his wife's death the author says that

One of the ties which bound him down to the gentle humanities of earth was loosened.

[1] Letter to Mrs. Greg, op. cit., p. lxiii.

[2] Another is defined only retrospectively; his early attempt to 'live Gospel-wise' and how he 'gave it up in despair, trying to make folks' actions square wi' th' Bible; and I thought I'd no longer labour at following th' Bible myself'. This is related only on his death-bed (ch. xxxv) and the delay is surely part of a deliberate avoidance of emphasis on his turning away from religion.

We watch others loosen, as his experience—the strike, its typical consequences in the Davenports' starvation and fever, the employers' arrogant isolation, the failure of the petition—seems to show that the world reckons them of no account. But, as he says on his deathbed after he has confessed the murder, 'All along it came natural to love folk, though now I am what I am . . . I did not think he'd been such an old man—Oh! that he had but forgiven me.' And even as he lies there, his enemy Mr. Carson sits in his library over the family Bible, unable to hate his son's murderer so vehemently now that he has seen him—'something of pity would steal in for the poor, wasted skeleton of a man'. He does forgive, and John Barton dies in the arms of the man whose son he has murdered. And this points to the book's true theme: not this or that feature of industrial society is being criticized, but its whole principle, excluding any human contact between masters and men; and the hope of betterment lies not in this or that reform, but in the persistence, against all odds, of humanheartedness. It is as simple, and as remote from 'political economy' as that; the moral content of *Mary Barton*, as distinct from all its accretion of specific, documentary detail, is also that of *Dombey and Son* and of *Past and Present*. 'What's money? It isn't cruel, is it?' 'Isolation is the sumtotal of wretchedness to man. . . . It was not a God that did this: no!' 'John Barton's overpowering thought . . . was rich and poor; why are they so separate, so distinct, when God has made them all? It is not His will that their interests are so far apart.

Whose doing is it?'[1] It is through John Barton, his experience, his honest, confused reflections, his deterioration and his fateful actions, that Mrs. Gaskell gives 'utterance to the agony which . . . convulses the dumb people; the agony of suffering without the sympathy of the happy'.

§ 3

Mary, John Barton's daughter, who gave the book its perhaps more marketable title,[2] nevertheless appears less prominently even than Florence Dombey; and like her, she subsides at times into the novel-heroine of the period—though the greater freedom of her class gives her more scope for action. Her emergence as active and heroic heroine after the murder, in her sensational pursuit of the missing witness in order to prove Jem Wilson innocent, makes her dominate the narrative for the latter half of the novel; but her relation to its theme seems too weakly developed. The rivalry of her two lovers, the master and the man, and her vacillation between them, her relation to her father, the threatening parallel between her and Esther, all have thematic possibilities that are only roughly suggested. It may be a concession to novel-convention that Mary alone of the working-class characters usually speaks ordinary English, not

[1] Ch. xv.
[2] Presumably Chapman and Hall insisted on this. They also demanded, when the novel was in the press, several extra pages to fill out the second volume (letter to Mrs. Greg, op. cit., p. lxiv). These are said, I do not know on what authority, to have been added in chs. xxxiii, xxxiv, and especially in ch. xxxvii (Thomas Seccombe, Introduction to Everyman edition).

dialect; but it has its dangers. 'Now I scorn you, sir, for plotting to ruin a poor girl'[1] flattens a climax of the narrative into a stage situation and is far removed from the Old Testament dignity of John Barton's utterances. Mary draws her importance from the story, where John Barton gives out strength to it; in her alone of the characters one sees the prentice hand. She could not have been a Margaret Hale; but she might have been a Sylvia Robson.

§ 4

More is contributed to the unity of the novel by what is indicated in its sub-title—'a tale of Manchester life'. It is the diversity and density of Manchester life, and the figure of John Barton rising craglike above it, that is built up before our eyes in the slow-moving expository opening chapters. They needed to be slow, because of the novelty of the material; they needed also to be reassuring.[2] The author had to enlist the reader's sympathy for her hero; she could not abruptly introduce him as a Trades Union man, a Chartist, an advocate and perpetrator of violence; and it would indeed be foreign to her purpose, which is not to demand approval or condemnation, but interest and understanding. With instinctive craftiness, she does not at once demand sympathy for hardship, but gently engages

[1] Ch. xi.

[2] 'Our readers need not be alarmed at the prospect of penetrating the recesses of Manchester. The king's daughter, washing the linen of the Phæacian palace, is scarcely more unsuggestive of anything like vulgarity, than are these descriptions' (*North British Review*, August 1951, p. 426).

the reader's participation in a simple family outing to Greenheys Fields and a north-country high tea in a basement kitchen.[1] The contrasts are so far unsensational; but there is light and shade—the back-to-back houses with their open drains, the firelit glow of the interior and the clever contrivances of small-scale housekeeping; the ripples of domestic gossip meeting sudden conversational rocks, and making us aware of such past events as little Tom's death and Esther's disappearance. John Barton's outburst, rooted in its context in the first chapter, gives out the theme and forecasts his relation to it:

'Thou never could abide the gentlefolk', said Wilson, half amused at his friend's vehemence.

'And what good have they ever done me that I should like them?' asked Barton, the latent fire lighting up his eye. . . . 'Don't think to come over me with the old tale, that the rich know nothing of the trials of the poor. I say, if they don't know, they ought to know. We are their slaves as long as we can work; we pile up their fortunes with the sweat of our brows; and yet we are to live as separate as if we were in two worlds. . . .[2]

Precarious present happiness, shadowed by past and future, is the 'note' of the opening chapters. But, though precarious, it yet recurs and persists, not for all characters, but as an uncovenanted hope; throughout the tribulations of the narrative, we are kept aware of another world than Manchester, another world than the two worlds of rich and poor. Its light falls on Greenheys Fields, on the recollected Cum-

[1] Ch. ii; 'A Manchester tea-party' is the title in the collected edition.
[2] Ch. i.

berland childhood of old Alice (a fully substantiated 'poor Susan'), on a chance-met child's face in the street, the blind girl's singing, Job Legh's absorption in his collection of insects, Mary's desperate courage at the trial, her face haunting an onlooker like 'some wild sad melody, heard in childhood'. Its broader radiance is perhaps best seen in a passage which may at first sight seem an excrescence, an interlude; in the chapter later called 'Barton's London experiences'.[1] John Barton has returned from London, and tells Mary, Job, and Margaret the story of the Chartists' march through the West End with their petition, in ironic juxtaposition to the carriage procession for the Queen's drawing-room. The actual rejection of the petition is too bad to be spoken of:

'I canna tell of our down-casting just as a piece of London news. As long as I live, our rejection that day will bide in my heart; and as long as I live I shall curse them as so cruelly refused to hear us; but I'll not speak of it no more.'

So, daunted in their inquiries, they sat silent for a few minutes.

The social point has been made (the description of the march is full of bitter detail) and there a propagandist might stop. But equally a part of Mrs. Gaskell's world view are 'the gentle humanities of earth'. From them springs the transition:

Old Job, however, felt that someone must speak, else all the good they had done in dispelling John Barton's gloom was lost. So after a while he thought of a subject, neither suffi-

[1] Ch. ix.

ciently dissonant from the last to jar on the full heart, nor
too much the same to cherish the continuance of the gloomy
train of thought.

'Did you ever hear tell,' said he to Mary, 'that I were in
London once?'

There follows the story of how many years ago he
planned a Whitsuntide visit to his married daughter
in London, only to hear from her father-in-law that
both she and her husband were stricken with fever.
The two men had gone to London together, to find
daughter and son dead, leaving a young infant; then
he tells at length, in garrulous yet reticent Lancashire style, of their journey north with the child, and
all their bewildered expedients. Falling into that
context, this narrative, with its basis of hardship,
the implicit tenderness of the two men's purpose,
and the comic awkwardness of the situation, is more
than a temporary relief to gloom. There is no simple
contrast; Job Legh's experience shares the common
ground of poverty with John Barton's grievances, but
its unembittered tone supplies an unconscious correc-
tive, a suggestion of values beyond the frustrations
of political action. And because it is something past
and safely lived through, it stands for hope.

That funeral cost a mint o' money, but Jennings and I
wished to do th' thing decent. Then we'd the stout little babby
to bring home. We'd not overmuch money left; but it were
fine weather, and we thought we'd take th' coach to Brummagem, and walk on. It were a bright May morning when I
last saw London town, looking back from a big hill a mile or
two off. And in that big mass o' a place I were leaving my
blessed child asleep—in her last sleep. Well, God's will be

done! She's gotten to Heaven afore me; but I shall get there at last, please God, though it's a long while first.

The babby had been fed afore we set out, and th' coach moving kept it asleep, bless its little heart. But when th' coach stopped for dinner it were awake, and crying for its pobbies. So we asked for some bread and milk, and Jennings took it first for to feed it; but it made its mouth like a square, and let it run out at each o' the four corners. 'Shake it, Jennings', says I; 'that's the way they make water run through a funnel, when it's o'er full; and a child's mouth is broad end of the funnel, and th' gullet th' narrow one.' So he shook it, but it only cried th' more. 'Let me have it', says I, thinking he were an awkward oud chap. But it were just as bad wi' me. . . . Well, poor babby cried without stopping to take breath, fra' that time till we got to Brummagem for the night [a chambermaid feeds and quiets the child] It looked so quiet and smiling, like, as it lay in her arms, that we thought 'twould be no trouble to have it wi' us. I says 'See, Jennings, how women folk do quieten babbies; it's just as I said.' He looked grave; he were always thoughtful-looking, though I never heard him say anything very deep. At last says he—'Young woman! have you gotten a spare nightcap? . . . Th' babby seems to have taken a mind to yo', and may be in th' dark it might take me for yo if I'd getten your nightcap on. . . .' Such a night as we had on it! Babby began to scream o' th' oud fashion, and we took it turn and turn about to sit up and rock it. My heart were very sore for the little one, as it groped about wi' its mouth; but for a' that I could scarce keep fra' smiling at th' thought of us two oud chaps, th' one wi' a woman's nightcap on, sitting on our hinder ends for half the night, hushabying a babby as wouldn't be hushabied.

They tramp through another day and night, and next day are helped by a cottage woman who has lost her own child.

'Last look I had o' that woman she were quietly wiping her eyes wi' the corner of her apron, as she went about her husband's breakfast. But I shall know her in heaven.'

He stopped to think of that long-ago May morning, when he had carried his grand-daughter under the distant hedgerows and beneath the flowering sycamores.

'There's nought more to say, wench,' said he to Margaret, as she begged him to go on. 'That night we reached Manchester, and I'd found out that Jennings would be glad enough to give up babby to me, so I took her home at once, and a blessing she's been to me.'

The return to the present, to the grown granddaughter, and John Barton with his daughter asleep at his knee, is unstressed; no moral is drawn; it is the reader, rather than John Barton, who is effectively reminded of 'the gentle humanities'. In the next chapter, the present closes over him; its opening words are 'Despair settled down like a heavy cloud'. As a Chartist delegate and Trades Union man, he can find no work; his rooms are stripped to buy food:

He would bear it all, he said to himself. And he did bear it, but not meekly; that was too much to expect.[1]

The ninth chapter points the significance of Job Legh, who is more than a minor character; he is the point of rest in the narrative, and in the theme, the embodiment of 'the gentle humanities of earth' and of the practical possibilities of the Christian ethic. Almost inactive in events until then, it is thus appropriate that it should be he who appeals for Mr. Carson's forgiveness, he who presses home the social and spiritual lesson after John Barton's death: 'I'm clear

[1] Ch. x.

about this, when God gives a blessing to be enjoyed, He gives it with a duty to be done; and the duty of the happy is to help the suffering to bear their woe.'

A novelist of narrower purpose might have didactically emphasized the difference between Job Legh and John Barton. But Mrs. Gaskell holds the balance fairly between John Barton's bitter protest and Job Legh's acceptance of his lot; resignation to the power of the masters and to the divine will are not confused. The lesson that Job Legh presses home is that of John Barton's terrible act, without which Mr. Carson's eyes could not have been opened, and for which the masters must share the responsibility. Even by Job, John Barton's failure as a Christian is almost extenuated:

'You see he were sadly put about to make great riches and great poverty square with Christ's Gospel. . . . For he was a loving man before he grew mad with seeing such as he was slighted, as if Christ himself had not been poor',[1]

whereas Mr. Carson's failure provokes the severest of the author's rare comments:

Oh! Orestes! you would have made a very tolerable Christian of the nineteenth century![2]

She makes no equivalent condemnation of the murder; and Job's summing up emphasizes the chain of cause and effect:

'The masters has it on their own conscience,—you have it on yours, sir, to answer for to God whether you've done, and are doing all in your power to lighten the evils, that seem

[1] Ch. xxxvii.   [2] Ch. xviii.

always to hang on the trades by which you make your fortunes. . . . John Barton took the question in hand, and his answer to it was NO! Then he grew bitter and angry, and mad; and in his madness he did a great sin, and wrought a great woe; and repented him with tears as of blood, and will go through his penance humbly and meekly in t'other place, I'll be bound. . . .'[1]

§ 5

These two men, John Barton and Job Legh, may perhaps stand not only for different yet related aspects of 'Manchester life', different responses to life's hardships, but for the defiant courage and persistent loving-kindness that are seen now colliding, now co-operating, in all Mrs. Gaskell's novels. Courage to give utterance to unfamiliar points of view——that of the workman driven to violence; of the stern self-made factory-owner; of the seduced girl and the parson who protects her; but always with the purpose, unconscious perhaps, of promoting sympathy, not sharpening antagonisms; between regions, classes, sexes, generations; on the quiet assumption that to know is to understand, to forgive, and even to respect.

Not even George Eliot shows such reverence for average human nature as Mrs. Gaskell; and this is evident from her earliest work. It helped to teach her the art which her later novels perfected; helped to guide her instinctive tact in avoiding the over-emphases of sentimentality and sensationalism, even in situations that tempt towards them. For she

[1] Ch. xxxvii.

accepts, and not ruefully, the ordinariness of people and the dailiness of life. Already in her first novel the minor characters (such as the boy Charley, Mrs. Wilson, Sally Leadbitter) are solid and distinct; each character, however small, has its scale of moral values, and its social medium; all are closely associated with the domestic detail of their surroundings. (Her explicit descriptions are mainly of what people use or make themselves at home in.) This unheightened truthfulness establishes confidence, so that we are ready to accept her 'big scenes'—the chase down the Mersey, the murder trial; like the bank failure in *Cranford*, they seem simply emergencies which must occasionally arise in ordinary life and which test character. And more: this almost pedestrian truthfulness is already accompanied by something spacious: her common flowers of human nature are rooted in earth, but over them arches 'the divine blue of the summer sky'.[1]

It would be better then to remove from *Mary Barton* the old tag of 'novel with a purpose', implying social, extra-artistic purpose. It was indeed, more perhaps than any other of the time, a novel with a social *effect*; but Mrs. Gaskell wrote, then as always, not with her eye on the effect, but as one possessed with and drenched in her subject:

I *can* not (it is not *will* not) write at all if I ever think of my readers, and what impression I am making on them. 'If they don't like me, they must lump me', to use a Lancashire

---

[1] Henry James, speaking not of this quality but of the completeness of the world in *Wives and Daughters* (review, 1866; *Notes and Reviews*, 1921, p. 154).

proverb. It is from no despising my readers. I am sure I don't do that, but if I ever let the thought or consciousness of them come between me and my subject I *could* not write at all.[1]

[1] *Letters of Mrs. Gaskell to Charles Eliot Norton* (1932), p. 20 (letter of 1858).

VANITY FAIR

§ 1

THACKERAY'S first full-length novel began to appear when he was thirty-five; it represents a fresh start in his literary career, and the emergence of such a novel as a 'first' novel has something of the miraculous. Behind him lay ten or twelve years of miscellaneous journalism—writing verses, sketches, reviews, and tales, works most of which seemed in comparison 'jokes, and schoolboy exercises as it were'.[1] He had written under many disguises—Charles Yellowplush, Ikey Solomons, Fitz-Boodle, Our Fat Contributor, Michael Angelo Titmarsh, and over a dozen more; the multiplicity suggests an unwillingness to commit himself, an awareness that he had not yet found his medium. 'Pen and Pencil Sketches of English Society', the original title, and later sub-title, of *Vanity Fair*, well describes the main mass of his earlier writing, but is ludicrously inadequate to the novel. There is common material, a common preoccupation with snobs and humbugs; but there is in these writings little preparation for a work so large in scale, so complex in organization or so mature in outlook, as *Vanity Fair*. Some preparation for its deeper tone may be found in Thackeray's private life; in the new stability of his *ménage*,[2] his change from Bohemianism to domesticity, and the

---

[1] *Letters*, ii. 316; letter to A. Hayward, 5 September 1847.

[2] In June 1846 he took a house in Kensington and in the autumn brought his young daughters to live with him.

greater assurance of his view of life and of the writer's function.[1] It is possible by such means to account for one change that is manifest in *Vanity Fair*: the enfolding of the satirist within the moralist. For the first time, Thackeray is openly the preacher.

And while the moralist, who is holding forth on the cover (an accurate portrait of your humble servant), professes to wear neither gown nor bands, but only the very same long-eared livery in which his congregation is arrayed: yet, look you, one is bound to speak the truth as far as one knows it, whether one mounts a cap and bells or a shovel-hat; and a deal of disagreeable matter must come out in the course of such an undertaking.[2]

The firm planning and complex unity of the novel must be partly explained by long preliminary reflection; such an interval for premeditation, unlikely for any earlier work, being here allowed by the early false start and the publishers' rejections. *Vanity Fair*, more than any later novel save *Esmond*, bears the marks of what Trollope called 'forethought . . . the elbow-grease of the novelist'; and more than any, it has at the same time the buoyant improvisation in detail arising from the practised skill of the journalist.[3]

---

[1] Cf. *Letters*, ii. 234, 255–6, 282–3; the letter of 24 February 1847, defining his change of view, is quoted above, p. 11.

[2] Ch. viii, which opens No. III. What are now chs. i–ix were originally written early in 1845. See above, p. 44.

[3] The buoyancy is also that of good health (which Charlotte Brontë regarded as indispensable equipment for a serial-writer), and contrasts with the intermittent lassitude of the later novels. Thackeray was never really well after the serious illness of 1849, which interrupted the publication of *Pendennis*.

But the earlier writings contribute one important connecting thread to the 'figure in the carpet' of Thackeray the novelist. That is, Thackeray's constant *criticism* of novel-conventions, seen especially in his many reviews and his burlesques. For many years before the publication of *Vanity Fair* he had been clearing the ground for himself and his readers by indicating the kinds of novel he would never write. He had taken his full share in *Fraser's* campaign against Bulwer;[1] in 1844–5 he was reviewing novels by Mrs. Trollope, Lever, and Disraeli; his *Catherine*, as we have seen,[2] was directed against the 'Newgate novels' of the thirties, especially Bulwer's *Eugene Aram* and Ainsworth's *Jack Sheppard*. There is a more affectionate teasing of historical romances in *A Legend of the Rhine* (1845) and *Rebecca and Rowena*, *A Romance upon Romance*;[3] and in the same year as *Vanity Fair* he produced his most specific and exuberant burlesques, in *Punch's Prize Novelists*, where the unmistakable targets are Bulwer Lytton, Disraeli, Lever, G. P. R. James, Mrs. Gore, and Fenimore Cooper.[4] Here he proclaims his rejection especially

---

[1] e.g. *Yellowplush Papers*, viii (*Works*, i. 315–33).

[2] See p. 75 above.

[3] This was first planned in 1841; the first version appeared in *Fraser's* in 1846, the revised version as a 'Christmas Book' in 1849.

[4] They were collected, with some omissions, in *Miscellanies*, ii (1856) under the title *Novels by Eminent Hands*. The separate titles are *George de Barnwell*, by Sir E. L. B. L., Bart.; *Codlingsby*, by D. Shrewsberry, Esq.; *Phil Fogarty a tale of the Fighting Onety-oneth*, by Harry Rollicker; *Barbazure*, by G. P. R. Jeames, Esq., &c.; *Lords and Liveries*, by the authoress of *Dukes and Déjeuners, Hearts and Diamonds, Marchionesses and Milliners*, &c., &c.; *The Stars and Stripes*, by the author of *The Last of the Mulligans*. See also *Crinoline*, by Jeames de la Pluche; and 'A Plan for a Prize Novel' (1851), in which the 'novel with a purpose' is mocked.

of pretentiousness of style,[1] of sham romance, of the pseudo-heroic, and all the stereotypes through which the novelist evades his responsibility for giving both an impression and an interpretation of life. These burlesques bear the same serious relation to Thackeray's own creative work as do Chaucer's *Sir Thopas* and Jane Austen's *Volume the First* and *Love and Freindship* to theirs; there is the same half-delighted familiarity with the original to weight and yet soften the attack, the same steady discrimination between the fake and the genuine. And like Chaucer and Jane Austen, Thackeray continues this criticism obliquely in his own narratives. In *Vanity Fair* even the method of burlesque survives in an early chapter.

We might have treated this subject in the genteel, or in the romantic, or in the facetious manner. Suppose we had laid the scene in Grosvenor-square, with the very same adventures—would not some people have listened? Suppose we had shown how Lord Joseph Sedley fell in love, and the Marquis of Osborne became attached to Lady Amelia, with the full consent of the Duke, her noble father: or instead of the supremely genteel, suppose we had resorted to the entirely low, and described what was going on in Mr. Sedley's kitchen;—how black Sambo was in love with the cook, (as indeed he was), and how he fought a battle with the coachman in her behalf; how the knife-boy was caught stealing a cold shoulder of mutton, and Miss Sedley's new *femme de*

It was Thackeray's intention to include Dickens, but he was dissuaded by Bradbury and Evans. Lever and Disraeli were the authors most offended, and both retaliated with satirical portraits of Thackeray (in *Roland Cashel* and *Endymion*).

[1] Cf. letter to Lady Blessington, 1848 (*Letters*, ii. 485): 'there are [in Lytton's novels] big words which make me furious, and a pretentious fine writing against which I can't help rebelling.'

chambre refused to go to bed without a wax candle; such incidents might be made to provoke much delightful laughter, and be supposed to represent scenes of 'life'. Or if, on the contrary, we had taken a fancy for the terrible, and made the lover of the new *femme de chambre* a professional burglar, who bursts into the house with his band, slaughters black Sambo at the feet of his master, and carries off Amelia in her night-dress, not to be let loose again till the third volume, we should easily have constructed a tale of thrilling interest, through the fiery chapters of which the reader should hurry, panting.[1]

This is perhaps overweighted; more effective is a passing side glance at the conventions, as in the opening of the Waterloo number:

We do not claim to rank among the military novelists. Our place is with the non-combatants. When the decks are cleared for action we go below and wait meekly. We should only be in the way of the manœuvres that the gallant fellows are performing overhead.[2]

So much for the authors of *Phil Fogarty* and *The Last of the Mulligans*.

But such parenthetic comments are merely incidental to the pervasive and positive criticism offered by *Vanity Fair*. One of Thackeray's most perceptive critics writes of it that

Coming as it did into the world of fiction occupied by the writers burlesqued in the 'Novels by Eminent Hands', its substitution of truth for convention had something almost fierce in it.[3]

[1] Ch. vi. The burlesque is much fuller in the first edition, where Thackeray went on to give actual samples of the rejected modes. See *Works*, xi, Appendix, pp. 882–4.

[2] Ch. xxx.

[3] W. C. Brownell, *Victorian Prose Masters* (1902), p. 33.

Its difference from popular novels—a difference concealed under intermittent and teasing similarities —and the author's seeming contempt for popular taste struck Thackeray's early readers more than we realize. He takes cunning advantage of the serial-writer's confiding relation with his public, but his attitude is not as friendly as Dickens's. Deliberately he defeats conventional expectation; he is at pains to warn his readers in the opening chapter that 'Amelia is not a heroine', and often employs her as a medium for mockery at the sweet insipid contemporary novel-heroine. It is indeed part of his object to exclude heroism:

holding that the Art of Novels is . . . to convey as strongly as possible the sentiment of reality as opposed to a tragedy or poem, which may be heroical.[1]

This exclusion is again proclaimed in the sub-title given to the novel when it appeared in volume form: 'A Novel without a Hero'.[2] His intention was not, as some have thought, to substitute for a hero a heroine with masculine resourcefulness; nor yet to strip the semblance of novel-hero from George Osborne in order to reveal unsuspected heroism in the uncouth Dobbin. He refuses the role to Dobbin too.

This history has been written to very little purpose if the reader has not perceived that the Major was a spooney.[3]

---

[1] Letter of May 1851 (*Letters*, ii. 772–3).
[2] The phrase appears in the letters as early as March 1846: *Letters*, ii. 233.
[3] Ch. lxvi.

He rejects heroism in the name of morality as well as of 'reality'.

> My object . . . is to indicate, in cheerful terms, that we are for the most part an abominably foolish and selfish people . . . all eager after vanities. Everybody is you see in that book,— for instance if I had made Amelia a higher order of woman there would have been no vanity in Dobbins falling in love with her, whereas the impression at present is that he is a fool for his pains[,] that he has married a silly little thing, and in fact has found out his error . . . I want to leave everybody dissatisfied and unhappy at the end of the story—we ought all to be with our own and all other stories.[1]

This rejection of heroism, this conveyance of the 'sentiment of reality', was recognized as a novelty by contemporary readers. Their response might be approving or otherwise. Mrs. Procter found it a relief that the 'characters [were] neither devils nor angels . . . neither appear through a trapdoor, nor change their father and mother in the third volume';[2] *Fraser's* reviewer was repelled by 'a loathsome truth, like that of Hogarth in *Gin Lane*'.[3] The revulsion of some readers of Thackeray lent itself to images of nausea; Ruskin said that he 'settled like a meat fly on whatever one had got for dinner and made one sick of it';[4] Whately was more elaborate:

> If you were to serve up a dinner with top dish a roasted fox, stuffed with tobacco and basted with train oil, and at

---

[1] Letter to Robert Bell, September 1848 (*Letters*, ii. 423.)

[2] Letter to Abraham Hayward, 23 July 1847 (*Letters*, ii. 312–13).

[3] Compare the *Times* reviewer who remarked on a story illustrated by the author that he preferred the sketches, because 'he cannot *draw* his men and women with their skins off'.

[4] *Fors Clavigera*, ii, letter xxxi.

bottom an old ram goat, dressed with the hair on, and seasoned with assafoetida, the side dishes being plain boiled rice, this would give an idea of what his fictions are to my taste.[1]

By these admittedly extreme examples we may gauge the general level of defeated expectation in Thackeray's readers. They found 'the established usages of novels . . . entirely set aside';[2] they were cheated even of a neat ending. The curtain does not fall either on a death-bed or wedding bells, both of which had in the past been the objects of Thackeray's mockery:

It is much better to look at the end of a novel; and when I read 'There is a fresh green mound in Brentford Church-yard, and a humble stone, on which is inscribed the name of "Anna Maria"' . . . I shut the book at once, declining to agitate my feelings needlessly.[3]

You, dear young ladies, who get your knowledge of life from the circulating library, may be led to imagine that when the marriage business is done, and Emilia is whisked off in the new travelling carriage, by the side of the enraptured Earl; or Belinda, breaking away from the tearful embraces of her excellent mother, dries her own lovely eyes upon the throbbing waistcoat of her bridegroom—you may be apt, I say, to suppose that all is over then, that Emilia and the Earl are going to be happy for the rest of their lives in his Lordship's romantic castle in the north, and Belinda and her young

[1] Letter to Nassau Senior, 12 January 1853; E. Whately, *Life and Correspondence of Richard Whately* (1866), ii. 263–4. *Vanity Fair* was the only one of the novels that Whately had 'been able to get through'.

[2] *Fraser's* (September 1848), p. 332.

[3] 'Jérôme Paturot. With considerations on novels in general'; *Fraser's* (September 1843; *Works*, vi. 321).

clergyman to enjoy uninterrupted bliss in their rose-trellised parsonage in the west of England. . . .[1]

The early arrival of Amelia's marriage (in the eighth number) must in itself have made readers suspicious; and Thackeray's comment draws attention to his divergence:

As his hero and heroine pass the matrimonial barrier, the novelist generally drops the curtain, as if the drama were over then: the doubts and struggles of life ended: as if, once landed in the marriage country, all were green and pleasant there: and wife and husband had nothing to do but to link each other's arms together, and wander gently downwards towards old age in happy and perfect fruition.[2]

When the return of Dobbin brings the situation within sight of conventional sentiment, a dramatized comment is ready to hand.

'There they are,' said Miss Polly. . . . She was a confidante at once of the whole business. She knew the story as well as if she had read it in one of her favourite novel-books—'Fatherless Fanny', or the 'Scottish Chiefs'.[3]

But Dobbin does not win his Amelia (nor Laura her Pendennis) until some illusions have been lost on both sides. Within sight of the end of *Vanity Fair* Thackeray produces his 'fake' conclusion, puncturing its sentiment by a single word:

This is what he pined after. Here it is—the summit, the end—the last page of the third volume. Good-bye, Colonel—God bless you, honest William!—Farewell, dear Amelia—Grow green again, tender little parasite, round the rugged old oak to which you cling!

---

[1] *Rebecca and Rowena*, ch. i (*Works*, x. 499–500).
[2] *Vanity Fair*, ch. xxvi.   [3] Ch. lviii.

to be followed on the actual last page by the true conclusion:

the Colonel seizing up his little Janey, of whom he is fonder than of anything in the world—fonder even than of his 'History of the Punjaub'.

'Fonder than he is of me,' Emmy thinks, with a sigh. But he never said a word to Amelia that was not kind and gentle; or thought of a want of hers that he did not try to gratify.

Ah! *Vanitas Vanitatum!* . . .

So too does Thackeray evade obvious 'poetic justice', the slick 'nemesis' on which Charley Tudor's editor insisted;[1] Carker may be cut to pieces by an express train, but our last sight of Becky is as a wealthy and charitable lady hanging about Bath and Cheltenham and arranging stalls at Fancy fairs. (Though this is perhaps the most fitting retribution for her—to be driven to 'religion', the social climber's last resource.)

In *Vanity Fair*, though not always in his later novels, Thackeray also avoids, as Mrs. Procter points out, startling and sensational turns of plot: what he was later to call 'the professional parts of novels', choosing an instance with rueful self-mockery:

Ask *me*, indeed, to pop a robber under a bed, to hide a will which will be forthcoming in due season![2]

The most nearly 'professional' situation in *Vanity Fair* is Rawdon's discovery of Becky and Lord

---

[1] See above, p. 116.

[2] *Roundabout Papers*, 'On a Peal of Bells'. This paper appeared in the *Cornhill* in September 1862, and *Philip*, in which a hidden will is finally discovered, had been concluded in August. Compare the mystery about Blanche's parentage in *Pendennis*.

Steyne, which approaches the stock scene of the penny theatres:

> There is always a wicked lord kicked out of the window.... Enter sturdy Blacksmith.—Scuffle between Blacksmith and Aristocratic minion: exit wicked Lord out of the window.[1]

But the divergence of Becky from the penny theatre's innocent victim is decisive.

The ironic use of stereotyped novel-material would also be evident to contemporaries in the opening situation and its development through the novel. The varying fortunes and contrasted characters of two closely associated young women was a stock pattern in novels, and indeed traditional in romance. Good girl and bad (often also blonde and brunette) were paired in numerous novels, as sisters, twins, half-sisters (preferably unaware of their kinship), cousins or friends.[2] But never, surely, with such subtleties and surprises as in *Vanity Fair*.

§ 2

Thackeray turns away, then, from heroes and heroines, from the conventional ending, from the

[1] 'Charity and Humour', 1852 (*Works*, x. 624). In 'Before the Curtain' Lord Steyne is referred to as the 'Wicked Nobleman'.

[2] A few closely contemporary instances are Miss Jewsbury's *The Half-Sisters* (1848), Lady Georgiana Fullerton's *Grantley Manor* (1847), Mrs. Gore's *The Diamond and the Pearl* (1849). Hannah Maria Jones in *The Curate's Daughter, or the Twin Roses of Arundale* (n.d.; 1830's?) had made great play with the sensational if implausible situation of identical twins, indistinguishable in appearance but as different in character as wolf and lamb. *Sense and Sensibility* makes its original use of the contrasted-sister pattern; and there is even something like the Amelia-Becky contrast in *Mansfield Park*.

'professional parts of novels'. And he evades the contemporary categories: *Vanity Fair* is not a novel of low life (its lowest level is the apartments at Fulham, or—unexpectedly—the elder Sir Pitt's *ménage* in Great Gaunt Street), nor of high life (the highest level is the ball at Gaunt House, which would contain some surprises for the devotees of Mrs. Gore);[1] it is not a military novel, despite Waterloo, nor a domestic novel, despite the number of family scenes. It is not historical, although it is a novel about the past; the period in which it is set is robbed of its usual glamour, and the past is strangely interpenetrated by the present. Thackeray's preface, 'Before the Curtain', illustrates his almost malicious way of teasing expectation:

There are scenes of all sorts; some dreadful combats, some grand and lofty horse-riding, some scenes of high life, some of very middling indeed: some love-making for the sentimental, and some light comic business; the whole accompanied by appropriate scenery, and brilliantly illuminated by the Author's own candles.

He promises variety; but he also gives unity, and not only by the continuous presence of the 'author's own candles'. The principles of organization in *Vanity Fair* must next be considered: the positive truth which Thackeray substitutes for the conventions of fiction.

By choosing as his field 'the debatable land between the middle classes and the aristocracy'[2] he takes a

[1] Mrs. Procter said, 'He has avoided the two extremes in which so many of our popular writers delight' (*Letters*, ii. 313).

[2] Review-article by W. C. Roscoe in *National Review* (January 1856); collected in *Poems and Essays* (2 vols., 1860).

social area which, though less extensive than Dickens's, gives him considerable vertical range. All the characters are seen in relation to 'society', living in it or on it; for each character he defines the rung on the ladder, the place on the slippery slope, the rocky ledge where they hang by finger-tips. None are unplaced; which means that the 'other nation' is excluded—it was not beyond his ken, but he chose to ignore it here.

There is less scope for oddity than in Dickens's world, for Vanity Fair is a world in which it is important to conform. Those who give up the pretence of conforming, like Sir Pitt Crawley or Lord Steyne, show that Thackeray can provide his own grotesques, with only the monstrosity which actual life provides. Specific comparison with Dickens illustrates Thackeray's different attitude to reality: the observed reality is often the same, but Thackeray mines into it, where Dickens makes it a springboard into fantasy. Even in his names Thackeray wishes 'to convey the sentiment of reality'. Dickens's may be actual, but they are chosen for their oddity and comic appropriateness, while Thackeray masks his satire in plausibility, preferring a subtle suggestiveness; as in 'Steyne', with its pun and its relation to Regency Brighton; or the contrast, rich in association, of the liquid and romantic 'Amelia Sedley' with the hinted racial astuteness of 'Rebecca Sharp'.

Thackeray's characters exist in a denser context than perhaps any characters in fiction. They are aware of past time; they draw on childhood memories.

'Am I much better to do now in the world than I was when I was the poor painter's daughter, and wheedled the grocer round the corner for sugar and tea? Suppose I had married Francis who was so fond of me. . . .'[1]

It is the only time we ever hear of 'Francis'. In the shadow, just beyond every character, but ready to catch the spotlight for a single instant when needed, seem to be all the people the character has ever met. Here is the sole appearance of Edward Dale:

the junior of the house, who purchased the spoons for the firm, was, in fact, very sweet upon Amelia, and offered for her in spite of all. He married Miss Louisa Cutts (daughter of Higham and Cutts, the eminent corn-factors) with a handsome fortune in 1820; and is now living in splendour, and with a numerous family, at his elegant villa, Muswell Hill.[2]

Odd corners of their houses, or possessions, may similarly light up at a touch. Their ancestries and family histories may be given; the baptismal names of the Crawley ancestors, according well with their surname, epitomize the political vanities of two centuries. And no single paragraph about Lord Steyne tell us more about him and his society, or about vanity in high places, than that list of titles and honours in his 'obituary':

the Most Honourable George Gustavus, Marquis of Steyne, Earl of Gaunt and of Gaunt Castle, in the Peerage of Ireland, Viscount Hellborough, Baron Pitchley and Grillsby, a Knight of the Most Noble Order of the Garter, of the Golden Fleece of Spain, of the Russian Order of Saint Nicholas of the First Class, of the Turkish Order of the Crescent, First Lord of the Powder Closet and Groom of the Back Stairs, Colonel

---

[1] Ch. xli.   [2] Ch. xvii.

of the Gaunt or Regent's Own Regiment of Militia, a Trustee of the British Museum, an Elder Brother of the Trinity House, a Governor of the White Friars, and D.C.L. . . .[1]

Such fullness of documentation, never introduced heavily, but ready to be drawn on where it is needed, is significant of Thackeray's emphasis on character in its social relations. This has been noted by all his critics, and best defined by Brownell:

Thackeray's personages are never portrayed in isolation. They are a part of the *milieu* in which they exist, and which has itself therefore much more distinction and relief than an environment which is merely a framework. How they regard each other, how they feel toward and what they think of each other, the mutuality of their very numerous and vital relations, furnishes an important strand in the texture of the story in which they figure. Their activities are modified by the air they breathe in common. Their conduct is controlled, their ideas affected, even their desires and ambitions dictated, by the general ideas of the society that includes them.[2]

But it would be wrong to see Thackeray as a fatalist about character. That Becky believes she might have been a good woman on five thousand a year is itself part of her character ('Becky consoled herself . . .');[3] some virtues may be accidental, but 'circumstance only brings out the latent defect or quality, and does not create it'.[4] Thackeray is not optimistic enough about human nature (less so, for example, than George

---

[1] Ch. lxiv.
[2] W. C. Brownell, op. cit., p. 29.
[3] Ch. xli.
[4] *Pendennis,* ch. lix; and cf. *Esmond,* Book II, ch. i.

Eliot) to have much belief in the power of people to change themselves:

> We alter very little. . . . Our mental changes are like our grey hairs and our wrinkles—but the fulfilment of the plan of mortal growth and decay.[1]

His characters are so mixed, so often on a moral borderland, so subject to time, and also so gradually unfolded—often with unpredictable detail—that they do not give the impression of being static. But they are not shown as evolving, nor do they undergo much inward conflict; and so the unity given to a novel by dominating or developing characters is not found. Only one of Thackeray's novels—*Pendennis* —is even formally built upon the fortunes of a single character; and Arthur Pendennis is less an interesting individual than a nineteenth-century variant of Everyman.

§ 3

Without recourse to obvious devices, without a hero or heroine or any single central figure, without any 'inward' study of development in character, Thackeray nevertheless makes us feel *Vanity Fair* a unity. This has sometimes been underestimated, and the novel apologized for as loose, rambling, and casual, though admitted to be rich and comprehensive: the apology may even lay the blame on the serial form. But the serial novel, serially written, is, as I have already suggested, really the less likely to

[1] *Pendennis*, ch. lix.

be loose and rambling; only some degree of fore-thought makes such writing even possible; and the reader's interest, spread over a year and a half, will not be held unless there is a genuine continuity and a firm centre of interest. It is a contention of this whole study that both novelists and critics of this time were interested in 'unity'; we may recall that Lytton claimed that 'composition' should be recognized in novels as in paintings, and *Fraser's* critic of 1851 says firmly:

> One of the great achievements... in the art of the novelist is unity. If we cannot get that, the next best thing is progress.[1]

A more reputable critical view, one indeed that is insidiously tempting, is that Thackeray's formal purpose is a 'picture' of society. This view, so persuasively set forth in Lubbock's *Craft of Fiction*, does admit of composition, even if 'picture' is extended to 'panorama'; but it accounts only for a part of *Vanity Fair*. For it allows too little for our fascinated sense of progression; too little also for Thackeray the moralist.

The clear and obvious line of progression in the novel is surely also, when closely considered, the chief of its unities: that is, the converging and diverging, parallel and contrasting fortunes of the two girls, Rebecca Sharp and Amelia Sedley.[2] In narrative terms, the basis of the contrast is simple (the moral contrast, on the other hand, is ironic and

---

[1] See above, p. 41.

[2] The point has of course been made by several critics, from *Fraser's* (September 1848, p. 347) to our own day, but I think with insufficient sense of the subtlety of Thackeray's intentions.

complex); it is that Rebecca attempts actively to shape her own fortunes, while Amelia passively accepts hers. They begin with 'the world before them', on their last day at Minerva House Academy in Chiswick Mall. Their manner of leaving Miss Pinkerton's differentiates them at the outset in character as well as social status. Rebecca is nineteen and Amelia sixteen, but Rebecca has never been a child (Thackeray refers early to her 'dismal precocity') and Amelia is never to grow up. But throughout the first number (chapters i to iv) their similarity as well as difference is emphasized; both are occupied with the 'vanity' of husband-hunting (the title of chapter ii is 'In which Miss Sharp and Miss Sedley prepare to open the campaign'); Rebecca is laying her snares for Jos Sedley, Amelia sighing and smiling at George Osborne. In the closing number, after seventeen years, Amelia at last consents to forget George, and Rebecca at last has Jos inescapably in her toils. Throughout the narrative a balance of interest between Amelia and Rebecca is steadily maintained; in every number there is something of both, and when they are apart the juxtaposition of chapters defining the progress in their histories still forms a pattern. In Number V (chapters xv to xviii) Rebecca is thrown out of favour with the Crawleys when her marriage to Rawdon is revealed; Mr. Sedley has failed in business and George Osborne's defection is threatened, but there is a hopeful turn at the end to bring Amelia's marriage into sight and match the close of Number IV. In Number XIV (chapters xlvii to l) there is a simple contrast between the zenith of Becky's fortunes (presented at Court, dining at Gaunt House) and the nadir of Amelia's (in poverty, and parted from her son). In Number XVI comes Becky's 'fall', set beside the first hint of Amelia's 'rise', the number closing with Dobbin's return from India (chapter lvi). There are also the subtler running contrasts of Becky's treatment of her son Rawdon, Amelia's of George: subtle, because Thackeray is critical both of heartless neglect and passionate possessiveness. Or the likeness within difference of Amelia's stupid fidelity to her husband's memory, and Becky's stupid infidelity to Rawdon. Each is an egoist; Thackeray's comment when Dobbin leaves Amelia is pointed:

> She didn't wish to marry him, but she wished to keep him. She wished to give him nothing, but that he should give her all. It is a bargain not unfrequently levied in love.[1]

Outside its context, the second of these sentences would be taken as describing Becky.

But the structural ironies are clearest when the two histories converge and entangle:

> [Becky] was thinking in her heart, 'It was George Osborne who prevented my marriage'.—And she loved George Osborne accordingly.[2]

Her small revenge of malicious teasing in chapter xiv (where these words are echoed) is the prelude to her triumph at Brussels:

> [George] was carrying on a desperate flirtation with Mrs. Crawley. He . . . passed his evenings in the Crawleys' company; losing money to the husband and flattering himself that

---

[1] Ch. lxvi. [2] Ch. vi.

the wife was dying in love for him. It is very likely that this worthy couple never absolutely conspired, and agreed together in so many words: the one to cajole the young gentleman, whilst the other won his money at cards: but they understood each other perfectly well. . . .[1]

At the ball on the night before Waterloo she receives his note 'coiled like a snake among the flowers'—a note whose substance is not divulged until the closing number. The next day she visits the half-suspecting Amelia:

Amelia . . . drew back her hand, and trembled all over. 'Why are *you* here, Rebecca?' she said, still looking at her solemnly, with her large eyes. These glances troubled her visitor.

'She must have seen him give me the letter at the ball', Rebecca thought.

But Amelia's accusations are in general terms, and are so answered:

'Amelia, I protest before God, I have done my husband no wrong', Rebecca said, turning from her.

'Have you done *me* no wrong, Rebecca? You did not succeed, but you tried. Ask your heart if you did not?'

She knows nothing, Rebecca thought.[2]

The number ends with George Osborne's death on the battlefield; from this mid-point in the novel proceed Amelia's simple subsequent fortunes—ten years of widowhood sentimentally faithful to a mythical memory, and resistance to Dobbin's suit. The two converge again when Amelia, abroad with Jos and Dobbin, meets Rebecca, now disgraced and

[1] Ch. xxix. [2] Ch. xxxi.

outside the social pale, but resilient as ever. She re-
news her designs on Jos, and when Dobbin, at last
despairing of Amelia, returns to England, finds
Amelia in her way. She reproaches her for refusing
Dobbin:

'I tried—I tried my best, indeed I did, Rebecca,' said
Amelia deprecatingly, 'but I couldn't forget—'; and she
finished her sentence by looking up at the portrait.

'Couldn't forget *him*!' cried out Becky, 'that selfish humbug, that low-bred cockney dandy, that padded booby, who
had neither wit, nor manners, nor heart. . . . He never cared
for you. He used to sneer about you to me, time after time;
and made love to me the week after he married you.'

'It's false! it's false! Rebecca', cried out Amelia, starting up.

'Look there, you fool,' Becky said, still with provoking
good-humour, and taking a little paper out of her belt, she
opened it and flung it into Emmy's lap. 'You know his handwriting. He wrote that to me—wanted me to run away with
him—gave it me under your nose, the day before he was shot
—and served him right!' Becky repeated.[1]

Apparently then the wheel comes full circle: Becky
ending as she began, as Amelia's friend. But Thackeray has one more surprise in store: the revelation
is not decisive, for Amelia has already relented and
written to recall Dobbin. The inner necessity of the
scene is rather to leave no sham unexposed, and to
keep our moral attitude to the two 'heroines' complicated to the last. For Becky's is the true view of the
case, and her action righteous, though from mixed
motives. But Amelia's actions, although muddle-
headed, are to the last motivated by love.

[1] Ch. lxvii.

'Anyone who mistakes [Amelia] for a simple character has missed *Vanity Fair*.'[1] The mistake has been
common, and has in modern times taken the particularly silly form of regarding Amelia as the straight
representation of an ideal now outmoded. But even
apart from Thackeray's own view, writ large in phrase
after phrase, his contemporaries did not unanimously
applaud Amelia. Some went even too far in the other
direction: 'No woman resents Rebecca . . . but every
woman resents his selfish and inane Amelia.'[2] (It
was perhaps more gratifying to the woman of the
eighteen-forties, and certainly rarer, to see herself
presented in fiction as a clever rogue than as an amiable fool.) If Thackeray has an ideal in mind, then
Amelia and Becky are both far (though not equally
far) removed from it; of the disproportion between
heart and brain possible to the feminine character
they provide extreme instances. Some readers may be
more legitimately misled by the necessary difference in
treatment. The active Becky can be displayed, where
the suffering, yielding Amelia must be described.
The tone of the description is deliberately ambiguous, seeming often sentimentally protective, but with
enough impatience breaking through to show that
the author wishes to confuse and make fun of the
sentimental reader. It is not necessary to attribute
confusion to Thackeray himself; there is room with
such a character for genuine indulgence as well as
impatience. Besides, he has an ulterior, 'literary'

[1] Brownell, op. cit., p. 31.
[2] Mrs. Jameson, as quoted by J. W. Dodds, *Thackeray* (1941), p. 130;
Mrs. Brookfield, and Thackeray's mother made similar comments.

motive in Amelia: Becky is a wholly new kind of heroine, Amelia the old kind ironically exposed. It is possible that Amelia may sometimes be imperfectly disengaged from 'the unwritten part' of his novels, not quite free from her moorings in his own emotional life;[1] whereas Becky swims free in the pure element of art.[2] Becky is one of those characters—like Chaucer's Pardoner—who can fully engage our aesthetic sympathies while defying most of our moral ones; Thackeray is not less a moralist for allowing us to enjoy her as a spectacle, for his judgement of her is firm. Her attraction is partly that of the triumphant knave in a world of knaves and fools; enjoyment is not complicated by pity for the less successful knaves, like the younger Sir Pitt, nor yet for the fools, like Jos Sedley or even Briggs; these belong to the world of satirical comedy, where we have the freedom of feeling that 'fools are responsible for their folly'. The comic inventiveness of these triumphs provides some of the most brilliant flashes of the book:

She listened with the tenderest kindly interest, sitting by him, and hemming a shirt for her dear little boy. Whenever

---

[1] He told Mrs. Brookfield that she was 'a piece of Amelia—My Mother is another half: my poor little wife *y est pour beaucoup*' (30 June 1848; *Letters*, ii. 394). But it is difficult to take this seriously; the three women can have had little in common with each other or with Amelia except charm and obstinacy. Perhaps there is something of Jane Brookfield's faithfulness to a husband Thackeray was coming to think unworthy of her. But J. Y. T. Greig, who has pressed this interpretation furthest (in *Thackeray A Reconsideration*, 1950) seems to make his bricks of very little straw.

[2] There are two possible 'originals' for Becky, Sydney Morgan and Theresa Reviss; but they can have provided no more than the 'germ of the real'.

Mrs. Rawdon wished to be particularly humble and virtuous, this little shirt used to come out of her work-box. It had got to be too small for Rawdon long before it was finished, though.[1]

'How I have been waiting for you! Stop! not yet—in one minute you shall come in.' In that instant she put a rouge-pot, a brandy-bottle, and a plate of broken meat into her bed. . . .

. . . 'I had but one child, one darling, one hope, one joy . . . and they tore it from me;' and she put her hand to her heart with a passionate gesture of despair, burying her face for a moment on the bed.

The brandy-bottle inside clinked up against the plate which held the cold sausage.[2]

But Thackeray does not go too far in enlisting the reader's pleasure on the side of wickedness. For this he had criticized Bulwer and Ainsworth:

Don't let us have any juggling and thimble-rigging with virtue and vice, so that, at the end of three volumes, the bewildered reader shall not know which is which.[3]

For this he was even, unjustly, criticized himself:

Sin is fire; and Mr. Thackeray makes fireworks of it.[4]

But his judgement of Becky never falters, and it is made plain to the reader through one character in particular: Rawdon Crawley. The words in the 'discovery' scene are pointed: 'I am innocent,' says Becky. 'Was she guilty or not?' asks Thackeray, and apparently leaves it an open question. But the technical question is not the most relevant one: her essen-

[1] Ch. xliv.   [2] Ch. lxv.
[3] *Catherine*, ch. i (*Works*, iii. 31).   [4] Roscoe, loc. cit.

tial guilt rests in Rawdon's simple accusation: 'You
might have spared me £100, Becky; I have always
shared with you.' The words take us back to the
night before Waterloo, with Rawdon making his last
dispositions—'my duelling pistols in rosewood case
(same which I shot Captain Marker)'; and Becky
stands condemned of cold-hearted treachery.

The relation of these two is one of the main sources
of 'progression' in the novel, and is worth tracing.
'Rawdon's marriage', says Thackeray, 'was one of the
honestest actions which we shall have to record in any
portion of that gentleman's biography.'[1] Unlike
George Osborne (the contrast is firmly indicated) he
married for love; which puts him at an initial disadvantage with Becky, who married him in hopes of
his aunt's money.

Is his case a rare one? and don't we see every day in the
world many an honest Hercules at the apron-strings of
Omphale, and great whiskered Samsons prostrate in Dalilah's lap?[1]

Becky's contempt is masked at first:

'If he had but a little more brains,' she thought to herself,
'I might make something of him;' but she never let him perceive the opinion she had of him. . . .[2]

But not masked for long; not when Miss Crawley's
favour seems again within reach:

'You fool! you ought to have gone in, and never come out
again,' Rebecca said.

'Don't call me names,' said the big guardsman, sulkily,
'Perhaps I *was* a fool, Becky, but you shouldn't say so.'[3]

---

[1] Ch. xvi. [2] Ch. xvii.
[3] Ch. xxv.

Their relation is fully and picturesquely defined in the farewell scene before Waterloo; but its deterioration is also hinted, in the narrative that so lightly sketches the 'three or four years'[1] which follow. At first, Rawdon's illusions are still intact; 'He believed in his wife as much as the French soldiers in Napoleon'; and with as little grounds. We are left to infer that, his aunt having died and left him only £100, Rawdon is no longer an investment worth nursing. Becky is flying at higher game. The scene that marks the change is of the kind that lights up far more than itself: the evening scene in Curzon Street, Becky in the centre of a party of gentlemen including Lord Steyne. (It is our first introduction to Lord Steyne; Thackeray's method is to make us feel that he has been there a long time.) Rawdon is 'sitting silent without the circle', engaged in 'shearing a Southdown'. The closing words mark the grouping as typical:

'How is Mrs. Crawley's husband,' Lord Steyne used to say by way of a good day when they met; and indeed that was now his avocation in life. He was Colonel Crawley no more. He was Mrs. Crawley's husband. . . .

'Hang it, I ain't clever enough for her—I know it. She won't miss me,' he used to say: and he was right: his wife did not miss him.

Rebecca was fond of her husband. She was always perfectly good-humoured and kind to him. She did not even show her scorn much for him; perhaps she liked him the better for being a fool. He was her upper servant and *maître d'hôtel*.

Two years later he is 'more and more isolated every

[1] Chs. xxxiv, xxxvi, and xxxvii.

day . . . beat and cowed into laziness and submission. Dalilah had imprisoned him and cut his hair off, too.'[1]

The 'discovery' scene is led up to with great skill; Rawdon's arrest is sprung on the reader as on Rawdon himself, and only then does Thackeray wind back over past events to show how Lord Steyne with Becky's connivance had previously got rid of young Rawdon and the 'sheepdog' Briggs—'And so two of Rawdon's out-sentinels were in the hands of the enemy'.[2] It is as near as he comes to saying that the arrest was framed.

There is a moral comment in the fact that Becky's downfall comes through the relations that she most despised; it is the innocent and stupid who confound her. She calculates brilliantly, but, like Iago, not quite brilliantly enough. Her neglect of her son disturbed Rawdon. When she kissed the child at Queen's Crawley she had not thought that he might say, 'You never kiss me at home, mother.' Lady Jane 'never felt quite the same to Becky after that remark'. And Lady Jane's simple kindness defeats Becky's calculation, when she releases Rawdon from the spunging-house in time for him to find Lord Steyne at Curzon Street. This is Becky's true nemesis. Contempt for other people is necessary to successful villainy; but within it lie the seeds of its own defeat. The walls of egoism rise, in the end, too high. By suggesting all this, Thackeray does more than condemn Becky; he

[1] Ch. xlv.
[2] Ch. lii. Greig, missing the subtlety of method, remarks that this chapter 'is chronologically misplaced, and was probably an afterthought' (op. cit., p. 116).

gives a less pessimistic moral direction to his story.
Goodness is not wholly ineffectual.

§ 4

These, then, are some of the ways in which
Thackeray gives shape and purpose to his great pic-
torial mass; but the most important way has been
often undervalued by later readers, because misunderstood. The whole is 'brilliantly illuminated by the
author's own candles'; Thackeray is constantly
present, commenting on the action. Only in this
novel is it undisguised. Elsewhere he partly identifies
himself with a character—Pendennis, or Esmond; or
uses a character as narrator—Pendennis in *The Newcomes* and *Philip*, with Clive and Philip as further
'projections' within the story. (The latter device,
caught, he admitted, from the despised Lytton, was
purposeful: 'I shall be able to talk more at ease than
in my own person.')[1] In *Vanity Fair* there is no disguise; the author is present, with a varying range of
visibility. He talks to us, about the story and characters, or about something it reminds him of;[2] he is
frankly the manufacturer of the narrative ('there are
some terrific chapters coming presently'); he is the
'producer' of particular characters (especially of
Amelia, who can do so little for herself); he is by

[1] Letter of August 1853 (*Letters*, iii. 298). There is a hint of it in the
use of Tom Eaves in *Vanity Fair*, ch. xlvii.

[2] Sometimes with a journalist's sense for the immediately topical, as in
ch. lv: 'Fifine went off in a cab, as we have known more exalted persons of
her nation to do under similar circumstances.' This number appeared in
April 1848.

turns the responsible, omniscient narrator ('for novelists have the privilege of knowing everything'),[1] the irresponsible, baffled spectator ('Was she guilty or not?'), even the mere reporter (himself meeting the characters at Pumpernickel in 1830). Above all he is the moral commentator, the 'preacher in cap and bells', amused, melancholy, hortatory—and constantly barbing his shafts with a *de te fabula*. The atmosphere of his personality—not his private, but his artistic personality—envelopes the story.

Nowadays, apparently, this practice requires defence; and several lines of defence are valid. There is the historical defence. This method was not new or peculiar to Thackeray, save in extent and subtlety. Behind it lies the tradition of Fielding's role of epic poet, with such modifications as the 'comic epic in prose' requires; it is as comedy that Thackeray sees his own novels, and comedy always allows more room for the author. There is also the seeming casualness of Sterne, taking us behind the scenes, showing us the raw material of a novel in process of being worked up. There is also as we have seen the peculiar audience-relation of the serial-writer, reassembling his listeners, responding to their comments with his own. All this helped to make Thackeray's technique easily acceptable in his own time.[2] The average modern reader starts with a prejudice in favour of 'dramatic' presentment; the novel having, since Thackeray's time, foregone many of its advantages in favour of a

[1] Ch. iii.

[2] Contemporary objectors were rare; one was G. H. Lewes, in *The Leader* (21 December 1850), p. 929.

fancied 'objectivity', and the novelist having dwindled into invisibility. But to press the historical defence might be to admit a limited appeal: or to suggest that he adopted this method unthinkingly. The true justification lies in its appropriateness to his kind of novel.

Thackeray has often been called the novelist of memory; all his stories are seen retrospectively. 'Let us have middle-aged novels', he said in *Rebecca and Rowena*; it is what he gives us, with the light of irony or pathos playing on past fashions and the morning ideals of youth. His commentary is in part a bridge between past and present, suggesting what time changes, what it leaves unchanged; putting past and present alike in a longer perspective. And it is a moral perspective. Thackeray gives us what seems a whole world, densely peopled, varied in scene, with the miscellaneousness and wastage and loose threads of the actual world; but through his comments he makes it plain that he sees the 'tower on the toft' above the 'field full of folk'. The title itself is a comment, the title that came to him in the night 'as if a voice had whispered';[1] it suggests both the observer, and the preacher who 'cries his sermon'. Without Thackeray's own voice, the melancholy and the compassion of his attitude to Vanity Fair might escape us. It is needed merely as relief, from a spectacle that might otherwise be unbearably painful. And not only morally painful, but mentally impoverished. The characters, the best as well as the worst, are almost without ideas; the intellectual atmosphere of the novel is provided by the commentary.

[1] *Letters*, i, p. cxxvi.

Can the reader do all this for himself? If he can, and can do it as well as Thackeray does it for him, he may consider it surplusage.[1]

Thackeray does not escape into commentary from any weakness in presentation; *Vanity Fair* is particularly rich in single scenes which reveal his power of presenting characters and action without comment, through dialogue, grouping, and gesture. Nor is he impulsively allowing his stored reflections to overflow; the effect of casualness in the commentary is as calculated as in Sterne. The commentary is itself art, selective and economical. Thackeray never tells everything; he leaves much to be read between the lines; the tone of intimate confidence often masks a real reserve. He knows when not to comment directly at all. Much could have been said on the death of George Osborne; this is all that is said:

No more fighting was heard at Brussels—the pursuit rolled miles away. The darkness came down on the field and city, and Amelia was praying for George, who was lying on his face, dead, with a bullet through his heart.[2]

It is no simple statement; not only is the immediate reference magnified by the drawing together of Brussels and the battlefield, but its very brevity and the silence surrounding it mark its subject—not the death of one George Osborne, sufficiently shown as odious and contemptible, but Death, sudden, august, and mysterious. But all this is implicit. Yet equally impressive in its own way, and equally enlarged

[1] Brownell, op. cit., p. 7; and cf. pp. 9–10.
[2] Ch. xxxii, at the close of the ninth number. See p. 47, n. 1 above.

beyond the particular circumstance, is the leisurely commentary on the death of Mr. Sedley;[1] appropriate to a death that is not sudden, but long prepared for, domestic and not dramatic, enmeshed in practical circumstance, and apparently presented as a mere change in habitation. The one method is as essentially part of the novel's texture as the other.

The commentary springs also from Thackeray's wish to 'convey the sentiment of reality'. Through it he openly admits, as no modern novelist dare, *all* the relations of the novelist to his story. The novelist does write what he knows to be 'terrific chapters', he does construct and manipulate his characters, and he is also carried beyond his conscious self ('I have no idea where it all comes from').[2] He remembers, and observes; he is affected, as he writes, by what is happening around him—the 'unwritten parts' of novels. Thackeray's candour about all this is part of his love of truth. Believing in truth, he can afford to admit that what he writes is fiction. And the illusion is not thereby broken. When he calls his characters puppets, it is not their smallness, but their separateness from him, that strikes us; and perhaps his own largeness. 'Thackeray is a Titan . . . [his words] as solemn as an oracle.'[3]

Ah! *Vanitas Vanitatum!* Which of us is happy in this world? which of us has his desire? or, having it, is satisfied?— Come children, let us shut up the box and the puppets, for our play is played out.

---

[1] Ch. lxi.
[2] *Letters*, iii. 468 n.
[3] Charlotte Brontë, in a letter of 1848 (see below, p. 261).

The great picture is not the less great from our final awareness that we and the author stand outside its frame. The words are a recall to life and individual responsibility as the preacher lays his cap and bells aside.

JANE EYRE

§ I

OF the novels included here, *Jane Eyre* has the least relation to its time. That it has some relation (and more than *Wuthering Heights*) its contemporary success alone would show. But it is not, like *Dombey and Son* and *Mary Barton*, a novel of contemporary life,[1] nor, like *Vanity Fair*, a novel of a recent and specific past, impinging on the present. Such social commentary as it may offer is oblique, limited, incidental. It is both in purpose and effect primarily a novel of the inner life, not of man in his social relations; it maps a private world. Private, but not eccentric. *Jane Eyre* is now read by thousands who have no idea of its period, many of them even too young[2] or too unsophisticated for clear discrimination of past from present, imaginary from actual; who devour it, unaware of difficulties, unconscious of any need for adaptation to unfamiliar manners or conventions. And this is a part, perhaps the vital part, of the response of all its readers. The further enlightenment which the more conscious or conscientious may draw from close analysis, from knowledge of biography, social context, and literary

---

[1] See above, pp. 95–96.

[2] No Victorian novel is so apt to be read in early youth; and this has honourable precedent: Thackeray's daughters had 'taken it without leave, read bits here and read bits there, been carried away by [a] . . . whirlwind'; Saintsbury read it 'so early that I never seem to have read it for the first time'. (A. T. Ritchie, *Chapters from Some Memoirs*, 1894, p. 61; *B.S.T.*, vol. ii, pt. ix, p. 20).

history is valuable, but not indispensable.[1] A love-story, a Cinderella fable, a Bluebeard mystery, an autobiography from forlorn childhood to happy marriage: this novel makes its appeal first and last to 'the unchanging human heart'.

Nevertheless it belongs to the eighteen-forties. Its flying start[2]—extraordinary for the first publication of an unknown author—would have been inconceivable ten years earlier or later: it would have been too 'low' in social level for 1837, too outspoken for 1857.[3] In 1847 it had apparently not more novelty than was welcome; the 'new' was hooked not only to the 'natural', but to what was already becoming familiar in novels. A survey of reviews and private

[1] More valuable than some critics would allow; the following, not untypical, is perhaps too sweeping a rejection:

What have we to do with Charlotte Brontë's or her critics' 'Victorianism'? There is *Jane Eyre*; read it once more, and all such antiquarian considerations are consumed by the fire of its living art.

(Lascelles Abercrombie, 'The Brontës To-Day', address given 8 March 1924; *B.S.T.*, vol. vi, pt. xxxiv, p. 183).

[2] The contemporary fame of *Jane Eyre* has been misrepresented by some critics. But the evidence of sales (a second edition was published three months after the first, a third two months after that) and of early reviews, very numerous and almost wholly laudatory, is clear, even without the still more significant accumulation of such privately recorded facts as these: 'H. Milman . . . praised *Jane Eyre* exceedingly . . . I heard no news [at Mrs. Sydney Smith's] . . . except great praise of *Jane Eyre*' (28 November 1847; *Emma Darwin, a Century of Family Letters*, 2 vols., 1915, ii. 112); 'Fonblanque raves about *Jane Eyre*' (29 November 1847; *The Ladies of Alderley*, 1938, p. 174); '*Jane Eyre* was eagerly hailed by some of the resident fellows of Exeter College' (G. D. Boyle, *Recollections*, 1895, p. 131); 'It makes our old bachelor bones rattle' (letter of 14 November 1848, *Autobiography of Dean Merivale*, 1899, p. 177). Cf. the early impressions of Thackeray (*Letters*, ii. 318–19; letter of 23 October 1847) and of W. G. Clark (recalled in his review of *Shirley* in *Fraser's*, December 1849, p. 692). [3] See above, pp. 58–59, 83–84.

contemporary references shows that the average intelligent novel-reader (better represented, here as always, by the *Examiner* and *Fraser's* than the *Quarterly*)[1] acclaimed *Jane Eyre* as a work of genius; there is no sign that he was antagonized by the novelties of setting and social level; they were new but not startlingly so. He had, for example, encountered as novel-material oppressed childhood in *Oliver Twist*; the child working out moral problems, in *The Crofton Boys* and *The Fairy Bower*; Yorkshire schools and schoolmasters in *Nicholas Nickleby*, 'middling' provincial society treated without satire in *Deerbrook*;[2] and the deliberate deflation of heroic convention in Thackeray's early stories. For the devotee of older traditions of novel-writing, there were the obvious affiliations with Richardson and Mrs. Radcliffe, even Jane Austen and Maria Edgeworth.

The few attacks upon *Jane Eyre* are not directed against breaches of literary convention; indeed, they testify indirectly to its timeliness, hearing it as a voice from the dangerous north and the dangerous class of oppressed or 'outlawed' women; using it as a text on which to hang warnings about female emanci-

[1] Charlotte Brontë justly referred to the 'timorous or carping few' in the Preface to the second edition (January 1848). The article in the *Quarterly Review* appeared in December 1848, fourteen months after the novel was published and long after most other reviews. It is actuated not only by the political bias natural to the journal (and the date) and by a mischievous love of scandal (in the passage insinuating some link between Currer Bell and Thackeray) but by the less disreputable motive of counter-acting the consensus of eulogy.

[2] And two women (one a governess) whose love precedes, or is independent of, the hope of return. C. B. greatly admired *Deerbrook*; see below, p. 276, n. 4.

pation and a rebellious and un-Christian spirit in
society.[1] The influence of *Jane Eyre*, both social and
literary, also bespeaks its importance in its own time;
on the lower level, it started a vogue for plain heroines
and ugly masterful heroes;[2] on the higher, it affected
the autobiographic children in Dickens's later novels,[3]
and at least smoothed the path for Mrs. Gaskell,
Trollope, and George Eliot. The profounder explorations of *Jane Eyre* were new indeed to the novel; not
before in fiction had such continuous shafts of light

[1] 'Pre-eminently an anti-Christian composition . . . a murmuring
against the comforts of the rich and against the privations of the poor,
which, as far as each individual is concerned, is a murmuring against
God's appointment. . . . We do not hesitate to say that the tone of mind
and thought which has overthrown authority and violated every code
human and divine abroad, and fostered Chartism and rebellion at home,
is the same which has also written Jane Eyre' (*Quarterly Review*, December 1848, pp. 173–4)—ironic reading for C. B. as a hero-worshipper of
the Duke of Wellington and a devout churchwoman. See also *The Christian Remembrancer*, April 1848, xv, p. 397, which uses the words 'burns
with moral Jacobinism'; *English Review*, December 1849, p. 307, and
North British Review, August 1851, pp. 422–3—'an undue reliance on
self, unamiable . . . if not positively irreligious'. All these critics were
perhaps hitting back at the manifesto in the author's Preface to the second
edition (1848), in which she claimed to assail only conventionality and
self-righteousness, not morality and religion, 'things . . . diametrically
opposed . . . narrow human doctrines, that only tend to elate and magnify
a few, should not be substituted for the world-redeeming creed of Christ'.

[2] As testified by W. C. Roscoe, *National Review* (October 1858), and
Poems and Essays (1860), ii. 414, and Walter Bagehot, 'The Waverley
Novels' (1858) reprinted in *Literary Studies* (ii. 148); cf. *North British
Review* (August 1849), p. 488, on 'that class of young ladies . . . now
beginning to be known by the epithet of Jane Eyrish', ibid. (August
1851), p. 430, on 'the Jane Eyre style of physiognomy'; and for later
evidence, Robert Buchanan, *Fortnightly Review* (15 September 1866),
p. 299.

[3] David Copperfield was compared to Jane Eyre by at least one reviewer, and also, apparently, by W. S. Williams (*S.H.B.* iii. 20).

penetrated the 'unlit gulf of the self'—that solitary self hitherto the preserve of the poets. The relation of *Jane Eyre* to the literature of its time is seen more clearly if we include the poetry being read, and written—the poetry of Wordsworth and Byron, Arnold and Clough.

But that relation appears most clearly of all in the mutual recognition between Charlotte Brontë and Thackeray.

You mention Thackeray and the last number of 'Vanity Fair'. The more I read Thackeray's works the more certain I am he stands alone—alone in his sagacity, alone in his truth, alone in his feeling (his feeling, though he makes no noise about it, is about the most genuine that ever lived on a printed page), alone in his power, alone in his simplicity, alone in his self-control. Thackeray is a Titan, so strong that he can afford to perform with calm the most herculean feats; there is the charm and majesty of repose in his greatest efforts; *he* borrows nothing from fever, his is never the energy of delirium—his energy is sane energy, deliberate energy, thoughtful energy. The last number of 'Vanity Fair' proves this peculiarly. Forcible, exciting in its force, still more impressive than exciting, carrying on the interest of the narrative in a flow, deep, full, resistless, it is still quiet—as quiet as reflection, as quiet as memory; and to me there are parts of it that sound as solemn as an oracle. Thackeray is never borne away by his own ardour—he has it under control. His genius obeys him—it is his servant, it works no fantastic changes at its own wild will, it must still achieve the task which reason and sense assign it, and none other. Thackeray is unique. I *can* say no more, I *will* say no less.[1]

[1] Letter to W. S. Williams, 29 March 1848, *S.H.B.* ii. 201; the 'last number' would be the fifteenth (chs. li–liii), published at the beginning of the month. It is not known when she began to read the novel, but it

Here, in the most specific and unqualified of her
many tributes to Thackeray,[1] Charlotte Brontë indicates the nature of her own values in art; perhaps also
her sense of what she feared might be lacking in her
own work. The 'truth', 'genuine feeling', 'power',
and 'ardour' that she admired in *Vanity Fair* were
also hers, beyond all difference of territory and approach; but the 'calm', 'repose', and 'control'—
these she had to fight for. The way from 'fever' and
'delirium' to 'sane, deliberate, thoughtful energy',
from a genius with its own 'wild will' to a genius
directed by 'reason and sense' was for her an ascent
arduous and protracted. Only when its course is
traced through her own earlier writings is *Jane Eyre*
seen in true perspective.

§ 2

But Charlotte Brontë's noble judgement on Thackeray and indeed the whole history of her contact
with him as writer[2] and man lies on the hither side of
the watershed which *Jane Eyre* and its fame made in
her career. The woman who wrote that novel at the
age of thirty knew only four living writers; but these

cannot have been much before August 1847, since '"Jane Eyre" was
written before the author had seen one line of "Vanity Fair"' (*S.H.B.*
ii. 314). She cannot therefore have 'read the parts as they were published'
as W. Robertson Nicoll supposed (*Jane Eyre*, 1901, p. xi).

[1] For others, see Dedication and Preface to the second edition of *Jane
Eyre* (written December 1847 and printed January 1848) and many
passages in letters from October 1847 to the end of her life; the most
striking are *S.H.B.* ii. 150, 160, 184; iii. 60, 67, 314–15.

[2] She may have read his earlier work in *Fraser's* and perhaps *Punch*,
though she is unlikely to have identified the author at the time.

she had known intimately as writers from her childhood, for they were her father, her brother, and her
two sisters. There can be few writers for whom the
impulses to artistic creation, the intellectual influences, and intense family affections are so nearly
included in a single constellation. *Jane Eyre* is no
mysterious first-born offspring of adverse circumstance and untaught genius; it is the culmination of
years of writing by one of a family of five long-
practised writers. In her own words:

As [Thackeray] once said to Currer Bell with some bitter-
ness, 'I worked ten years before I achieved a real success'. . . .
Currer Bell had worked quite as long as Mr. Thackeray,
without publishing.[1]

This is the nearest she ever came to telling anyone
outside the family—except perhaps Mrs. Gaskell—
of that exotic hinterland of creative activity; and
even here its extent in time is halved. Of this her
contemporaries in general knew nothing; but in their
speculations on the number and relation of the Bells,
the likenesses and differences between them, they
had laid hold of an essential truth about the Brontës
which too much subsequent criticism has lost sight
of: the literary interdependence of the family. This
far outweighs in importance (and unusualness) the
supposed inadequacy of their experience of life; indeed, it directly counteracted such inadequacy, since
to a large extent each shared the experience of the
others, and it may be that the twofold act of sharing
emphasized that 'distancing' which personal experi-

[1] Letter to George Smith, 28 November 1851; *S.H.B.* iii. 294–5.

ence requires before it can be formed into art.[1] Whatever the family group's isolation from the world,
within it there was continuous stimulus and challenge, the complex interplay of literary and personal
influences, and even, for many years, the closest
possible co-operation.

> We wove a web in childhood[,]
>   A web of sunny air;
> We dug a spring in infancy
>   Of water pure and fair.
> We sowed in youth a mustard seed,
>   We cut an almond rod;
> We are now grown up to riper age—
>   Are they withered in the sod?[2]

Chance and change affected particular partner-
ships, the degree of interdependence varied, but the
pattern of the 'web' underlies all the work of the four:
it seems an association not merely lifelong, but ending only with the life of the last survivor. Periods of
separation and sharply disparate experience, both
actual and imaginative, and divergence in maturity,
exerted a pressure towards the individual solitari-
ness which is a condition of creation; but some part
of the web was still weaving, even in Charlotte's
latest, loneliest works, when she

almost despaired, because there was no one to whom to read
a line, or of whom to ask a counsel. 'Jane Eyre' was not

---

[1] 'Emily would never go into any sort of society herself, and whenever
I went I could on my return communicate to her a pleasure that suited
her, by giving the distinct faithful impression of each scene I had witnessed. When pressed to go, she would sometimes say, 'What is the use ?
Charlotte will bring it all home to me' (*S.H.B.* iii. 38).

[2] Poem written at Roe Head in 1835 (*S.H.B.*, *Poems*, 1934, p. 180).

written under such circumstances, nor were two-thirds of 'Shirley'.[1]

As four;[2] as two independent pairs;[3] and in the last and most creative phase, as three, they continued to further a common purpose—working now together, now separately, but rarely without constantly comparing, discussing, advising.[4]

[1] *S.H.B.* iv. 13 (on *Villette*, October 1852). Cf. ii. 327 (16 April 1849): 'Worse than useless did it seem to attempt to write what there no longer lived an "Ellis Bell" to read'; and iii. 23 (September 1849): 'The two human beings who understood me, and whom I understood, are gone.'

[2] The family pattern, as re-formed in 1825 (after the deaths of Maria and Elizabeth, and the return from Cowan Bridge) is made clearest in Charlotte's retrospective account of 'plays' in *The History of the Year* (1829) and Branwell's Introduction to *The History of the Young Men* (1830). June 1826 is the earliest date there specified for 'plays'; at that time Charlotte was ten, Branwell nine, Emily not quite eight, and Anne six and a half. Fourfold collaboration belongs to the period of the 'wooden-soldiers', and the first years of Angria, which lasted from 1826, or earlier, to 1831 or 1832; the concurrent 'secret plays' were carried out either in couples (Charlotte and Emily) or singly, and how they are reflected in the stories is unknown. The earliest stories and magazines date from 1829 and show Angria already well established.

[3] This was after Gondal had split off from Angria, probably during Charlotte's first absence at Roe Head (1831–2). Charlotte and Branwell continued in a loosening and somewhat stressful 'collaboration' over Angria until about 1839; Emily and Anne, who it seems had rebelled not against Charlotte's leadership but that of Branwell her deputy, formed a presumably firmer partnership over Gondal, which persisted until at least 1845, and probably until Emily's death (Birthday Notes; *S.H.B.* ii. 49–53).

The important critical point here is that the retreat from her dream-world was a pre-condition of Charlotte's self-discovery in creative art; but not so of Emily's. In the absence of Gondal prose-narrative, however, not too much can be built on this. The effective difference may perhaps be not that between Angria and Gondal, or Charlotte and Emily, but between their partners Branwell and Anne, extreme contrasts in balance and moral integration.

[4] Cf. Gaskell, ch. xv: 'They talked over the stories they were engaged

The father's part was not only to keep out of the way[1]—in which, indeed, he took a just pride:

> When my daughters were at home they read their manuscripts to each other and gave their candid opinions of what was written. I never interfer'd with them at these times—I judged it best to throw them upon their own responsibility. Besides, a clergyman, bordering upon the age of eighty years, was likely to be too cold and severe a critic to the efforts of buoyant and youthful genius;

nor to tell stories of his youth in Ireland, Cambridge, and Dewsbury, nor to supply, from his newspapers and conversation on current events, a wider context of public affairs for his children's curious dreamland. These things were important, but not in comparison with the one simple, often forgotten fact: that his was the inspiring, overarching example of achieved authorship, the sober intoxication of actual print. While they were children, the mere existence of his five printed volumes[2] would outweigh, perhaps even conceal, his lack of fame; later, their awareness of his personal disappointment, and his proportionate ambition for them, must have sharpened the conviction that nothing but the firm assurance of literary fame

upon, and described their plots. Once or twice a week, each read to the others what she had written, and heard what they had to say about it.'

[1] Gaskell, chs. iii, xv; the letter (to Mrs. Gaskell, 20 June 1855) was first printed in 1933, in *B.S.T.* viii, No. 2, pt. xlii, p. 90.

[2] *Winter-Evening Thoughts* (1810); *Cottage Poems* (1811); *The Rural Minstrel* (1813); *The Cottage in the Wood* (1815); *The Maid of Killarney* (1818). The first three are volumes of poems, the last two short tales. All but the first, and four later prose pieces, are reprinted, somewhat inaccurately, in *Brontëana* . . . ed. J. Horsfall Turner (Bingley, 1898). No biographer or critic has yet done justice to Patrick Brontë, whether as personal or quasi-literary influence on the writings of his daughters.

for his offspring would do to offer in return.[1] And it was offered, not only in pride and gratitude, but in consolation for his disappointed hopes and the loss, Absalom-like but long-drawn, of his only son.

Branwell's was the one final defection from the group; but in the end it drew the three sisters closer. The defection came, not from death or deliberate withdrawal, but from the thickening and darkening of his private dream, the final hopeless confusion on the borders of it and the world of action and moral responsibility. It was foreseeable; if a break was to come, this was the danger point, this the most vulnerable and dubious talent—but not less a shock to the affections. This is no place for case-history; but the concurrence of events is important. Briefly, by 1845 Branwell had collected and manufactured enough 'injustice' to last him the rest of his short life; out of it he built his ultimate prison and for three years is heard only battering at the bars. To this his sisters must listen. They were driven into isolation again— no pupils, no visitors even, were possible now. And in these years they wrote *Agnes Grey*, *Wuthering Heights*, *The Professor* and *Jane Eyre*, and moved the more rapidly towards their early deaths.[2]

[1] The often repeated story of how he was apprised of the publication and favourable reception of *Jane Eyre* is in Gaskell, ch. xvi; and cf. Ellen Nussey's notes, *S.H.B.* ii. 228. It first appears (as part of Lady Kay-Shuttleworth's information) in a letter of Mrs. Gaskell to Catherine Winkworth on the occasion of her first meeting with Charlotte in August 1850 (*S.H.B.* iii. 144; with the additional and often neglected detail, 'they never dared to tell him of the books her sisters wrote'). F. J. A. Hort had heard something to the same effect some months earlier (*Life and Letters*, 1896, i. 146–7; letter of March 1850).

[2] It is difficult not to sympathize with the burning and bitter feelings of

For the withering of one 'almond tree' hastened, against all odds, the fruitfulness of the others. The three sisters, impelled by circumstance and mutual affection into association as close as that of childhood, were once more re-formed into a group of writers by Charlotte's strengthened desperate purpose; and for the first time they together looked outwards, towards audience and fame. Some time after her sisters' death, feeling it a 'sacred duty'; to 'leave their dear names free from soil',[1] she gave a reticent outline[2] of this final phase of activity:

About five years ago, my two sisters and myself, after a somewhat prolonged period of separation, found ourselves reunited, and at home . . . we were wholly dependent on ourselves and each other, on books and study, for the enjoyments and occupations of life. The highest stimulus, as well as the liveliest pleasure we had known from childhood upwards, lay in attempts at literary composition; formerly we used to show each other what we wrote, but of late years this habit of com-

Mrs. Gaskell when she heard from Charlotte and later wrote the story of Branwell's last years; and difficult not to envy her, for she, unenlightened by the findings of twentieth century psychology, felt free to blame his moral weakness and (in her first edition, before the threats of legal action) the heartless villainy of Lady Scott. But at least modern readers need not, like some Brontë biographers, react so far as to pity the plumage and forget the dying bird. It cannot be too often emphasized that the three sisters had to suffer all the horrors that a psychopath, bound by ties of past affection and present moral obligation, can inflict; to suffer them in failing health, and unfortified by his tonics of drink and drugs and lies; and that while so suffering, they wrote their novels. There can be no clearer instance of the sanity of true genius.

[1] 'Biographical Notice' prefixed to the 1850 edition of *Wuthering Heights* and *Agnes Grey*; this was written in September and published in December.

[2] There is no reference to Branwell, save in the hint of Anne's motive in writing *The Tenant of Wildfell Hall*.

munication and consultation had been discontinued; hence it ensued, that we were mutually ignorant of the progress we might respectively have made. [*Then follows the well-known account of Charlotte's accidental discovery in the autumn of 1845 of Emily's poems, her eventual success in persuading her that they deserved publication, and the voluntary production of Anne's poems.*] We had very early cherished the dream of one day becoming authors. This dream, never relinquished even when distance divided and absorbing tasks occupied us, now suddenly acquired strength and consistency: it took the character of a resolve. We agreed to arrange a small selection of our poems, and, if possible, get them printed. . . . The bringing out of our little book was hard work. As was to be expected, neither we nor our poems were at all wanted. . . . Ill-success failed to crush us: the mere effort to succeed had given a wonderful zest to existence; it must be pursued. We each set to work on a prose tale [*Wuthering Heights, Agnes Grey,* and *The Professor*] . . . These MSS. were perseveringly obtruded upon various publishers for the space of a year and a half; usually, their fate was an ignominious and abrupt dismissal.

At last *Wuthering Heights* and *Agnes Grey* were accepted on terms somewhat impoverishing to the two authors. . . . As a forlorn hope, [Currer Bell] tried one publishing house more [*Smith and Elder, who rejected* The Professor, *but expressed readiness to see a three-volume novel*]. I was then just completing *Jane Eyre,* at which I had been working while the one volume tale was plodding its weary round in London: in three weeks I sent it off; friendly and skilful hands took it in. This was in the commencement of September 1847; it came out before the close of October following. . . .

§ 3

The 'web of childhood', which afforded so much 'stimulus' and 'pleasure', is here referred to as if it did no more than provide a precedent for co-operative literary effort. Its nature and extent were virtually unknown until the present century;[1] but even fragmentary knowledge and tentative understanding[2] have shown how closely and strangely it is related to the mature novels. But the relation is not one of straightforward development; however many themes and situations may be traced from the Angrian stories to *Jane Eyre*, the gulf between fantasy and creation remains, and the decisive leap was taken only with *The Professor*. The vast cycle of romances written between 1830 and 1840 remains as the dark hinterland of the novels, or the chaos from which they were formed. In two senses a chaos. Since they themselves issued from a corporate daydream, nothing ever needed to be explained; each piece assumed a knowledge not only of all the rest but of much that was 'made out' only in talk or solitary imaginings. As the amorphous mass swelled and sprawled, it became impossible to envisage 'outside' readers; the large

[1] Mrs. Gaskell borrowed 'a whole heap of minute writings' in 1856 (*S.H.B.* iv. 207) and printed a few extracts in ch. iv of her biography. The rest were purchased from Mr. Nicholls by Clement Shorter for T. J. Wise in 1894, and soon scattered in various collections. Not all have been published, but most have been seen by Miss Fannie E. Ratchford, whose book *The Brontës' Web of Childhood* (New York, 1941), is the sole authoritative critical study. The chief collections are *The Twelve Adventurers*, ed. C. W. Hatfield (1925), *Legends of Angria*, ed. Ratchford and De Vane (1933), and *S.H.B. Miscellaneous and Unpublished Writings* ...ed. Wise and Symington (1936). All subsequent critics and biographers of the Brontës have made some use of this material, and it is further illuminated in the studies of Laura B. Hinkley and Phyllis Bentley.

[2] Criticism must eventually seek the help of psychology, as Miss Bentley suggests; but as it must be help and not dictation, any fruitful issue may lie far in the future.

problems of structure, the delicate question of guiding the interest—in a word, of communication—were
never faced. There is no Angrian story that can be
read with the serene confidence that, whatever happens, the writer is in control. And further, the
Angrian world is a moral chaos: its heroes, especially
the dominating Duke of Zamorna, Byronic figures
lacking even the Byronic sense of sin, racked by
passion, revenge, cruelty, and madness, their utterance feverish and strident. In its massiveness and
distortion Angria was, as its chief creator[1] came to
see, dangerous to the claims both of art and life; a
Frankenstein monster. But it was to be conquered,
not fled from.

Her letters and some of her journal fragments in the
eighteen-thirties show her intermittently pursued by
qualms of conscience taking the form of general self-
accusation, religious melancholy and imaginations
'gloomy and frightful'.[2] More revealing, and more
pathetic, are the struggles of artistic conscience in the
stories themselves. A narrative will begin with
lowered tone, with even a contemporary English setting, an attempt at normal exposition in description
and dialogue;[3] new characters appear, and seem to
promise a re-centring of the romance or a shifting of

---

[1] The other, Branwell, let it devour him; his doom was to try to turn
life into an Angrian romance with himself as hero-victim.

[2] See the quotations in *S.H.B.* i, ch. vii; *Legends of Angria*, Introduction; *Brontës' Web of Childhood*, ch. xiv. The journal fragments of 1835
(when she was nineteen) show that the Angrian dreamland possessed her
to the point of hallucination.

[3] This is a tendency even in early examples; e.g. ch. i of 'The Foundling' (1833).

emphasis from aristocratic to humble life; there are repeated attempts to 'distance' Zamorna by the use of a sardonic critical observer. But as the story proceeds, the old tone reasserts itself, Zamorna dominates the situation and the emotional tempest rises, shrivelling the weak shoots of naturalism. Something was achieved; at least in the later stories the emphasis shifted from war and revolution and dynastic fortunes to personal rivalries and keener emotional analysis; but violence is thereby only more concentrated, not more ordered and controlled. To the last the writer seems hag-ridden by her own creations.[1]

Angria must be apparently rejected before it could be transformed in other terms. The proclamation of rejection[2] is decisive, if reluctant; its motive not, openly at least, any moral or artistic scruple, but satiety and exhaustion.

I have now written a great many books and for a long time

[1] One of the latest and most readable of the series, 'Caroline Vernon' (1839; reprinted in *Legends of Angria*) well illustrates the author's struggle to write more responsibly and her inevitable failure as soon as Zamorna dominates the scene. Caroline, Zamorna's ward and his rival's child, is a study in conflicting feelings, who does momentarily hesitate between passion and conscience; had she resisted, the approach to *Jane Eyre* would have been closer. This story so nearly becomes a true novel that its failure shows with especial clearness the fatal limitations of the Angrian world, with its disordered aristocratic passion and general remoteness from the writer's experience.

[2] The fragment is undated; the only dated item in the manuscript volume containing it (Bonnell collection, now at Haworth: described and quoted in *B.S.T.* 1924, vol. vi, pt. xxxiv, p. 229) bears the date 1838. The date assumed by Miss Ratchford and others following her is 1839, presumably on the grounds that no Angrian stories of later date are known. The whole fragment is quoted in *Legends of Angria*, pp. 315-16.

I have dwelt upon the same characters and scenes and subjects. . . . My readers have been habituated to one set of
features . . . but we must change, for the eye is tired of the
picture so oft recurring and now so familiar.

Yet do not urge me too fast, reader; it is not easy to dis-
miss from my imagination the images which have filled it so
long; they were my friends and my intimate acquaintances,
and I could with little labour describe to you the faces, the
voices, the actions, of those who peopled my thoughts by day,
and not seldom stole strangely even into my dreams by night.
When I depart from these I feel almost as if I stood on the
threshold of a home and were bidding farewell to its inmates.
When I strive to conjure up new images I feel as if I had
got into a distant country where every face was unknown and
the character of all the population an enigma which it would
take much study to comprehend and much talent to expound.
Still, I long to quit for a while that burning clime where we
have sojourned too long—its skies flame—the glow of sunset
is always upon it—the mind would cease from excitement and
turn now to a cooler region where the dawn breaks grey and
sober, and the coming day for a time at least is subdued by
clouds.

Thus, at twenty-three, she embarked on the journey
which, according to her later view of the ages of man,
she should have begun five years before.

At eighteen the true narrative of life is yet to be commenced. Before that time, we sit listening to a tale, a marvellous fiction; delightful sometimes, and sad sometimes; almost
always unreal. Before that time, our world is heroic; its
inhabitants half-divine or semi-demon. . . . At eighteen,
drawing near the confines of illusive, void dreams, Elf-land
lies behind us, the shores of Reality rise in front. . . . At
eighteen, the school of Experience is to be entered, and her

humbling, crushing, grinding, but yet purifying, invigorating lessons are yet to be learnt.[1]

In several ways the years 1837–9 mark a transition in her life. She left Miss Wooler's school, she witnessed Branwell's rapid degeneration, and she decided to go out as a private governess. Literary ambition had been checked by Southey's reply when she submitted poems to him; and he had especially discouraged 'the day dreams in which you habitually indulge'.[2] But her main motive for the decision was her gradual realization that Angria and Zamorna were retarding and not developing her imagination. Their stranglehold must be loosed and she must start afresh.

It is unfortunate that so few of the narratives that must have closely followed the 'farewell to Angria' have survived. One or two beginnings of novels, and a group of fragments, alone escaped her stern self-criticism;[3] for now she 'destroyed' her 'crude effort[s] almost as soon as she composed them'.[4] But at least in 1840 or early 1841 she had for the first time a specimen of prose narrative that she judged fit for an out-

[1] *Shirley*, opening of ch. vii.

[2] Her first letter (29 December 1836) is lost, so it is not known what she told him. For the rest of the correspondence, see *S.H.B.* i. 155–9.

[3] 'Mr. Ashworth,' or 'The Ashworths,' unprinted, but discussed in Ratchford, pp. 191–2, 208–9; and fragments of a story about Mr. and Miss Percy, Mr. West, and Miss Thornton (printed in *B.S.T.*, vol. x, pt. l, pp. 18–24). 'The Moores,' called by Miss Ratchford a discarded draft of *The Professor* (printed in W. Robertson Nicoll's *Jane Eyre*, 1901) seems to me maturer work, and probably an attempt to recast *The Professor* in 1847–8 (it can hardly be later than *Shirley*, because of the name Moore).

[4] Preface to *The Professor*.

side eye;[1] and its fragments (if rightly identified) suggest a domestic novel of manners, with a wealthy upper-middle-class Yorkshire setting.[2] We have her own word for it that in what she was writing for some years before *The Professor*, she 'got over such taste as I might once have had for ornamental and redundant composition, and came to prefer what was plain and homely';[3] that she 'restrained imagination, eschewed romance, repressed excitement . . . and sought to produce something which should be soft, grave, and true'.[4] She destroyed, because the imagination's farewell was still reluctant; even at the Pensionnat Héger in 1843—

in the evening when I am in the great dormitory alone . . . I always recur as fanatically as ever to the old ideas, the old faces, and the old scenes in the world below.[5]

But the 'scheme of a magazine tale' in the same year looks forward:

[1] All that survives of the correspondence is the draft of her second letter written on the wrapper in which her manuscript was returned, post-marked Ambleside. The recipient was almost certainly Hartley Coleridge, and not, as often stated, Wordsworth. (See C. W. Hatfield, *B.S.T.*, vol. x, pt. l, pp. 15–16).

[2] She has not found the right social angle; in *Jane Eyre* wealth is observed from below, but here the author pretends unsuccessfully to be of the same class and habits as her characters. Her discomfort on this point is suggested by the sardonic references (in her draft letter) to Richardson and the *Lady's Magazine,* and to the tendency of an imaginary world to produce 'books, thoughts and manners bordering on the idiotic'. The letter, however, is written so much 'in character' as to be dubious as evidence.

[3] Preface to *The Professor*, 1857; written 'shortly after the appearance of *Shirley*' (A. B. Nicholls's Preface).

[4] Letter to G. H. Lewes, 6 November 1847; *S.H.B.* ii. 152.

[5] *S.H.B.* i. 297 (letter to Branwell, 1 May 1843).

Time—from 30 to 50 years ago. Country—England.
Scene—Rural. Rank—Middle. Person—First. . . .

with a special memorandum on 'villains'—'N.B.
Moderation to be observed here'.[1]

Once the author had made up her mind to make
this change, she would find much in what she read,
observed, and experienced, to strengthen her resolu-
tion. It has been shown[2] that the tide was then setting
against novels of fashionable life: Charlotte Brontë's
access to contemporary literature might at this date
be limited, but she could read *Fraser's*,[3] where the
new trend was clearly reflected both in reviews and
stories, and may have read Harriet Martineau's
Deerbrook.[4] Her response to current experience is in
sharp contrast to that of a few years earlier. In her
letters of 1840–1 there is none of the old self-con-
suming melancholy, but a dry, vigorous, amused
analysis of the situations and persons around her,
which already forecasts the observation of the novels.
She was turning her imagination outward and feeding it upon ordinary life; she was therefore the more
able to meet the challenge of Brussels, which was not
ordinary, nor yet overlaid, like Haworth and Dewsbury Moor, by the web of dream.

---

[1] *B.S.T.* vol. vi, pt. xxxiv, p. 231.

[2] See above, pp. 73 ff.

[3] Her aunt had begun to take it in 1831 (*S.H.B.* i. 88). Many of
Thackeray's stories appeared there, including *Catherine* (1839–40), *A
Shabby Genteel Story* (1840) and *The Great Hoggarty Diamond* (1841).

[4] 'When C. B. first read *Deerbrook* he tasted a new and keen pleasure,
and experienced a genuine benefit. In his mind *Deerbrook* ranks with the
writings that have really done him good, added to his stock of ideas and
rectified his views of life' ('Currer Bell's' note to Harriet Martineau, in
1849; *S.H.B.* iii. 56).

Her two sojourns at the Pensionnat Héger[1] have a hidden interest which is surely greater than romantic biographers have imagined. Two desires and ambitions, writing and teaching, had hitherto run separate, even in conflict, in her life; a year after her return the first had absorbed the second, in terms both of her outer and her inner life. It was the second ambition that propelled her to Brussels; she went in order to study languages and so to make herself a real teacher instead of a drudging governess. But the other ambition, hinted in the 'Farewell' and by the act of submitting verse and prose to established authors, was only latent. And in Brussels the ruthless impersonal hunger of the artist recognized its true nourishment: not the heady wine of fantasy, from the alien kingdom of the 'world below', but the mixed bitter-sweet cup[2] of experience endured, observed, and extended in imagination. That experience was dominated by M. and Mme Héger, persons as strange and mysterious as any Duke of Zamorna or Lady Zenobia and of far less exhaustible interest. The role of M. Héger was perhaps somewhat other than it has been commonly pictured. She had gone to his establishment to learn: 'at this ripe time of life I am a schoolgirl, . . . and, on the whole, very happy in that capacity. . . . It is natural to me to submit.'[3] 'Nothing ever charms me more than when I meet my superior' said Shirley;[4] this charm was first accorded

---

[1] With Emily, from February to November 1842, and alone, from January to December 1843.

[2] The image is a favourite one with Charlotte. Cf. Preface to *The Professor*; *S.H.B.* ii. 271.

[3] *S.H.B.* i. 260.   [4] *Shirley*, ch. xii.

to Charlotte (outside her family) at the age of twenty-
five, and she submitted to learn from his example and
precept the two arts to which she aspired—to write
and to teach. He was 'Mon maître de litérature—[le]
seul maître que j'ai jamais eu'.[1] For the first time
she was mastering a new medium and submitting to
continuous criticism; constantly writing what would
be immediately read, and by an outsider, and one
whose judgement she admired. His criticism (of
which examples survive), while far from coldly ped-
antic, still emphasized always the need for clarity and
precision without which there can be no adequate
communication.[2] Thus, just when she needed help,
additional forces were· marshalled against the fatal
limitation of her earlier writing—its unconciliating
remoteness from readers. This, perhaps, is the core
of the Brussels experience in her development as an
artist; this what made it possible for her so soon to
transform even the more desolating aspects of that
experience into art, in her first novel.

The letters she wrote to M. Héger in 1844–5 after
her final return are primarily an attempt to renew that
special intimacy of master and pupil; she is once
again submitting her 'theme' for his criticism. Distance, and another language as medium, emphasized
the character of these letters as something 'made' as
well as a 'thinking aloud'; upon the basis of the actual

[1] *S.H.B.* ii. 11.

[2] For examples of corrected 'themes', see Gaskell, ch. xi, and *T.L.S.*,
19 July 1923 (reprinted in *B.S.T.* vol. vi, pt. xxxiv, pp. 239–46).
As she took some of her Angrian manuscripts to Brussels, and copied
some of her poems there, it is possible that these also were shown to
M. Héger.

relation and its potentialities[1] she has reared a super-structure that is half-way to art—half-way, at least, to William Crimsworth and his Frances, and the poem beginning 'He saw my heart's woe, discovered my soul's anguish'. But only half-way: true communication, either in life or literature, is not attained. In the deliberate dramatizing and intensifying of her emotion ('Vous direz encore que je suis *exaltée*')[2] there is again a breath from the burning clime of Angria; and perhaps the same sense of guilt about it —'c'est humiliant cela — de ne pas savoir maîtriser ses propres pensées . . . esclave à une idée dominante et fixe qui tyrannise son esprit.'[3]

These letters help to fill the gap in the literary documents of the years between Angrian romance and *The Professor*. The personal heart-hunger expressed in them had no future; her sense of the imaginative values of the situation had. How complete her self-detachment and projection soon became is evident in the first novel, told in the first person (and, in the Brussels chapters, convincingly so) by the

[1] In which M. Héger's marriage was a datum, in no sense a frustration but rather an encouragement; he was married, therefore he could, she thought, accept the ardent feeling she offered him, as belonging to a quite other kind of relation. The moment that he hinted that misinterpretation was possible, she ceased writing. The relation has been much misunderstood; C. W. Hatfield's note (Ratchford, pp. 164–5) seems the most perceptive comment; and see May Sinclair, *The Three Brontës* (1914), pp. 81–82 (written before the full text of the letters was known, but still valid).

[2] Letter of 8 January, 1845; *S.H.B.* ii. 22.

[3] Letter of 18 November, 1845; *S.H.B.* ii. 67. The fear of blindness mentioned in this and one earlier letter may be a hysterical extension of her habitual short-sightedness; there is no reference to it in letters to other correspondents.

'Master'[1] himself, but made English, Protestant, and poor, like her. Here the relation is expanded imaginatively, with the artist's calm and not the fever of the private fantasist. (To those who find here evidence of Héger's emotional implication, the best reply is Caroline Helstone's, 'Why should anyone have told me? Have I not an instinct? Can I not divine by analogy?')[2]

The last letter to Héger perhaps nearly coincides with the beginning of the novel.[3] It is one of many circumstances which converge on that one significant point of time, the end of 1845. The drab despair of the previous spring—

one day resembles another . . . life wears away—I shall soon be 30—and I have done nothing yet—Sometimes I get melancholy—at the prospect before and behind me—yet it is wrong and foolish to repine—and undoubtedly my duty directs me to stay at home for the present—There was a time when Haworth was a very pleasant place to me, it is not so now—I feel as if we were all buried here—[4]

[1] 'The Master' was the novel's first title (*B.S.T.* vol. viii, pt. iv, p. 196).

[2] *Shirley*, ch. xii.

[3] The evidence suggests that writing began seriously about January 1846, after the expensive agreement with Aylott and Jones had shown that little success was to be expected for the *Poems*. The prose tales are first referred to, as if nearly completed, in a letter to these publishers on 6 April 1846, about a month before the publication of the *Poems*. They were therefore 'perseveringly obtruded on publishers' for rather less than the 'year and a half' of the 'Biographical Notice', since *The Professor* returned from its last rejection in July 1847, by which time *Wuthering Heights* and *Agnes Grey* were already accepted.

But the incubation of *The Professor* may have been much longer; it may well be the book which she says in July 1844 she would like to write and dedicate to Héger (*S.H.B.* ii. 11). Frances Henri's poem was probably written in 1843.

[4] *S.H.B.* ii. 28.

had ended in the explosive events of the summer, when Branwell returned, dismissed, and soon to prove himself, in Emily's phrase, 'a hopeless being'. Charlotte anticipated, and justly, a domestic 'season of distress and disquietude';[1] but there was a stimulus in its very extreme and variety of misery. And the three sisters were reunited, and for ever. Together again, Emily and Anne compared their separated progress in writing; at the end of July, a week after the bad news had broken, Emily is 'comfortable . . . and . . . undesponding':

The Gondals still flourish bright as ever. I am at present writing a work on the First Wars. Anne has been writing some articles on this, and a book by Henry Sophonia. . . .

Anne cannot forget what she has seen at Thorp Green:—

I have had some very unpleasant and undreamt-of experience of human nature.

But

Emily is engaged in writing the Emperor Julius's Life. . . . She is writing some poetry, too. . . . I have begun the third volume of *Passages in the Life of an Individual*. . . .'[2]

It needed only the last chance of Charlotte's discovery of the poems, the overcoming of Emily's reluctance to disclose her private world to outside readers, and the three were engaged together selecting poems for the press. Then 'we each set to work

[1] *S.H.B.* ii. 43.
[2] Birthday Notes of Emily and Anne, 30–31 July, 1845; *S.H.B.* ii. 49–53.

on a prose tale'[1]—and these were the three tales that
led to *Jane Eyre*.

§ 4

Of the three *The Professor* is the least firmly
planned and has least unity of feeling. They begin
where they should: *Wuthering Heights* just before the
end of the story, *Agnes Grey* at the beginning. *The
Professor* is a single-track novel like *Agnes Grey*, mas-
querading as a more complex unity, and with raw
edges broken off from Angrian stories. The relation
between the Crimsworth brothers raises interest, but
leads nowhere, is dropped after seven chapters, and
never recurs; it is a vestigial appendix from the rivalries of Angrian characters.[2] The early chapters also
introduce a further false lead—more damaging to the
novel because it does recur, but quite ineffectively—
in Yorke Hunsden, a sharply etched character with
a misleading semblance of function; and even at
Brussels, M. Pelet is a too transparent device for
setting the main action in motion.[3] The fault of the

[1] Not, perhaps, in the sense of beginning afresh. Anne's three-volume
work may have been the Gondal 'book by Henry Sophonia', or the quarry
from which *Agnes Grey* was drawn; her title fits the novel. Emily's
solitude throughout 1843, the parallels with poems dated in that year,
suggest an early inception for *Wuthering Heights*, and its intricate
structure would seem to demand long consideration. On the other hand,
it is difficult to picture the Gondal chronicler embarking upon such a
work without publication in mind; and that seems unlikely before
Charlotte found the poems.

[2] e.g., the Percy Brothers (one a coarse manufacturer) as drawn by
Branwell in 'The Wool is Rising' (Ratchford, pp. 193–7). The Angrian
tone is most evident in ch. v.

[3] 'It is some time since I made any reference to M. Pelet' (ch. xx). It is
seven chapters, and the reader has forgotten him.

novel is that the real story occupies barely half its space; the rest is an awkward prologue. Here alone, in Crimsworth's wooing of Frances Henri, the devious delicate pursuit of one solitary by another, the first of Charlotte's many explorations of the master-pupil relation,[1] is the growing-point of her first novel. Indeed the love-story in the first person is here already perfected. The concentration on a single view, the gradual explication of a mysterious character, the emotional suspense, of this part of the novel, she equalled but never surpassed; not even in *Villette*, where so much of the outer material is reworked.[2] But these chapters, while perfect in scale and tone, are too slight for a novel; their context nearly destroys them, for the reader, hungering for recurrence and symmetry, is haunted by the expectation of something to develop from the incidents and characters introduced in the first half of the novel. All that those first twelve chapters achieve—the establishing of William Crimsworth as solitary, misfit, and rebel—could have been done in one chapter; even two years later she thought them 'very feeble'.

Because of its structural weakness, directly deducible to the unwillingness to give up Angrian characters entirely and the inability to combine them

[1] e.g., ch. xiv (second and third paragraphs). The poem 'I gave, at first, attention close' in ch. xxiii is probably earlier; it will be noted that its heroine's name is 'Jane'.

[2] In December 1847 she wished to recast *The Professor*, thinking 'the Brussels part' 'as good as I can write'. She offered it for publication again in February 1851; her answer to this rejection was the writing of *Villette*. Its posthumous publication, though fortunate, has caused it to be underestimated, through a comparison she could never have permitted.

with the rest, *The Professor* represents an imperfect victory over 'the world below'. Charlotte was perhaps deceived into thinking it complete because of her strenuous and indeed successful effort to avoid extravagance in situation and style, to lower the social tone into congruity with the scenes and characters she knew at first hand. Her pride in this self-denial and her sardonic sense of the irony of its failure to attract publishers[1] is a measure of what it cost her:

I said to myself that my hero should work his way through life as I had seen real living men work theirs—that he should never get a shilling he had not earned—that no sudden turns should lift him in a moment to wealth and high station; that whatever small competency he might gain, should be won by the sweat of his brow; that, before he could find so much as an arbour to sit down in, he should master at least half the ascent of 'the Hill of Difficulty'; that he should not even marry a beautiful girl or a lady of rank. As Adam's son he should share Adam's doom, and drain throughout life a mixed and moderate cup of enjoyment.

In the sequel, however, I found that publishers in general scarcely approved of this system, but would have liked something more imaginative and poetical—something more consonant with a highly wrought fancy, with a taste for pathos, with sentiments more tender, elevated, unworldly.[2]

Novelists should never allow themselves to weary of the study of real life. If they observed this duty conscientiously, they would give us fewer pictures chequered with vivid contrasts of light and shade; they would seldom elevate their heroes and heroines to the heights of rapture—still seldomer sink

---

[1] 'They all told me it was deficient in "startling incident" and "thrilling excitement" ' (*S.H.B.* ii. 152–3; letter to Lewes, 6 November 1847).
[2] Preface to *The Professor*.

them to the depths of despair . . . the man of regular life and rational mind never despairs.[1]

No golden halo of fiction was about this example [of 'romantic domestic treachery'], I saw it bare and real, and it was very loathsome . . . unlawful pleasure, trenching on another's rights, is delusive and envenomed pleasure—its hollowness disappoints at the time, its poison cruelly tortures afterwards, its effects deprave for ever.[2]

Not only such passages, but the whole tone of *The Professor*, show the completeness of her moral emancipation from the world of Angria, where 'romantic domestic treachery' was the norm. The emphasis upon the 'farewell' to the 'burning clime' may be at times aggressive; but the convinced preference for the 'shores of Reality' to 'illusive, void dreams' has been exemplified as well as asserted. It remained to discover the structure, the unity, which a whole novel demands; and, now safely anchored upon those shores, to rediscover the realm of dream. *The Professor* was a necessary stage; it set up a bare framework of 'working one's way through life' with a 'rational mind', a framework unknown to Angria, and from which none of her later narratives seriously departs; but it perhaps sacrificed too much to down-to-earth truthfulness in its conscientious avoidance of sudden turns of fortune and extremes of feeling. This is indeed a clime 'where the dawn breaks grey . . . subdued by clouds': and truthfulness need not be quite so grey to the senses as well as the emotions.[3]

---

[1] Ch. xix (opening).　　　[2] Ch. xx (last but one paragraph).

[3] May Sinclair (op. cit., p. 105) calls it 'a world where there is no sound, no colour, no vibration . . . the work of a woman who is not perfectly alive'.

Charlotte Brontë did not weary of the 'study of real life' in *Jane Eyre*; but there is room there for both rapture and despair; nor is unlawful pleasure seen as simply 'loathsome'.

§ 5

Jane Eyre is the completion of her victory; writing it, she was able to accept and keep in due subordination material from her fantasy world. There, Angria has become a positive value; for she has asserted her dominion, and the reader of this novel has never any doubt that she, and not any of her creatures, is in control. Like Lamb's true poet, she 'dreams, *being awake*', and 'treads the burning marl without dismay'.[1]

When the Angrian plot-material in *Jane Eyre* is recognized,[2] its subordination is seen to be a triumph of structure and emphasis. Had the story begun with the nodal situation, we should have been on a distant island (Spanish Town standing for Glass Town or Verdopolis) and have seen Rochester's father and elder brother entrapping him into marriage with a vicious lunatic. Instead, this situation is embedded in the main story, revealed retrospectively

---

[1] 'Sanity of True Genius,' in *Last Essays of Elia*. The whole essay is deeply relevant to Charlotte Brontë's progress.

[2] See Ratchford, pp. 200–14. I do not find all her parallels convincing, but there is certainly a reminiscence of Zamorna's wooing of Zenobia and her mad jealousy in Rochester's marriage to Bertha Mason, and also of the menacing hag Bertha in the deserted castle of 'The Green Dwarf'. Adèle Varens' parentage and past history recalls Caroline Vernon's, the Reed sisters recall Eliza and Georgiana Seymour, 'tall haughty blondes, proud of their accomplishments'.

only at its climax; it is there not for its sensational sake, but as precisely that situation which will make Rochester's deception most nearly excusable, and Jane's resistance most difficult, producing the maximum of conflict between conscience and compassion and holding the reader's sympathies in true balance. By holding its revelation in reserve the author keeps the two rising lines of suspense in the middle chapters ironically parallel; Jane draws nearer and nearer to the mystery of Thornfield, unaware that it holds the destruction of her growing love. More incidental Angrian material is usually distanced in time or space, even as Spanish Town, Madeira, and India lie out on the edges of the novel's world. It is disinfected of feverish emotion: Rochester's mistresses are recollected with moderate tranquillity, and Adèle, the dancer's illegitimate child, is almost visibly stripped of glamour. Only in Blanche Ingram and Rochester's deliberate use of her as a means of tormenting Jane is there any approximation to the Angrian tone. Elsewhere, radical differences belie a superficial similarity; a girl's arrival at a strange house, with an absent and mysterious master, is recurrent in Angria (as in all romance), but is not there accompanied by a solidly reassuring Mrs. Fairfax, nor by the heroine's rationality and courage and her concern to earn an honest competence. Mr. Rochester looms up at first like Zamorna; but, unlike him, he can be mocked, has wit, intellect, and a conscience dormant, not dead. He is at worst an outlaw, where Zamorna was despot of a lawless world. Jane, the steady centre of the narrative, represents what no Angrian heroine ever had:

an incorruptible heart. Angria storms behind locked doors; the walls between chaos and the world are thin, but they will stand.

'The first duty of an author is, I conceive, a faithful allegiance to Truth and Nature.' The statement, coming from Charlotte Brontë in 1848,[1] is no truism; for her, that allegiance was hard-won. And it was natural also for her to place second to it the duty of a 'conscientious study of Art'; that came second in order for her, and *Jane Eyre* is her first work to show it. *The Professor* contains art, but is not a total work of art; in design and control, thanks to the backward drag of Angria, it is a broken-backed whole. Its inferiority to *Agnes Grey* as well as to *Wuthering Heights*, and the startling advance in *Jane Eyre* suggest that she may have learnt from her sisters' novels, in this as in other ways.[2] Different as they are, both had the power to teach her an economy of construction which *The Professor* lacks and *Jane Eyre* has.

Anne's unassuming but forcible narrative may have shown Charlotte the possibilities of a first-person angle of vision approximating to the author's experience: that of the solitary governess, observant and stoical in the strange and uncongenial world of other people's houses. The emotional driving-force of Anne's tale is simple and single: it is homesickness, directed both to past and future. The subsidiary characters minister to this, and also (like the Reeds and Adèle) supply incidental morals on the upbring-

---

[1] *S.H.B.* ii. 243.   [2] The writing of *Jane Eyre* was wholly subsequent to that of *Wuthering Heights* and *Agnes Grey* (see below, pp. 290–1); a fact of which critics have made too little.

ing of children. There is no mystery or conflict, and very little suspense; it is a linear narrative, without depth. But it is not desultory; its line defines a genuine and self-sustaining world of circumstance and feeling, and a world which at times suggests the stormier terrors of *The Tenant of Wildfell Hall*.[1] To *Jane Eyre*, *Agnes Grey* could contribute the courage of its simple, honest adaptation of form to substance; and its sober truthfulness was a salutary antidote to Angria. .

Wuthering Heights, on the other hand, could contribute the courage of its passion[2] and some part of its elaboration of structure.[3] Perhaps its most useful lesson was that it employed a device of exposition, not used before by Charlotte, which makes for a satisfying complexity: a present mystery is gradually illuminated by the unfolding of the past. In *Jane Eyre* this is done mainly by retrospection; whereas Emily displays two or three levels of time, bridged by a common observer. But both novels must have been planned backwards, and with a close regard for chronology; and that is the prosaic kind of planning which one might suppose very likely to be discussed.

[1] A full critical study of the Brontë novels would need to show how this in its turn was influenced by *Wuthering Heights* and *Jane Eyre*.

[2] 'It is not possible that Charlotte, of all people, should have read *Wuthering Heights* without a shock of enlightenment; that she should not have compared it with her own bloodless work; that she should not have felt the wrong done to her genius by her self-repression' (May Sinclair, p. 125. Miss Sinclair was writing before the Angrian writings were known, so that the contrast between the first two novels seemed still more inexplicable.)

[3] Though not, of course, its most remarkable feature, and the one most alien to the narrative modes of the time: the presentation of the narrative from the points of view of two onlookers, Lockwood and Nelly, and therefore the invisibility of the author herself.

Further, one of Emily's larger purposes is reflected, though differently achieved, in *Jane Eyre*: that is, to show the pressures of childhood experience in the full-grown character, with artfully contrived recurrences and contrasts. The conflicts of character in the two novels are not comparable; for Emily, the visionary, by-passes the moral world, rising straight from the jungle of childhood love-and-hate to the spiritual world and seeing them as one. Nor are the settings, the sense of place and season, alike; but there is the same 'exaltation of the senses'[1] whose absence has been remarked in *The Professor*. *Wuthering Heights* may have shown Charlotte that she need not deny her poetic imagination for the sake of allegiance to Truth. The 'more vivid interest' which she had 'endeavoured to impart' to *Jane Eyre*[2] was surely stimulated not only by her reading of her sister's novel, but by each successive rejection of *The Professor*.[3]

[1] Sinclair, pp. 121-2.

[2] Letter of 6 August 1847, Gaskell, ch. xvi. (Not in *S.H.B.*)

[3] And perhaps finally by the rejection which presumably accompanied Newby's acceptance of *Wuthering Heights* and *Agnes Grey*. It seems fair to assume that Charlotte was not offered even his 'somewhat impoverishing terms' (Emily and Anne, or more probably Anne on behalf of both, made an advance of £50; *S.H.B.* iii. 160). It is possible that Charlotte would regard this as rejection, but I think she would in that case have told us so.

Mrs. Gaskell's statement about separate submission of the tales cannot be taken seriously. In its context (ch. xv), it is irreconcilable with facts; she says that the 'three tales [after trying] their fate in vain together', 'were sent forth separately, and for many months with still-continued ill-success', *The Professor* returning from one such journey in *August* 1846. But the earliest possible date for first submission of the 'tales' is late April 1846, and we know they were submitted together to Colburn on 4 July 1846 (*S.H.B.* iv. Appendix ii). And 'separately' could not mean what it would appear to mean, since *Wuthering Heights* and *Agnes Grey* were

When *Jane Eyre* was begun is not certainly known; but it was 'nearly completed' (in 'three volumes') by 6 August 1847, and had been worked at while *The Professor* was 'plodding its weary round'.[1] The evidence points to bursts of writing spread over about a year. It was accepted as it stood, at the end of August; on the 16th October it was on sale.

'*Jane Eyre: an Autobiography*. Edited by Currer Bell' was its title.[2] 'An Autobiography': the choice of this form is of vital importance to the structure of the novel. Not, however, because the author is ever transcribing experience. The criticism of the Brontë novels is so overlaid with biographical conjecture that it is well at the outset to recall Charlotte's explicit disclaimer;

'Jane Eyre' was naturally and universally supposed to be Charlotte herself; but she always denied it, calmly, cheerfully, and with the obvious sincerity which characterised all she said.

clearly accepted together by Newby, and so, eventually, published. She was perhaps confused by the authors' offering each publisher the choice of one three-volume or three one-volume publications.

The date of Newby's acceptance was probably May or June 1847; it is controlled by Charlotte's statement that 'the first proof-sheets were already in the press at the commencement of August' (*S.H.B.* ii. 154).

[1] Letter of 6 August, and 'Biographical Notice'. Mrs. Gaskell, writing from memory of what Charlotte told her, specified the beginning of writing precisely, as 25 August 1846, the day of Mr. Brontë's operation in Manchester; she also quotes Harriet Martineau's story of Charlotte 'writing incessantly' at the Thornfield chapters for 'three weeks'. But she speaks also of Anne's having worked at *The Tenant* 'ever since the completion of . . . *Agnes Grey*' and of regular evening discussion of their stories, thus implying that the writing of three more tales began as soon as the first three had been sent out. (For possible evidence that Emily wrote a second novel, see *S.H.B.* ii. 187–8; and cf. 'Biographical Notice'—'They were both prepared to try again'.)

[2] The word 'edited' was dropped in the second edition.

The basis was no more than this: she determined to take, in defiance of convention, a heroine 'as small and as plain as [her] self' who should nevertheless be 'interesting'.

'Hence, "Jane Eyre"', said she in telling the anecdote; 'but she is not myself, any further than that.'[1]

The crucially different circumstance—and to the common novel-reader's view, the 'interesting' one—is, of course, Jane Eyre's lack of family.[2] The whole of Charlotte's life was conditioned by her duties as daughter and sister; Jane is free of all ties. She is also ignorant. To enter the being of Jane Eyre, the author deliberately discarded much of her own knowledge, quantitatively at least, of men: of father, brother, employers, curates, brothers of friends. Jane knows only three men, who indeed form the novel's pattern—Mr. Brocklehurst, Mr. Rochester, and St. John Rivers. What Charlotte Brontë used from her own experience was feeling, not fact; especially feeling drawn from its most detached and solitary phases —for example, the feeling of a young child at boarding-school, dumb sufferer and witness of harshness towards others; and of the governess at a family party:

the miseries of a reserved wretch . . . thrown at once into the midst of a large family—proud as peacocks and wealthy

[1] Harriet Martineau, obituary in the *Daily News*, April 1855 (*S.H.B.* iv. 182). Other implications of the story are less acceptable, for Jane's plainness is not new. Frances Henri was 'not beautiful', though not plain either; Agnes Grey looked in the glass and 'could discover no beauty in those marked features, that pale hollow cheek, and ordinary brown hair'.

[2] The significance of this is further explored in W. Robertson Nicoll's Introduction to *Jane Eyre*, 1902.

as Jews—at a time when they were particularly gay, when the house was full of company—all strangers, people I had never seen before.[1]

Her heart had been touched by the helplessness of a strong man 'his countenance . . . a lamp quenched, waiting to be relit';[2] she had known, and used, the powerless despair felt in witnessing 'a phase of insanity which may be called moral madness . . . all seems demonized'.[3]

We only suffer reality to *suggest*, never to *dictate*.[4]

Charlotte said this of *Shirley*; but the suggestions are even less specific in *Jane Eyre*. 'She is not myself, any further than that'; it is an *illusion* of identification that is produced by the use of feminine first-person narrative.

She had not attempted it before[5] and its novelty for her was no doubt an advantage; it imparts a warmth and confidence to the passages of self-analysis lacking in *The Professor*. The way it is used may be influenced by her sisters' example, in *Agnes Grey*, and in parts of *Wuthering Heights*; and also perhaps by *Pamela*, whose central situation *Jane Eyre* reproduces with a difference.[6] It was the method of

[1] Letter to Ellen Nussey from Stonegappe, 30 June 1839 (*S.H.B.* i. 180).

[2] *Jane Eyre*, ch. xxxvii. In 1843 Charlotte returned from Brussels to find her father nearly blind.

[3] Letter of 4 January 1848 (*S.H.B.* ii. 173–4), defending the character of Mrs. Rochester as 'but too natural'. Branwell, though of course unmentioned, is clearly in her mind.

[4] Letter of 16 November 1849 (*S.H.B.* iii. 37).

[5] The first-person narratives in the Angrian cycle are all masculine, as in *The Professor*.

[6] See above, p. 149.

narrative that suited her best; her unease without it is manifest in *Shirley*, which lacks a single centre of interest, and disposes its much greater masses of material without informing them with unity.[1]

For the peculiar unity of *Jane Eyre*, the use of the heroine as narrator is mainly responsible.

All is seen from the vantage-ground of the single experience of the central character, with which experience the author has imaginatively identified herself, and invited the engagement, again even to the point of imaginative identification, of every reader.[2] For both author and reader the threads of actual common experience are unbreakable, if slender; and they lead into the realms not of daydream, but of art. Only ingenuousness or assured mastery would choose such a method; to charge its limitations with the utmost significance, to avoid all its pitfalls, is the fortunate achievement of very few. The single point of view may be easily held at the circumference of the narrative and the emotional interest; but Jane continually, quietly, triumphantly occupies the centre, never receding into the role of mere reflector or observer—as does David Copperfield for several chapters at a time. Nor is she ever seen ironically, with the author hovering just visibly beyond her, hinting at her obtuseness and self-deception; an effect well-contrived, for example, by Dickens, notably in the Steerforth scenes of *David Copperfield*, and almost pervasively in *Great Expectations*; by Mrs. Gaskell in

[1] The unity she was groping after there was perhaps that of a social microcosm, seen in *The Newcomes* and *Middlemarch*.

[2] See above, p. 20.

Cousin Phillis; and by Stevenson in *Kidnapped*. These are masterpieces of first-person narrative, but they all sacrifice something that *Jane Eyre* retains; the ironic hovering sets the reader at a further distance from the central character—invited to understand it better than it does itself, he admires it, and identifies himself with it, a shade the less. But the reader of *Jane Eyre* at best keeps pace with the heroine, with her understanding of events (it would be a safe assumption that every reader shares her suspicions of Grace Poole) and of character, including her own. A special difficulty of presenting a central character in first-person narration (and one more incident to heroines, since custom allows women less latitude here) is that of combining enough self-description and self-analysis to define, with enough self-forgetfulness to attract. This difficulty also Charlotte Brontë circumvents; Jane is not tediously egotistical like Pamela, nor so transparently useful to the author as Esther Summerson, uncomprehendingly recording the compliments paid to her. Jane is self-critical, but also self-respecting; her modesty attracts while never making the reader take her at her own initial valuation. We watch a personality discovering itself not by long introspection but by a habit of keeping pace with her own experience. It is from her own explicit record that we are convinced both of her plainness and her charm, her delicacy and her endurance, her humility and her pride. Contrivance is never obtrusive and on a first reading probably unnoticed as such; in the rapid current of the narrative the deliberate contribution of others' view of her is accepted unconsciously as part of our picture of Jane. 'If she were a nice, pretty child, one might compassionate her forlorn- ness; but one really cannot care for such a little toad as that.' The speaker (Abbot, the commonplace heartless servant, deflecting Bessie's first stirrings of pity) is just enough defined for the testimony to be given due but not excessive weight. Five chapters and a few weeks later, in the sweep of Helen Burns's impassioned sermon, comes this, 'I read a sincere nature in your ardent eyes and on your clear front';[1] again, we know the witness and can weigh the testi- mony. At Thornfield, Mr. Rochester's half-irritated speculations on Jane's appearance and nature build up a still clearer definition; but we are so much occupied in discovering his own still more mysterious character and attitude that we hardly notice *how* we are being helped to see Jane.

'Eight years! . . . No wonder you have rather the look of another world. . . .'[2]

'By my word! there is something singular about you', said he: 'you have the air of a little nonnette; quaint, quiet, grave, and simple, as you sit with your hands before you, and your eyes generally bent on the carpet (except, by-the-by, when they are directed piercingly to my face; as just now for instance). . . .'[3]

Even when, disguised as the gipsy fortune-teller, he describes and interprets her character at length,[4] the situation justifies it; as the gipsy's testimony, it is accepted as the oracular revelation of the true Jane; as Mr. Rochester's, it is evidence alike of his love and

[1] Ch. viii.   [2] Ch. xiii.
[3] Ch. xiv.   [4] Ch. xix.

understanding, and of the 'finest fibre of [her] nature';
as yet not consciously realized by him. All that has
gone before and follows in the novel is embedded in
his concluding words:

'The forehead declares, "Reason sits firm and holds the
reins, and she will not let the feelings burst away and hurry
her to wild chasms. The passions may rage furiously, like
true heathens, as they are; and the desires may imagine all
sorts of vain things: but judgment shall still have the last
word in every argument, and the casting vote in every decision. Strong wind, earthquake shock, and fire may pass by:
I shall follow the guiding of that still small voice which interprets the dictates of conscience."'

Their irony is only in his unawareness that this very
reason, judgement, and conscience will frustrate him.

Jane keeps no journal and writes no letters; she
simply re-enters her experience, and even the vision
of herself as retrospective recorder is rare and deli-
cately timed:

What a consternation of soul was mine that dreary afternoon! How all my brain was in tumult, and all my heart in
insurrection! Yet in what darkness, what dense ignorance,
was the mental battle fought! I could not answer the ceaseless
inward question—*why* I thus suffered; now at the distance of
—I will not say how many years, I see it clearly.

I was a discord in Gateshead-hall: I was like nobody there:
I had nothing in harmony with Mrs. Reed or her children,
or her chosen vassalage. . . .[1]

I was almost as hard beset by him now as I had been once
before, in a different way, by another. I was a fool both times.
To have yielded then would have been an error of principle;
to have yielded now would have been an error of judgment.

[1] Ch. ii.

So I think at this hour, when I look back to the crisis through the quiet medium of time: I was unconscious of folly at the instant.[1]

Rarely in self-analysis, though more often in description, are we aware of 'the quiet medium of time'; the tense of most of the novel is the just-after-present; many chapters—especially in the Thornfield section —could be letters of Pamela's, and the angle of the Gateshead chapters is more often that of *David Copperfield* than of *Esmond*. Truth to immediate experience extends to minutest detail; the description of Miss Temple is partly retrospective—'round curls, according to the fashion of those times . . . watches were not so common then as now . . .' but it ends with a quiet return to the child's view—'Miss Temple—Maria Temple, as I afterwards saw the name written in a prayer-book entrusted to me to carry to church'.[2]

The consistency and flexibility of the first person method is unusual, and its use in a narrative of childhood perhaps an absolute novelty in fiction. The novel would have lost incalculably had it started later in Jane's life—say, at her setting out for Thornfield. The early chapters are no mere prologue; they expound a situation, introduce and partly account for a character, and initiate the major themes of the whole novel. Presented as a child, she engages interest, sympathy, and admiration, which is yet kept clear (as not wholly with the Dombey children) of a too generic compassion. The author who launches hero or heroine early in life can count on a special kind of goodwill

[1] Ch. xxxv.　　　　　　　　　[2] Ch. v.

in the reader—which is perhaps defined by merely citing the instances of Fanny Price, David Copperfield, Henry Esmond, Pip, Maggie Tulliver, and Molly Gibson. And by representing typical experiences and responses, the author also draws upon everyone's recollections of early consciousness; we are all Wordsworthians at heart.

Who that remembers early childhood, can read without emotion the little Jane Eyre's night journey to Lowood? How finely, yet how unconsciously, are those peculiar aspects of things which cease with childhood developed in this simple history!—that feeling of unlimited vastness in the world around—that absence of all permanent idea of the extra-visible, which leaves everything not actually seen in outer fog, where all things are possible. . . . This 'I', that seems to have no inheritance in the earth, is an eternity with a heritage in all heavens. . . Is there not something awful in these 'I's' and 'me's'? They go about the page with a kind of veiled divinity.[1]

But, beyond all other examples in the novel, *Jane Eyre* arrests attention in its opening chapters by disclosing an individual character enmeshed in, yet independent of, unusual circumstances. And it is the opening of a poetic novel; season, scene, and character are interpenetrated:

There was no possibility of taking a walk that day. We had been wandering, indeed, in the leafless shrubbery an hour in the morning; but since dinner (Mrs Reed, when there was no company, dined early) the cold winter wind had brought with it clouds so sombre, and a rain so penetrating, that further outdoor exercise was now out of the question. . . .

[1] Sydney Dobell, *The Palladium* (September 1850); quoted in *The Life and Letters of Sydney Dobell*, 2 vols., 1878, i. 179–80.

... At intervals, while turning over the leaves of my book, I studied the aspect of that winter afternoon. Afar it offered a pale blank of mist and cloud; near, a scene of wet lawn and storm-beat shrub, with ceaseless rain sweeping away wildly before a long and lamentable blast.

It is November—a season which is to recur nine years later in the novel just when the last particulars of Jane's early history are disclosed.[1]

An indoor scene on a winter's day; a child in disgrace, excluded from the family circle, reading a book in a curtained window-seat; a creature dependent, captive, yet with the liberty of adventure in imagination—a window to look out of, a book to read and pictures on which to build fancies. The double impression of constraint and freedom is burnt into the mind in those first few paragraphs; it is accompanied by the symbol (to become recurrent) of the window. From this retreat we see her dragged out, bullied, insulted; she is a terrified cornered animal—but one that fights back, with intellectual and imaginative resourcefulness.

The cut bled, the pain was sharp: my terror had passed its climax; other feelings succeeded.

'Wicked and cruel boy!' I said. 'You are like a murderer—you are like a slave-driver—you are like the Roman emperors!'

I had read Goldsmith's History of Rome, and had formed my opinion of Nero, Caligula, &c. Also I had drawn parallels in silence, which I never thought thus to have declared aloud.

John Reed's taunts skilfully conceal a piece of formal

---

[1] Chs. xxxii–xxxiii; the date, 5 November, is specified.

exposition, in which the outline of Jane's situation is conveyed to us—a child without status or adult protector. Not until the second chapter is her actual relation to the Reed family stated, and the details of her origin wait until the third, where she overhears the servants' gossip. Meanwhile the terrors of imagination increase the agony of her imprisonment in the Red Room. But yet the tone is kept low, with no overt bid for pity; her captors are not monsters, their point of view is a valid one ('I was a discord in Gateshead-hall'); Bessie pities her for a moment, before roast onion supervenes; and the large gestures of romance are explicitly avoided:

No severe or prolonged bodily illness followed this incident of the red-room. . . .

'No; I should not like to belong to poor people. . . .' I was not heroic enough to purchase liberty at the price of caste.[1]

(Even so, later, a full-dress death-bed repentance for Mrs. Reed is avoided; and Hannah, turning the stranger from the door in the storm, acts not from cruelty but well-intentioned loyalty to her employers). Another opportunity for heightening is balked in the interests of deeper truthfulness at the child's verbal triumph over Mrs. Reed:

I was left there alone—winner of the field. It was the hardest battle I had fought, and the first victory I had gained. . . . First, I smiled to myself and felt elate; but this fierce pleasure subsided in me as fast as did the accelerated throb of my pulses. A child cannot quarrel with its elders as I had done; cannot give its furious feelings uncontrolled play, as I

[1] Ch. iii.

had given mine; without experiencing afterwards the pang of remorse and the chill of reaction.[1]

And this sense of the victory of impulse turning to ashes is a part of the novel's theme.

The deliberate dryness of tone and accompanying self-criticism make the early chapters less harrowing than they could have been—and than the Murdstone chapters of *David Copperfield* are. The facts are terrible enough; how terrible is quietly indicated at the appearance of the apothecary Mr. Lloyd as she revives from her fainting fit:

I felt an inexpressible relief, a soothing conviction of protection and security, when I knew that there was a stranger in the room; an individual not belonging to Gateshead, and not related to Mrs. Reed.[2]

But they are counterbalanced by our sense of a character growing from its own inward strength, like grass pushing up between stones. This growth is reflected in the clear shallow pool of Bessie's

'You little sharp thing! you've got quite a new way of talking. What makes you so venturesome and hardy?'[1]

The impact of Mr. Brocklehurst is the more terrifying from the precise use of the physical child's-eye view ('I looked up at—a black pillar'); but under moral and theological bullying the animal again fights back:

'And what is hell? Can you tell me that?'
'A pit full of fire.'
'And should you like to fall into that pit and to be burning there for ever?'

[1] Ch. iv.   [2] Ch. iii.

'No, sir.'

'What must you do to avoid it?'

I deliberated a moment; my answer, when it did come, was objectionable: 'I must keep in good health, and not die.'

'And the Psalms? I hope you like them.'

'No, sir.'[1]

The colloquy has more than one echo; the less obvious is the more valuable in revealing part of the novel's pattern:

'But', was slowly, distinctly read, 'the fearful, the unbelieving, &c., shall have their part in the lake which burneth with fire and brimstone, which is the second death.'

Henceforward, I knew what fate St. John feared for me.[2]

'You examine me, Miss Eyre; do you think me handsome?'

'No, sir.'[3]

The savagery and reserve, sensitiveness and sharp-wittedness that we are to know in Jane at eighteen are hers at ten. 'Never was anything at once so frail and so indomitable.'[4] She is as tough in happiness as in misery:

'I like you more than I can say; but I'll not sink into a bathos of sentiment; and with this needle of repartee I'll keep you from its gulf too.'[5]

Figures in the pattern recur; Lady Ingram will remind Jane of Mrs. Reed, as a worldly cold-hearted mother of conventionally attractive daughters, who personifies the same threat to her happiness. The two sisters are indeed three times repeated, as the Brockle-

[1] Ch. iv.   [2] Ch. xxxv.   [3] Ch. xiv.
[4] Ch. xxvii.   [5] Ch. xxiv.

hursts, Ingrams, and Riverses. Most significantly, the image used for Mr. Brocklehurst is repeated for St. John Rivers—'at the fireside, . . . a cold cumbrous column, gloomy and out of place'.[1] He gathers into himself the cousinship of John Reed, the formidable religious sanctions of Mr. Brocklehurst, and the desire for possession of Mr. Rochester: it takes more than Jane's mature powers of resistance for her to fight back at this final enemy; supernatural aid is hers.[2]

Above all, in these early chapters there is gradually disengaged from the generic impression of a child robbed of its birthright the individual figure of a heart hungering for affection. Save for a few unconsciously dropped crumbs from Bessie, at Gateshead her bread is stones; in the choric words of Bessie's song 'Men are hard-hearted', and the assurance that 'Kind angels only Watch o'er the steps of the poor orphan child' is as yet barren of comfort; there are no angels in Mr. Brocklehurst's religion. Lowood opens inauspiciously, with still harsher physical discomfort —not merely piercingly actual (the taste of the burnt porridge, the starved arms wrapped in pinafores) but symbolic of a loveless order of things.[3] In Helen Burns and Miss Temple appear the first shadowings of hope; the warm fire and the cake from the cup-

---

[1] Ch. xxxiv. This image was probably in Swinburne's mind when he called St. John 'this white marble clergyman (counterpart, as it were, of the "black marble" Brocklehurst)'. *A Note on Charlotte Brontë* (1877), p. 69.

[2] See below, p. 312.

[3] Compare the emphasis on hunger in her flight from Thornfield (Ch. xxviii).

board in Miss Temple's room are assertions of individual loving-kindness, though also of its limited
power; and Helen's comfort in injustice reaches her
as from another world:

. . . She chafed my fingers gently to warm them, and went
on:—

'If all the world hated you, and believed you wicked, while
your own conscience approved you, and absolved you from
guilt, you would not be without friends.'

'No; I know I should think well of myself; but that is not
enough: if others don't love me, I would rather die than live—
I cannot bear to be solitary and hated, Helen. . . . ¹

Helen's religious assurances bring calm—but with
'an alloy of inexpressible sadness'. For she has spoken
as one facing towards death; and she dies, her message of endurance and trust (the message of *Rasselas*)
only half accepted; at her deathbed Jane asks 'Where
is God? What is God?'

The vehement, impulsive hunger of her nature is
not satisfied at Lowood; it is only assuaged. Summing
up eight years of Miss Temple's influence, she says:

I had imbibed from her something of her nature and much
of her habits: more harmonious thoughts; what seemed better
regulated feelings had become the inmates of my mind. I had
given an allegiance to duty and order; I was quiet; I believed
I was content: to the eyes of others, usually even to my own,
I appeared a disciplined and subdued character.²

Miss Temple leaves: the adventurous spirit reawakes.

I went to my window, and looked out. . . . I tired of the
routine of eight years in one afternoon. I desired liberty; for

¹ Ch. viii.   ² Ch. x.

liberty I gasped; for liberty I uttered a prayer; it seemed scattered on the wind then faintly blowing. . . .

Or if not liberty, 'at least a new servitude'.[1]

The next twelve chapters, the longest stretch of the novel, belong to Thornfield; with one significant exception—the visit to Gateshead at Mrs. Reed's death, where the return to the theme of the first movement marks the passage of time and Jane's own progress, as well as satisfying poetic justice. At Thornfield, saturation in the present is at its most intense; a whole year passes, each season marked, from autumn to summer. Through vicissitudes of doubt, jealousy, unsolved mystery, we are brought with Jane to the verge of satisfaction of her long heart's-hunger, on Midsummer Eve. Then, at her marriage, in the very church, the existence of Bertha Rochester is revealed: 'a Christmas frost had come at midsummer.'

The long chapter that follows,[2] in which 'conscience, turned tyrant, held passion by the throat', is the true centre of the novel, to and from which all else leads; the crisis of event, character, and spirit, culminating in Jane's final resistance and her flight from Thornfield. She resists not only her love and Mr. Rochester's, but her compassion and the human sense of justice aroused by his history; and resists, not through any sense of social convention, or shocked morality:

'Is it better to drive a fellow-creature to despair than to transgress a mere human law—no man being injured by the breach? . . .'

[1] Ch. x. [2] Ch. xxvii.

This was true: and while he spoke my very Conscience and Reason turned traitors against me, and charged me with crime in resisting him. They spoke almost as loud as Feeling: and that clamoured wildly. 'Oh, comply!' it said. 'Think of his misery; think of his danger—look at his state when left alone: remember his headlong nature; consider the recklessness following on despair—soothe him; save him; love him; tell him you love him and will be his. Who in the world cares for *you*? or who will be injured by what you do?'

Still indomitable was the reply—'*I* care for myself. The more solitary, the more friendless, the more unsustained I am, the more I will respect myself. I will keep the law given by God; sanctioned by man. . . .'

Her resistance belongs to a world beyond that of human love; a world whose presence has lain across the whole novel, if only half-perceived. Helen Burns is its spokesman:

'Hush, Jane! you think too much of the love of human beings; you are too impulsive, too vehement: the sovereign hand that created your frame, and put life into it, has provided you with other resources than your feeble self, or than creatures feeble as you. Besides this earth, and besides the race of men, there is an invisible world and a kingdom of spirits: that world is around us, for it is everywhere; and those spirits watch us, for they are commissioned to guard us. . . .'[1]

It is hinted in the terrors of the Red Room (recalled at this very crisis), in Bessie's song, in Jane's 'look of another world'. To that world indeed belong incidents which would be unacceptable in an ordinary domestic novel: the seeming coincidence of Jane's meeting with the Rivers family, who prove to be her

[1] Ch. viii.

cousins; and to that world belongs the miraculous voice which recalls her to Mr. Rochester. Part of the novel's inclusiveness and unity comes from Jane's spiritual growth: her individual religion—sharply distinguished from the loveless creeds of Mr. Brockle-hurst, Eliza Reed, and St. John Rivers—is fully discovered only in this crisis; but it has been prepared for, even as early as the first long conversation with Mr. Rochester:

'I know what my aim is, what my motives are; and at this moment I pass a law, unalterable as that of the Medes and Persians, that both are right.'

'They cannot be, sir, if they require a new statute to legalise them.'

'They are, Miss Eyre, though they absolutely require a new statute: unheard-of combinations of circumstance demand unheard-of rules.'

'That sounds a dangerous maxim, sir; because one can see at once that it is liable to abuse.'

'Sententious sage! so it is: but I swear by my household gods not to abuse it.'

'You are human and fallible.'

'I am; so are you—what then?'

'The human and fallible should not arrogate a power with which the divine and perfect alone can be safely entrusted.'

'What power?'

'That of saying of any strange, unsanctioned line of action, —"Let it be right".'[1]

There is a warning a few weeks before the marriage-day, emphasized by its placing at the end of a chapter:[2]

My future husband was becoming to me my whole world; and, more than the world: almost my hope of heaven. He stood

[1] Ch. xiv.   [2] Ch. xxiv.

between me and every thought of religion, as an eclipse inter-
venes between man and the broad sun. I could not, in those
days, see God for his creature: of whom I had made an idol.

When therefore in her deepest despair 'One idea only
still throbbed life-like within me—a remembrance of
God' and 'begot an unuttered prayer'[1] it is no merely
rhetorical gesture. This is not to counter the attacks
of the *Quarterly Review* by claiming *Jane Eyre* as a
Christian novel; though it expresses, more directly
than any other novel, the convictions of many creed-
less Christians in the eighteen-forties;[2] the conviction that 'not a May-game is this man's life, but a
battle and a march, a warfare with principalities and
powers'.[3] The master-influence of the decade is
audible when Jane asserts to Rochester, 'We are
born to strive and to endure'.

That the reader is aware of the 'other world', into
whatever formulae he may choose to translate it, and
that Jane's progress is one of spiritual growth as well
as emotional adventure, is perhaps made most evident
if one imagines the alternative issue. If Jane had
yielded,[4] the novel would still be 'serious'; a novel
with a purpose indeed, striking a blow for insurgent

---

[1] Ch. xxvi.

[2] Sydney Dobell commends Charlotte Brontë's 'unshaken faith'—a
faith 'positive and energic . . . united with a vigour of private judgment,
without which there is nothing for it but famine in these days' (*Palladium*,
September 1850).   [3] Carlyle, *Past and Present*, iv. 7.

[4] As George Eliot seems to have wished:

> I have read 'Jane Eyre', and shall be glad to know what you admire
> in it. All self-sacrifice is good, but one would like it to be in a some-
> what nobler cause than that of a diabolical law which chains a man soul
> and body to a putrefying carcase

(Letter to Charles Bray, June 1848; Cross, ch. iii.)

feminism, the anarchy of passion, and the reform of the divorce laws. But it would have been smaller and narrower, and would have violated its own moral pattern.

It would also have lost had it ended with renunciation. The phase which ends with Jane's resistance and flight is in fact the third Act; there are ten chapters—nearly a third of the novel—before we reach harbour with, 'Reader, I married him'. They are the least appreciated part of the novel: but an essential part of its unity, knitted alike to the Thornfield and the Lowood chapters. For they show Jane becoming calm after suffering, again giving 'allegiance to duty and order', again studying, again teaching in a school, submitting to virtue in lovable form, as she had once submitted to Miss Temple. They also show her tempted by and withstanding the opposite temptation to Mr. Rochester's—that of duty and virtue which take no account of passion, personified in St. John Rivers, in appearance and manner Rochester's antithesis, with his 'Greek face, very pure in outline' and his 'firmness and self control'—'the material from which Nature hews her heroes . . . a steadfast bulwark . . . but at the fireside, too often a cold, cumbrous column, gloomy and out of place'. His religion seems more noble than any Jane has yet encountered; but something is wanting; there is 'an absence of consolatory gentleness'; St. John 'pure-lived, conscientious, zealous as he was', has, she thinks, not yet found 'that peace of God that passeth all understanding'.[1]

[1] See above, p. 303, for the echo of Mr. Brocklehurst. There is a

Nearly another year elapses at Marsh End and Morton; the seasons are marked as before. But instead of progress, there is quiescence; what St. John at first appeared, so he remains. Reason, duty, cousinly affection lead to his proposal—of marriage and a life of devoted service as missionaries in India. The service she would accept, but not the marriage:

... as his wife—at his side always, and always restrained, and always checked—forced to keep the fire of my nature continually low, to compel it to burn inwardly and never utter a cry, though the imprisoned flame consumed vital after vital —*this* would be unendurable.[1]

She offers him 'a comrade's constancy . . . a neophyte's respect and submission to his hierophant: nothing more—don't fear'. He misses the sardonic conclusion. ' "It is just what I want," he said, speaking to himself; ". . . we *must* be married . . . and undoubtedly enough of love would follow upon marriage to render the union right even in your eyes." ' Jane is ready with the most emphatic of her negatives.

'I scorn your idea of love', I could not help saying; as I rose up and stood before him, leaning my back against the rock.

(For of course this wooing too is out of doors; but on the open heath, not in a garden.)

'I scorn the counterfeit sentiment you offer: yes, St. John, and I scorn you when you offer it.'

But this is not the final test; that comes a week later, when he speaks to her as a man of God:

his look was not, indeed, that of a lover beholding his mistress;

Calvinistic strain in both, contrasted with the Arminianism of Helen Burns. [1] Ch. xxxiv.

but it was that of a pastor recalling his wandering sheep—
or better, of a guardian angel watching the soul for which he
is responsible. . . . I felt veneration for St. John. . . . I was
tempted to cease struggling with him. . . .

She draws the parallel:

I was almost as hard beset by him now as I had been once
before, in a different way, by another. I was a fool both times.

A fool, that is, to feel temptation. But she is beset
now, it seems, by the very world which gave her
strength to resist before:

Religion called—Angels beckoned—God commanded. . . .
The dim room was full of visions.

'Could you decide now?' asked the missionary. The inquiry
was put in gentle tones: he drew me to him as gently.

It was

almost as if he loved me (I say *almost*—I knew the difference,
—for I had felt what it was to be loved . . .).

She waits only for a sign from Heaven; it comes, and
it is the voice of Mr. Rochester, borne by the wind.
The invisible world has spoken.

She makes her last journey—'like the messenger-
pigeon flying home'; first to Thornfield, the burnt-
out shell of the past, and at last to Ferndean and Mr.
Rochester, blind and desolate, a 'caged eagle'. The
stage is set for the conventional happy ending; but
the 'needle of repartee' still keeps us from the 'gulf of
sentiment'. The uses of St. John Rivers are not exhausted; the tables must be turned, and she mocks
her one-time tormentor, in a long, provocative, teasing dialogue. It is the most artful reconciliation

possible—not only of Jane and Rochester, but of the different kinds of love threaded through the novel; and the appropriate assurance of future happiness to these so articulate lovers—after ten years' marriage she can still say, 'We talk, I believe, all day long'. The spiritual pattern is also resolved; not only by his new dependence on her, but by the disclosure that at the moment of the miraculous voice, he was calling to her, in penitence and prayer. 'I kept these things, then, and pondered them in my heart.' But the true climax, the justified superlative, is the last proposal:

'Jane suits me: do I suit her?'
'To the finest fibre of my nature, sir.'

with the typically practical consequence:

'The case being so, we have nothing in the world to wait for; we must be married instantly.'

The discovery and revelation of that fineness of fibre is this novel's triumph. There is no character in any novel of the eighteen-forties whom the reader knows as intimately as Jane Eyre: and it is an intimacy at all levels—alike with the fiery spirit and the shivering child.

With *Jane Eyre*, the novel that everyone knows, this study comes full circle. And here, in the words of the most famous of all literary conclusions,

I rejoice to concur with the common reader; for by the common sense of readers uncorrupted with literary prejudices, after all the refinements of subtilty and the dogmatism of learning, must be finally decided all claim to poetical honours

—and also to the honours of the novelist.

APPENDIX I

From *Master Humphrey's Clock*, No. LXXIX, October 1841
(*Barnaby Rudge*, ch. LXV).

TO THE
READERS OF 'MASTER HUMPHREY'S CLOCK'

DEAR FRIENDS,

NEXT November, we shall have finished the Tale, on which we are at present engaged; and shall have travelled together through Twenty Monthly Parts, and Eighty-seven Weekly Numbers. It is my design, when we have gone so far, to close this work. Let me tell you why.

I should not regard the anxiety, the close confinement, or the constant attention, inseparable from the weekly form of publication (for to commune with you, in any form, is to me a labour of love), if I had found it advantageous to the conduct of my stories, the elucidation of my meaning, or the gradual development of my characters. But I have not done so. I have often felt cramped and confined in a very irksome and harassing degree, by the space in which I have been constrained to move. I have wanted you to know more at once than I could tell you; and it has frequently been of the greatest importance to my cherished intention, that you should do so. I have been sometimes strongly tempted (and have been at some pains to resist the temptation) to hurry incidents on, lest they should appear to you who waited from week to week, and had not, like me, the result and purpose in your minds, too long delayed. In a word, I have found this form of publication most anxious, perplexing, and difficult. I cannot bear these jerking confidences which are no sooner begun than ended, and no sooner ended than begun again.

Many passages in a tale of any length, depend materially for their interest on the intimate relation they bear to what has gone before, or to what is to follow. I sometimes found it difficult when I issued thirty-two closely-printed pages once a month, to sustain in your mind this needful connexion; in the present form of publication[1] it is often, especially in the first half of a story, quite impossible to preserve it sufficiently through the current numbers. And although in my progress I am gradually able to set you right, and to show you what my meaning has been, and to work it out, I see no reason why you should ever be wrong when I have it in my power, by resorting to a better means of communication between us, to prevent it.

Considerations of immediate profit and advantage, ought, in such a case, to be of secondary importance. *They* would lead me, at all hazards, to hold my present course. But, for the reasons I have just now mentioned, I have, after long consideration, and with especial reference to the next new Tale I bear in my mind, arrived at the conclusion that it will be better to abandon this scheme of publication, in favour of our old and well-tried plan, which has only twelve gaps in a year, instead of fifty-two. . . .

[1] The weekly numbers of *Barnaby Rudge* consisted of twelve pages, including illustrations.

APPENDIX II

Dickens's Letter Outlining *Dombey and Son*

I WILL now go on to give you an outline of my immediate intentions in reference to *Dombey*. I design to show Mr. D. with that one idea of the Son taking firmer and firmer possession of him, and swelling and bloating his pride to a prodigious extent. As the boy begins to grow up, I shall show him quite impatient for his getting on, and urging his masters to set him great tasks, and the like. But the natural affection of the boy will turn towards the despised sister; and I purpose showing her learning all sorts of things, of her own application and determination, to assist him in his lessons: and helping him always. When the boy is about ten years old (in the fourth number), he will be taken ill, and will die; and when he is ill, and when he is dying, I mean to make him turn always for refuge to the sister still, and keep the stern affection of the father at a distance. So Mr. Dombey—for all his greatness, and for all his devotion to the child—will find himself at arms' length from him even then; and will see that his love and confidence are all bestowed upon his sister, whom Mr. Dombey has used—and so has the boy himself too, for that matter—as a mere convenience and handle to him. The death of the boy is a death-blow, of course, to all the father's schemes and cherished hopes; and 'Dombey and Son', as Miss Tox will say at the end of the number, 'is a Daughter after all'. . . . From that time, I purpose changing his feeling of indifference and uneasiness towards his daughter into a positive hatred. For he will always remember how the boy had his arm round her neck when he was dying, and whispered to her, and would take things only from her hand, and never thought of him. . . . At the same time, I shall change *her* feeling towards *him* for one of a greater desire to love him, and to be loved by him; engendered in her compassion for his loss, and her love for the dead boy whom, in his way, he loved so well too. So I mean to carry the story on, through all the branches and off-shoots and meanderings that come up; and through the decay and down-fall of the house, and the bankruptcy of Dombey, and all the rest of it; when his only staff and treasure, and his unknown Good Genius always, will be this rejected daughter, who will come out better than any son at last, and whose love for him, when discovered and understood, will be his bitterest reproach. For the struggle with himself, which goes on in all such obstinate natures, will have ended then; and the sense of his injustice, which you may be sure has never quitted him, will have at last a gentler office than that of only making him more harshly unjust. . . . I rely very much on Susan Nipper grown up, and acting partly as Florence's maid, and partly as a kind of companion to her, for a strong character throughout the book. I also rely on the Toodles, and on Polly, who, like everybody else, will be found by Mr. Dombey to have gone over to his daughter and become attached to her. This is what cooks call 'the stock of the soup'. All kinds of things will be added to it, of course.[1]

[1] Forster, vi. 2; letter of 25 July 1846. The marks of omission are Forster's.

APPENDIX III

Table Showing Part-issues of *Dombey and Son* and *Vanity Fair*

	Dombey and Son Chapters	Numbers	Date	Vanity Fair Chapters	Number
1846	i–iv	1	Oct.		
	v–vii	2	Nov.		
	viii–x .	3	Dec.		
1847	xi–xiii	4	Jan.	i–iv	1
	xiv–xvi	5	Feb.	v–vii	2
	xvii–xix	6	Mar.	viii–xi	3
	xx–xxii	7	Apr.	xii–xiv	4
	xxiii–xxv	8	May	xv–xviii	5
	xxvi–xxviii	9	June	xix–xxii	6
	xxix–xxxi	10	July	xxiii–xxv	7
	xxxii–xxxiv	11	Aug.	xxvi–xxix	8
	xxxv–xxxviii	12	Sept.	xxx–xxxii	9
	xxxix–xli	13	Oct.	xxxiii–xxxv	10
	xlii–xlv	14	Nov.	xxxvi–xxxviii	11
	xlvi–xlviii	15	Dec.	xxxix–xlii	12
1848	xlix–li	16	Jan.	xliii–xlvi	13
	lii–liv	17	Feb.	xlvii–l	14
	lv–lvii	18	Mar.	li–liii	15
	lviii–lxii	19–20	Apr.	liv–lvi	16
			May	lvii–lx	17
			June	lxi–lxiii	18
			July	lxiv–lxvii	19–20

INDEX

PRINTED IN GREAT BRITAIN AT THE UNIVERSITY PRESS, OXFORD
BY CHARLES BATEY, PRINTER TO THE UNIVERSITY